POTENT PASTIMES

Books by the same author

Fighting their own war: South African blacks and the First World War (1987)

Die Hendsoppers en Joiners: Die rasionaal en verskynsel van verraad (1999)

The Dynamics of Treason: Boer collaboration in the South African War of 1899–1902 (2006)

Radelose rebellie?: Dinamika van die 1914–1915 Afrikanerrebellie (with Sandra Swart) (2009)

POTENT PASTIMES
Sport and leisure practices in modern Afrikaner history

ALBERT GRUNDLINGH

Protea Book House
Pretoria
2013

Potent Pastimes: Sport and leisure practices in modern Afrikaner history
Albert Grundlingh

First edition, first impression in 2013 by Protea Book House

PO Box 35110, Menlo Park, 0102
1067 Burnett Street, Hatfield, Pretoria
8 Minni Street, Clydesdale, Pretoria
protea@intekom.co.za
www.proteaboekhuis.com

Editor: Danél Hanekom
Proofreader: Martjie Bosman
Cover design: Hanli Deysel
Indexer: Dawie Malan
Front cover image: Thinkstockphotos
Typography: 10.5 on 12.75 pt Times New Roman by Ada Radford
Printed and bound: Creda Communications

© 2013 A. Grundlingh

ISBN: 978-1-86919-861-9 (printed book)
ISBN: 978-1-86919-862-6 (e-book)

All rights reserved. No part of this book may be reproduced or transmitted in any form or by any electronic or mechanical means, including photocopying and recording, or by any other information storage or retrieval system, without written permission from the publisher.

Images on pp. 80 and 121 used with the kind permission of Rapport/Media24.

Contents

Introduction   *7*

Chapter 1:
  Dogs, *dominees* and the Afrikaner working class: Cultural politics of greyhound racing on the Rand, 1932–1949   *14*

Chapter 2:
  Holidays at Hartenbos: Sand, sea and sun in the construction of Afrikaner cultural nationalism, c 1930–c 1961   *34*

Chapter 3:
  Playing with purpose: Rugby and its wider significance in Afrikaner society, c 1900–c 1989   *54*

Chapter 4:
  From international isolation to inclusion: The quest for rugby respectability, 1969–1994   *93*

Chapter 5:
  Explaining euphoria: The 1995 Springbok Rugby World Cup victory and its impact   *128*

Chapter 6:
  Rugby, rands and religion: Ramifications of the professionalisation of the game, 1995–2013   *155*

Chapter 7:
  Diffusion and depiction: How Afrikaners came to play cricket in twentieth-century South Africa   *192*

Afterword   *219*

Acknowledgements   *221*

Glossary:
  Abbreviations of rugby bodies mentioned in this study   *222*

Sources   *223*

Index   *237*

To my late father, Mauritz Grundlingh, who taught me to appreciate and critically appraise sport, and encouraged me to read.

Introduction

This book deals with activities which many Afrikaners have indulged in, even more have watched, but relatively few have reflected upon seriously. It has been selective in its choice of subject matter, believing that an in-depth analysis of specific topics during the twentieth century has the potential to be more rewarding than an encyclopaedic sweep of a variety of leisure practices and sporting codes. Hence, the focus is on the attraction of dog racing in the 1930s in Johannesburg, the lure of the beach at Hartenbos in the southwestern Cape, the enduring obsession with rugby and the evolving interest in cricket.

Whilst generally historians have focused a great deal on formal Afrikaner politics, black resistance movements and of course apartheid and many of its ramifications, other dimensions of life as manifested through leisure pursuits and sport have not attracted the same kind of academic attention or been foregrounded to the same extent. It is true that popular books about sport abound, particularly of the autobiographical kind or those focusing on specific teams and sports tours, but with some notable exceptions sustained academic analyses have lagged behind.[1]

---

[1] Over the past 30 years or so academics who have been consistent in producing work on sport history in South Africa have been restricted to: André Odendaal, John Nauright, Douglas Booth, Peter Alegi, Christopher Merrett and Floris van der Merwe, Ashwin Desai and Goolam Vahed. For a full historiographical overview see A. Odendaal, "Sport and Liberation: The Unfinished Business of the Past" in C. Thomas (ed.): *Sport and Liberation in South Africa: Reflections and Suggestions* (University of Fort Hare, Pretoria, 2006), pp. 11–38.

Part of the reason may be that given South Africa's turbulent history and the dramatic way in which opposing political forces squared up against one another, sport and leisure appeared as rather trivial phenomena, best left to amateurs and not the kind of topics to be taken serious by guild historians. The field may even have appeared frivolous, outside the domain of serious intellectual endeavour, sport historians being hardly more than "fans with typewriters practising their esoteric craft with little contact with the historical mainstream."[2] Such an attitude can, however, be misleading. Writing in a South African cultural studies volume, Rita Barnard has elaborated on the significance of the apparently insignificant:

> it is precisely in the most trivial, the most hopelessly flawed manifestations of any given genre or cultural form that the operations of ideology are most clearly and characteristically displayed. A critical reader of culture should therefore prick up her ears when a text, idea, or practice is habitually and as a matter of course dismissed as silly, uninteresting, or *passé*; for it is in the fertile loam of the marginal that we may find the structures of power revealed in peculiarly fascinating ways.[3]

This is nowhere more apparent than in dealing with the issue of sport and politics. Only those who do not wish to probe any deeper can believe the assumption that sport and politics are completely separate domains. In South Africa, even more so than in most other countries, despite the best protestations of some, separation was never possible as the sporting boycotts during apartheid strikingly revealed.

But apart from formalised sport politics as conducted for example by the anti-apartheid movement, sport separation can also be regarded as a form of "deep politics" in which "social traditions and attitudes are expressed through recreational practises." Tony Collins, the British author on the history of rugby has reminded us that all "sports that have mass appeal reflect the preferences and prejudices of those sections of society that nurture them."[4] It is for the sport historian to ferret out the precise significance and meanings of a par-

---

2   Quoted in D. Booth: "Escaping the past? The Cultural Turn and Language in Sport History" in *Rethinking History*, 8, 1, (2004), p. 103.
3   R. Barnard: "Contesting Beauty" in S. Nuttal and C.A. Michael (eds), *Senses of Culture: South African Cultural Studies* (University of Cape Town Press, Cape Town, 2000), p. 347.
4   T. Collins: *A Social History of English Rugby Union* (Routledge, London, 2009), p. 213.

ticular sport over time in a changing context and to establish how these interconnect with other relevant forces in the rest of society. These linkages, of course, must be proven and cannot simply be assumed or assigned. Nor can their outcome be considered as preordained. Jeremy MacClancy has made the salutary point that any "particular sport is not intrinsically associated with a particular set of meanings or social values. What it is meant to represent is not laid down like some commandment etched in stone." Accordingly, sport is rather "an embodied practice, in which meanings are generated, and whose representation and interpretation are open to negotiation and contest."[5]

It is equally important for the academic historian of sport and leisure to be constantly aware of his or her moorings in the wider historiographical landscape. South African historiography over the past 40 years or more has exhibited certain distinct traits: from an Afrikaner interpretation of history which foregrounded white nationalistic interests to a liberal version usually emanating from white English speakers who emphasised "wrong turnings" and premised upon notions of individual agency within a free-market economy, through to an oppositional neo-Marxist frame which included a strong social history tradition, and more recently, an unalloyed Africanist perspective at odds with the preceding points of departures. Within such a stark characterisation there are of course many overlaps and nuances.

Over and above these developments in South Africa, there has been a wider emergence of post-modernist views, questioning some of the assumptions of historical narratology and also setting their sights on the mode in which sports history is generally produced.[6]

The precise impact of such critiques is still to be seen, but social history as an analytical frame had till recently an uncontested and proven record as a fertile point of departure to pursue the wider connections between sport, leisure and society. Tony Collins writing in 2007 has little doubt about its salience: "It remains the case today

---

5   J. MacClancy: "Sport, Identity and Ethnicity" in J. MacClancy (ed.), *Sport, Identity and Ethnicity* (Berg, Oxford, 1996), p. 4.
6   In terms of sport history see for example M. Phillips (ed.), *Deconstructing Sport History: A Postmodern Analysis* (State University of New York Press, Albany, 2006). For an overview of theoretical frames see D. Booth; "Theory" in S.W. Pope and J. Nauright (eds) *Routledge Companion to Sports History*, (Routledge, London, 2010).

that the most interesting work published on sport and leisure history is produced by historians working with the methods of and asking the questions originally posed by social historians."[7]

Although the term "social" in social history has not always been defined with precision, three main features can be discerned. First, it can be seen as a synthetic notion, interrogating those spheres which at first glance may appear as distinct but which may actually be intricately interwoven. Second, as opposed to focusing only on individual agency, it foregrounded systemic forces usually rooted in, but not necessarily axiomatically restricted to material considerations, as the encapsulation of the "social". Third, social history declared a strong focus on the everyday lives of "ordinary people".[8] These elements were sufficiently flexible to incorporate a cultural practice such as sport or leisure and infused expositions with an understanding that the "cultural" cannot operate in isolation. Writing on these developments in a Western context, Nancy Struna has emphasised that in the term sport *and* society the conjunctive indicated equal attention. Therefore, "one of the goals of this kind of social history is the telling of a 'large' story about the nature, fit and meanings of sporting practices as these were embedded in society; hence the common focus on the making of sporting life as an inextricably linked dimension of the making of a nation, a people or a sub-period"[9]. These considerations present the historian of sport and society with a clear set of challenges.

The unifying theme that runs through this book is the different ways in which sport and leisure practices during certain historical eras were connected with wider concerns in Afrikaner society. "Sport," according to the British historian Richard Holt, "is not only a physical activity; it has heroic and mythical dimensions and can be viewed as a story we tell ourselves about ourselves."[10] Elements

---

7   T. Collins: "Work, Rest and Play: Recent Trends in the History of Sport and Leisure" in *Journal of Contemporary History*, 42, 397 (2007), p. 399.

8   Compare D. Posel: "Social History and the Wits History Workshop" in *African Studies*, 69, 1 (2010), p. 30.

9   N. Struna: "Social History and Sport" in J. Coakley and E. Dunning (eds), *Handbook of Sport Studies* (Sage publications, 2000), p. 3. (Electronic version, Accessed 13 September 2011)

10   R. Holt: *Sport and the British: A Modern History* (Oxford University Press, Oxford, 1990), p. 3.

of this sport story can be adapted over time, but its core is likely to show remarkable durability. In this respect it differs from formal political discourses which are more vulnerable and exposed; a change in political regime usually renders the legitimising disquisitions of the earlier incumbents suspect if not completely obsolete. Understandings of sport, though, partly because they are not primarily perceived to be in the political frontline, have a longer shelf life. Standard nationalistic interpretations of Afrikaner political history, for example, have withered away since the advent of the African National Congress in 1994, but in rugby the story of the fame and glory of the Springboks and their grounding in Afrikaner historical memory has carried on largely uninterrupted.

Rugby has had a firm grip on the imagination of many an Afrikaner. A former Springbok rugby captain, Wynand Claassen, has evocatively captured the pervasive influence of the game: "Rugby holds a special fascination in South Africa. In every little town, at every little school, a rugby field can be found, and the goalposts alongside a corrugated iron pavilion are just as familiar as the church towers in these towns."[11] It is this allure that has sparked the cluster of questions in this book relating to the history of the game in Afrikaner circles. These questions concern the way in which rugby has come to assume pride of place in Afrikaner popular culture; the nature of the "deep play" between rugby and Afrikaner nationalism; the connecting tissues between the game and a specific assertion of masculinity; responses to the sporting boycott under apartheid; the euphoria that accompanied the Springbok victory during the World Cup tournament in 1995; and the impact of the professionalisation of the game on its politics and supporters since 1995.

But the book is about more than rugby. In the 1930s and 1940s a sport like dog racing, now largely forgotten, held many Afrikaners in the working class and poorer suburbs in thrall. The fate of this sport and the way in which it was dispelled from the cultural landscape bear testimony to the central thrust of the overall analysis pertaining to the interconnectedness of the Afrikaner political project and what was regarded as appropriate leisure practices. While dog racing disappeared, other leisure pursuits were foregrounded, such as the de-

---

11   W. Claassen: "Is it Worth Being a Springbok?" *Rugby*, 15, 2, 5 (1992), p. 4.

velopment of an Afrikaner seaside holiday resort at Hartenbos in the southwestern Cape. This exposition examines the processes through which Hartenbos was established in 1936 and imbued with a specific form of Afrikaner culture. The successful outcome of this endeavour entailed the navigation of ideological rapids to ensure that Afrikaner leisure time was spent in safe nationalistic waters. At the other end of the spectrum is cricket. Afrikaners were relatively late entrants to the game during the final four decades of the twentieth century and the *leitmotif* of the book also finds expression in an attempt to analyse the forces which deterred as well as attracted Afrikaners to the game.

Finally, one needs to reflect briefly on how historical writing on Afrikaners can be approached nineteen years after the National Party government has surrendered. As noted, grandiose ethnocentric versions dealing with the political past, which at one point historically fed into nationalist ideology, were well eroded even before 1994. While a certain sense of nostalgia in the public sphere, linked to remembrances of experiences when Afrikaner power seemed unassailable may well emerge intermittently, there is a strong general consensus that formal state power has been irrevocably lost and that the underlying historical ideology has been severely compromised. The corollary of this is that the further Afrikaner memory in the present recedes and becomes detached from the formal notions of power which had held sway under an earlier generation, the greater the chances that interest in and association with "softer" versions of power as expressed through sport – which as we have suggested has better long-term memory potential for the rank and file than politics *per se* – and other forms of cultural expression such as music may become apparent.

Hermann Giliomee, one of South Africa's most prolific historians who has written extensively on the Afrikaners, is of the opinion that despite the negative impulses mainly related to apartheid coursing through Afrikaner history, there remains much of worth to be rediscovered and reconsidered.[12] In this respect it may be helpful to turn one's gaze slightly away from the structured realm of formal politics

---

12 H. Giliomee: "Die Soeke na 'n Sinvolle Afrikaanse Verlede" in J. Tempelhoff (ed.), *Historical consciousness and the future of the past* (Kleio Publishers, Vanderbijlpark, 2003), p. 40.

to the processes which helped to shape a specific social and cultural world of sport and leisure in which Afrikaners asserted themselves in various ways. These manifestations, although they cannot always claim to be redemptive in nature, were, as will become clear, potent pastimes indeed.

Writing this kind of history is a tight-rope act. It involves constant mediation between a set of knowledges emanating from within the group and carrying their imprint, and a more clinical detachment enabling the material to be refracted through an acceptable academic frame. Welding these elements into as near as possible seamless whole has been one of the challenges in producing this book.

1
Dogs, *dominees* and the Afrikaner working class: Cultural politics of greyhound racing on the Rand, 1932-1949

One of the central threads of Afrikaner social history is that of urbanisation. It was a rapid process: from about 3% in 1890 to 50% in 1936.[13] The transition from the slow pace of the "platteland" to the cauldron of city life called for substantial adaptations, especially as many ill-educated arrivals entered the labour market on the lower rungs, that is to say if they could find work at all. The needs of daily survival and the demands of coping in a new melting-pot environment had the potential of eroding ethnic identity. Afrikaner middle-class cultural entrepreneurs such as ministers of religion, teachers and others were alert to this possibility and the political importance of preventing de-ethnicisation. "If the Afrikaner," it was argued in church circles, "first start thinking, feeling and acting like an urban dweller, then his whole outlook on life is compromised, then he becomes a replica, a caricature of the foreigner."[14]

The project of Afrikaner political mobilisation during the 1930s and 1940s has been amply documented, but accounts tend to focus on formal politics or the blandishments of nationalist politicians and their cultural counterparts which often cast the experience of recently urbanised Afrikaners in terms which deny them agency. A

---

13 H. Giliomee: *The Afrikaners: Biography of a People* (University of Virginia Press, Virginia, 2003), p. 323.
14 J.R. Albertyn (et al.): *Kerk en Stad: Verslag van Kommissie van Ondersoek oor Stadstoestande* (Pro Ecclesia, Stellenbosch, 1948), p. 218. (Translation)

contemporary church commission emphatically sketched the lot of the newly urbanised Afrikaner:

> He was looked down upon, he had to come with his hat in hand, and he had to be satisfied with the crumbs which fell from the tables of the rich. To make any sort of progress, however little, he had to beg the English oppressor and had to obey his every command. Any job that was offered him, however humiliating, dangerous and lowly paid it might have been, he had to accept with gratitude. He and his family had to be satisfied with the worst living conditions in the dirty ghettoes. The door to well-paid occupations was firmly closed. His erstwhile independence was reduced to humiliating servitude and bondage.[15]

While this was not necessarily misleading in factual terms, underlying this discourse was the impulse of having to "rescue" such helpless souls for the *volk*. The newly arrived proletariat, as will become apparent, in some respects carved out a social world and constructed a cultural map of the city which bear testimony to their adaptability. Poor as they were, or more accurately precisely because they were poor, they incorporated those cultural dimensions of the city, such as dog racing, which they perceived to be enabling in a new environment.

The world of greyhound racing which attracted many Afrikaners is a vanished subculture today, despite the fact that the "new" South Africa has embraced gambling with gusto, but does provide us with a glimpse of wider social processes. It is then through the lens of leisure that we seek to understand more of the interface between class and emerging Afrikaner cultural nationalism on the Rand.

Origins, diffusion and control of dog racing

In its elementary form, dog racing as practised in Britain can be traced back to the 1830s. Particularly in the northwest of England, what was known as 'coursing' was a regular pastime. 'Coursing' involved the release of a hare in an open field to be set upon by a pack of greyhounds after the hare had made some 50 yards. This was accompanied by betting which dog would first devour the unfortunate hare. Rather perversely it carried genteel associations as it was likened to fox hunting.

---

15 Albertyn (et al.): *Kerk en Stad*, pp. 216–217. (Translation)

Working classes adapted the activity and gave it even more of an edge as rabbits were used as bait in a confined space with whippets leading the charge. Anti-animal cruelty organisations claimed that in addition to the ordeal of rabbits when caught, so-called referees were also known to poke out a rabbit's eye in order to blind it and force it towards the side of the dog the bookmaker wished to win. On one occasion it was alleged that during a ten-day rabbit 'coursing' meeting near Liverpool, 128 dogs claimed 700 rabbits.[16] With the need to adapt the leisure activity to increasingly cramped urban conditions and in the face of anti-cruelty criticism, the use of artificial bait became more common. The period after the First World War saw the building of floodlit stadiums and the introduction of the mechanical hare from America.

The end of the First World War proved to be a boom period in the popularity of dog racing in the United Kingdom. The general sense of psychological release after the Armistice fuelled a need for entertainment, and the war spawned more of a devil-may-care attitude than before which fed into gambling. In addition, workers had more leisure time at their disposal as weekly working hours dropped from 65 to 48 and they also earned more as real wages increased by 20 per cent. Whereas horse racing was seen as the sport of kings, dog racing was regarded as a working man's sport. Unlike horse racing which usually took place outside the city limits, charged relatively high entrance fees and demanded a certain dress code, dog-racing tracks were more conveniently accessible in urban areas, fairly cheap to attend in any kind of attire, and allowed for bets in a variety of small denominations. Five or more 30 second races at nearby tracks provided short, intensive thrills and an attractive diversion for many working-class people.[17]

Even the worldwide depression of 1929–1933 failed to dent the popularity of dog racing. On the contrary, the pastime seemed to have benefited from the deep slump as desperate punters sought to improve their financial circumstances through gambling. The attendance at licensed tracks in the United Kingdom increased from about

---

16   M. Clapton: *A Bit of a Flutter: Popular Gambling and English Society, c 1823–1961* (Routledge, London, 1998), pp. 138–43.
17   Clapton: *A Bit of a Flutter*, p. 144.

6,5 million in 1928 to nine million in 1932.[18] In those hard times, a keen follower of the dogs has recollected years later, "dog racing sang its siren song to the working man and helplessly he followed".[19] For many it was also a night out in a festive atmosphere. One enthusiast commented: "The brilliantly lit track stood out sharply from the surrounding darkness, in which the seething crowds of excited people could hardly be distinguished. It was reminiscent of a fête in some continental city, for rarely is such an all-pervading spirit of enjoyment found in sober England".[20]

Given the upsurge of interest it was an appropriate time for the industry to expand to other areas of the empire, and the Witwatersrand – the industrial heartland of South Africa – appeared an attractive option. The first official licence for dog racing and betting was granted to the African Greyhound Racing Association in 1932, followed by the Union Greyhound Racing Association and the East Rand Greyhound Racing Association. In time the Union Association proved to be the strongest of these companies. Tracks were built at the Wanderers, Wembley and Dunswart on the East Rand. The managers of these tracks came from Britain and the organisation of the races, not surprisingly, was largely patterned on the British model. Meetings usually took place on Friday evenings – deliberately timed to coincide with the weekly payment of working men's wages. It was a lucrative industry. Between 7000 and 10 000 people attended the weekly races at the Wanderers and the average profits were between 24 503 and 31 525 pounds per week in 1941. Those who had bought shares in the Union Association in 1932 would have seen their 10 pounds share climb to 180 pounds in 1940.[21]

Organised dog racing came to South Africa under a cloud. It carried with it the reputation it had gained in the United Kingdom as

---

18 S.G. Jones: *Workers at Play: Social and Economic History of Leisure, 1918–1939* (Routledge & Kegan Paul PLC, London, 1986), p. 38.
19 L. Thompson: *The Dogs: A Personal History of Greyhound Racing* (Summersdale Publishers, London, 1993), p. 18.
20 F.C. Clarke: *Greyhounds and Greyhound Racing: A Comprehensive and Popular Survey of Britain's Latest Sport* (London,1934), p. 22.
21 E.L.P. Stals: *Die Geskiedenis van die Afrikaner aan die Witwatersrand, 1924–1961* (Pretoria, 1987), p. 33; "Hondewedrenne", *Die Kerkbode*, March 1940; Transvaal Archives (hereafter TA), C.58 Dog Racing Commission, 1942, evidence of M.H. Coombe, pp. 1835–1836.

a crass and corrupt commercial enterprise. Regardless of the validity of such claims, it was a difficult image to shed. As late as the 1950s, when dog racing had already entrenched itself as a pastime with a huge following in Britain, considerable antipathy remained. The British Broadcasting Corporation (BBC) had strong reservations about broadcasting race meetings as the sport was considered to bear an "anti-social character", was not "a desirable or sociologically useful sport", and to give exposure to such an activity "would lower BBC standards".[22] Barely concealed class prejudices clearly entered the equation. Nevertheless, it was early on deemed necessary by the dog-racing fraternity in Britain to introduce an independent Board of Control to try and stamp out possible illegal practices. Members of the Board assumed overall control for what happened on the race tracks and in the betting halls, and they also had to ensure that each race was fairly graded and that all the dogs in one race had an equal chance of winning. Such officials, working in an environment where money could easily change hands, had to be irreproachable and above suspicion of bribery. Indeed they were "expected to have the morals of saints, and the willpower of a mule that refuses to step aside, in order that the public could have a square deal".[23]

In South Africa such checks and balances were not in place. Overall control of race meetings and procedures at the tracks rest squarely with the two race managers, F.C. Meeser of the African Association and R.H. Haswell of the Union Association. They received their authority from companies which had to report to their shareholders. Despite opposition to the sport and although it was a system more open to abuse than in Britain, it was never proven that race managers acted improperly in the years that dog racing existed in South Africa.[24]

It is true though that the public had no real way of ascertaining the validity of what happened on the track. As one critic of dog racing explained:

---

22 G. Whannel: *Fields in Vision: Television Sport and Cultural Transformation* (London, 1992), p. 18.
23 A.S. Baker: *Greyhound Racing with the "Lid Off"* (Routledge, London, 1953), p. 3.
24 TA, C 58 Dog Racing Commission, 1942, evidence of M.H. Coombe, 1836. Haswell later became the doyen of South African boxing promoters. *Beeld*, 28 February 1995.

> Six greyhounds are paraded before a race. All may be brindle, or they may be mixed colours. I would say, at a conservative estimate, that not more than one per cent of the public know, except by reference to the race-card ... whether the greyhound in the striped jacket is Plug Ugly, Our John, Silly Point or Masked, to name a few top-class greyhounds at the tracks, or whether they are in racing parlance, 'ringers'. And I would stress this firmly that the public has no means of finding out, under present conditions that all is as it should be. The public goes along, pay their money, and take what is offered them in the manner of the boy who shuts his eyes, opens his mouth and waits hopefully.[25]

However, such reservations did not act as a deterrent for enthusiastic betting on the dogs. While on-course betting was legal, off-course betting was not. Off-course betting nevertheless took place on a huge scale and it was estimated that 14 000 agencies for such betting, also known as bucket shops, existed on the Reef in 1940. These were usually run by Greek café owners or Chinese, Indian and African storekeepers. They employed runners who were assigned to collect bets in African townships, poor white neighbourhoods and industrial centres. This system allowed those who were too poor to attend the races in person, to participate in the betting. The owners of the bucket shop profited by taking their share of the bet off the top.[26]

Bucket shop betting had the potential to fleece unsuspecting gamblers even more than those who placed their bets personally at the races. The fact that it was illegal and that bucket shop owners ran the risk of incurring a heavy fine, seemed to have had little effect on the practice. Also, as in the case of on-course betting, the public did not appear to have been unduly concerned by loopholes in the system. To some degree, tolerance of possible chicanery had its own logic. It was a face-saving device for those gamblers who invested considerable pride in their much-vaunted ability to pick winners; if the opposite happened, failure could be explained as a result of crookedness. "Men plug the dikes of their most needed beliefs with whatever mud they can find," the anthropologist, Clifford Geertz, has noted.[27]

---

25 TA, C.58 Dog Racing Commission, 1942, evidence of M.H. Coombe, p. 1837.
26 TA, C.58 Dog Racing Commission, 1942, evidence of A. Quenet, p. 3460 and evidence of D.N. Murray, p. 200.
27 C. Geertz: *Local Knowledge: Further Essays in Interpretative Anthropology* (New York, 1983), p. 80. Information on public responses to bucket shop system from M.C. Edmonds who worked for a bucket shop owner in 1945, interview in Pretoria, 25 July 2000.

Explaining the attraction

The expression "gone to the dogs," which emanates from dog racing has become deeply embedded in the English language and carries strong overtones of moral and financial ruination. However, the expression is less than useful in trying to explain why people actually did go to the dogs. In order to account for the appeal of dog racing, one has to disaggregate the crowds at race meetings and also analyse the wider social purpose of dog racing in the community.

A small minority was interested in the event as such. They delighted in the grace and pace of well-trained animals which they regarded as "one of the most beautiful sights". Apart from the aesthetic enjoyment, they also marvelled at the "excitement and emotion that could be compressed into less than a minute".[28] Race meetings indeed created an atmosphere of heady anticipation. None other than Leslie Blackwell, member of parliament, described it as "an extremely pleasant way of passing an evening – and if you want an evening's amusement with plenty of colour and life you cannot get it more pleasantly than at such a meeting".[29]

Betting, of course, was the main reason for such animation. "It created a love of excitement and a false idea that wealth can easily be won in this way," one critic explained. As the evening wore on, some of these expectations evaporated and for the majority who had lost money on the dogs "the atmosphere is rather one in which the predominant note is one of disgust and disappointment".[30] But central to the gambling culture was the prospect that the losses of one week could be recouped the following week. The disappointment was therefore seldom enduring and each Friday came ripe with the renewed hope of a major win.[31]

Dog racing attracted a variety of gamblers. "At the Wanderers alone," an observer commented, "there are some 7000 patrons, young and old, some with money to burn, some who cannot afford to gamble, some wary and well-balanced, some unstable and immature."[32] In broad terms, the gambling fraternity at the races can be divided into four categories. First, and in the minority, were the

---

28 Clarke: *Greyhounds and Greyhound Racing*, p. 23.
29 *House of Assembly Debates*, 1 Mar. 1940, par. 2646.
30 TA, C.58 Dog Racing Commission, 1942, evidence of D.N. Murray, pp. 22, 24.
31 TA, C.58 Dog Racing Commission, 1942, evidence of A. Quenet, p. 3466.
32 TA, C.58 Dog Racing Commission, 1942, evidence of A. Quenet, p. 3466.

professional gamblers for whom gambling was work. They had an in-depth knowledge of all aspects pertaining to the game and only placed their bets within fixed limits, based upon carefully calculated permutations. Next were the semi-professionals who kept their regular employment, but also studied the form of the dogs assiduously and were more inclined to bet fairly substantial sums. Third came the sporting type, who regarded the tracks as a hobby and attended regularly, but did not bet too much. Not too far removed from this group were the casual racegoers in groups of families or friends who attended occasionally, for a bit of flutter or the night out. Then, in the majority, was the rowdy band of proletarian gamblers for whom the outcome of the race meant much more as it could have a significant effect on their available cash.[33] This group comprised mainly elements of the white working class of the Witwatersrand who earned at most three pounds a week and could easily lose a third or more of that at the races, or in the unlikely event of a win, could boost their finances substantially.

Dog racing had its most dedicated followers in areas such as Booysens, Fordsburg, Mayfair and Braamfontein, and in particular Vrededorp. Many of these residents were recently or fairly recently urbanised Afrikaners. What is remarkable is the extent to which dog racing pervaded the everyday lives of these communities. An Afrikaner social worker in Vrededorp found that although there was a reluctance on the part of individuals to talk about dog racing to outsiders, this leisure pursuit was well established. She explained:

> The neighbours were only too willing to give information about gambling and the whole neighbourhood knows exactly who attends dog races. I was absolutely amazed to find to what a large scale dog racing is participated in and what a real knowledge 99% of the residents have of the "sport".[34]

Similarly, Ben Schoeman, National Party member of parliament for Vrededorp and later a prominent member of the cabinet, testified in 1942 that "he invariably found that the one subject which all could discuss, and in respect of which they knew every detail, was dog

---

33 Compare Clapton: *A Bit of a Flutter*, 149; TA, C.58 Dog Racing Commission, 1942, evidence of D.N. Murray 21. Interview with M.C. Edmonds, Pretoria, 25 July 2000.
34 TA, C.58 Dog Racing Commission, 1942, evidence of J. Terburgh, p. 1511.

racing".[35] It was even a lively topic of discussion at schools where on Monday mornings those youngsters whose fathers were fortunate enough to have won on Friday night could boast to their friends about the *gelukkie wat Pappie gehad het* ("the piece of good luck Daddy had").[36] Winning dogs became household names: "Jack the Giant Killer" and "Last Hope" evocatively expressed the wishes and yearnings of those who placed bets on them.

Enthusiasm for dog racing cut across gender divides. From the East Rand it was reported that an army depot that employed a number of women in clerical positions came to a standstill on Fridays: "Wherever you go, whichever office you go into, it is nothing else but dog racing and sweeps."[37] Wartime anxieties, with many male breadwinners away on active service, contributed to a need for psychological release, which some women found at the races. In Vrededorp the participation of women in gambling was a matter of particular concern for a social worker who argued: "that when gambling takes hold on a woman, she loses her equilibrium more easily that the man and goes as far as to sell the kitchen utensils in order to obtain money to bet".[38]

Moving away from such stereotypes and into a broader social analysis of working-class women's involvement in gambling, it is instructive to look at the popularity of bingo in the United Kingdom. It can be argued that the attraction of bingo was similar to that of dog racing. Bingo, it has been explained,

> is played by those in the least powerful positions in British society. In one sense the game parodies the socio-economic situation in which many players found themselves, in their lack of economic power and reliance on luck or patronage. It clearly demonstrates who is controlled and who is controlling. However, it can also be seen that working-class women have taken the opportunity to fashion this activity in positive ways which suit them, and which offer some recreation for themselves, with the constraints which restrict their leisure options.[39]

---

35 TA, C.58 Dog Racing Commission, 1942, evidence of B. Schoeman, p. 467.
36 TA, C.58 Dog Racing Commission, 1942, evidence of J.F. du Toit, p. 947.
37 TA, C.58 Dog Racing Commission, 1942, evidence of G.D. Kotze, p. 1577.
38 TA, C.58 Dog Racing Commission, 1942, evidence of J .Terburgh, p. 1511.
39 R. Dixey: "Bingo in Britain: An Analysis of Gender and Class", in J.C. McMillan, *Gambling Cultures: Studies in History and Interpretation* (Routledge, London, 1996), p. 147.

The contradictions inherent in the gambling culture shed light on the underlying dynamics which propelled women to the race tracks, despite the real risks of inflicting greater hardship.[40]

The brief excitement of dog racing on Friday nights also helped some working-class men to offset the tedium and monotony of a menial job during the week.[41] But it was, of course, more than purely recreational; the primary concern was to improve their financial position. Although it was an extremely risky way of spending hard-earned cash, it was not entirely reckless and unthinking behaviour. There was a certain logic as to why the urban poor regularly wound their way to the tracks.

Gambling made more sense than saving; a small and often irregular income did not encourage prudence and the anticipation of a better future. Saving at best implied delayed gratification, if at all, and vague promises of a better future which many could hardly begin to imagine. Gambling at least had the immediate potential and the promise, however illusionary, of enhancing their financial circumstances. Given this context, it can even appear as a rational act. For many it was "the only possibility of actually making a decision, of a choice between two alternatives, in a life otherwise prescribed in every detail by poverty and necessity". Betting generated its own patterns of serious reflection, as one spent "one's time in discussion, analysis and decision making with a seeming sense of purpose" and possible achievement.[42] Regardless of one's losses, betting on the dogs provided a fleeting sense of control and importance.

Dog racing and the politics of leisure time

Dog racing gained its hold on impoverished Afrikaner communities during a period of increased urbanisation. Mainly as a result of the Great Depression of the early 1930s, 6500 Afrikaners on average annually found their way to the Witwatersrand between 1926 and 1936. The trek to the Rand was further fuelled by wartime industrialisation, which opened up greater employment opportunities. In the

---

40 Compare, for example, Dutch Reformed Church (hereafter DRC) Archives, Pretoria, Synod Documents, p. 178, Selected Testimonies of Women on the Financial Implications of Betting on the Dogs, 1943.
41 TA, C.58 Dog Racing Commission, 1942, evidence of B. Schoeman, p. 2631.
42 Compare R. McKibbin: "Working Class Gambling in Britain, 1880–1939", *Past and Present*, 82 (1979), pp. 169–70.

late 1940s Afrikaners constituted almost 36% of the white inhabitants of Johannesburg.[43]

While the transition from the countryside to the city was undoubtedly a painful one, particularly given the low level of skills of those who sought to enter the job market, the Afrikaner working class was not entirely hapless victims of forces beyond their control. They might have found it difficult to cope with a demanding work environment, but they had a well-developed sense of possible benefits that city life could offer. Impoverished whites are on record as telling welfare officers: "Why should we not come to Johannesburg? Look at what we are offered. Johannesburg has free hospitals, homes for babies, school clinics and a chance to bring children to be educated, physically treated and get a good many things free."[44] Certainly, in the area of leisure as we have noted, the alacrity with which they supported dog racing creates the impression, contrary to the general belief, that they blended in very well with the new urban social landscape.

However, the enthusiasm displayed for dog racing did not meet with the approval of the emergent Afrikaner middle-class cultural entrepreneurs who, during the 1930s and 1940s, played such a major role in ethnic mobilisation. This class, consisting of clergy, university lecturers, social workers and other professionals, regarded themselves as the interpreters (and manufacturers) of Afrikaner culture and its endeavours found expression in a number of organisations. Cultural politics became an increasingly important area where discourses around notions of the *volk*, a legitimising "sacred history" and appropriately sober mores and conduct were deftly woven into the fabric of an overarching Afrikaner ideology.[45] This also included the way in which leisure time was spent.

---

43 E.L.P. Stals: *Die Geskiedenis van die Afrikaner in die Goudstad* (HAUM, Johannesburg, 1986), pp. 10–11; J.R. Albertyn (et al.): *Kerk en Stad* (Johannesburg, 1965), p. 51.

44 Quoted in E. Brink, "'Maar 'n Klomp Factory Meide': Afrikaner Family and Community on the Witwatersrand during the 1920s", in B. Bozzoli, (ed.), *Class, Community and Conflict: South African Perspectives* (Ravan Press, Johannesburg, 1987), p. 183.

45 D. O'Meara: *Volkskapitalisme: Class, Capital and Ideology in the Development of Afrikaner Nationalism, 1934–1948* (Cambridge University Press, Cambridge, 1983), pp. 55–56; H. Adam and H. Giliomee: *The Rise and Crisis of Afrikaner Power* (D. Philip, Cape Town, 1979), pp. 112–114; I. Hofmeyr: "'Building a Nation from Words': Afrikaans Language, Literature and Ethnic Identity, 1902–1924", in S. Marks and S. Trapido, (eds), *The Politics of Race, Class and Nationalism in Twentieth Century South Africa* (Addison-Wesley Longman Ltd, London, 1987), pp. 95–123.

It was the clergy in particular who singled dog racing out as a manifestation of what they regarded as the moral decay that followed in the wake of Afrikaner urbanisation. Annual church synods did not hesitate to make this clear.[46] There was little doubt in the mind of Reverend William Nicol of Johannesburg, prominent in church and cultural circles, that what he regarded as "the moral and spiritual deterioration of the Afrikaner people was to a large extent attributable to dog races".[47] On religious grounds Afrikaner clergy were opposed to gambling as it was seen to undermine the Biblical injunction of having to "earn one's bread by the sweat of one's brow"; diligence as opposed to chance was the prescribed way to try and alter one's circumstances.[48] Gambling was simply incompatible with a pious lifestyle.

However, in publicly voicing their opposition against dog racing, Afrikaans clergy shied away from using explicit religious arguments. They preferred the charge that betting encouraged working-class people to fritter away their money and that it gave rise to a variety of domestic problems. While betting on the dogs undoubtedly contributed to greater poverty and dissolute behaviour in some individual cases, it is problematic to single out dog racing as the sole variable that impacted negatively on working-class lives. Nevertheless, it was the stock-in trade of clergymen opposed to dog racing. A comprehensive inquiry into dog racing was launched in Johannesburg in 1942 and after more than 4000 pages of evidence, the commissioner, E. Beardmore, had this to say on the submissions made by ministers of religion:

> [S]peaking broadly they had no accurate knowledge of the extent of the social evils of betting on the dogs among their own people, or among the general public, and their evidence against dog racing was based rather on ethical ... grounds. It was in keeping with this attitude of mind that one expressed the view that one single case of social evil attributable to dog racing would, in his opinion, justify the closing of the tracks.[49]

---

46 DRC Archives, General Synod Minutes, 1942; Albertyn (et al.), *Kerk en Stad*, p. 327.
47 Quoted by B. Schoeman in *House of Assembly Debates*, 1 March 1940, par. 2630.
48 D. du Preez: "Die Calvinistiese Beskouing van Arbeid", *Koers*, 14, 2 (Oct. 1946), p. 53.
49 TA, C.58, Dog Racing Commission Report, 1944, p. 15.

It was not a preoccupation peculiar to Afrikaner clergymen. Ross McKibbin, writing on working-class gambling in Britain between 1880 and 1939, pertinently observed that Protestant churches were quick to make extravagant claims: "... families pauperised, industries ruined, a class corrupted – even an empire lost. Why was this?" According to him the Protestant clergy "had a vocational interest in the perpetuation of sin" and if it "could be demonstrated that gambling had *material* consequences as well as spiritual, so much the better."[50]

Afrikaner clergymen might also have exaggerated the "evils" of dog racing, but their motives for doing so cannot readily be connected with the notion of the professional proclamation of sin being in their own narrow vocational interest. In their case, and also among other Afrikaner leaders, opposition to dog racing and invoking it as "a social evil", related more directly to their conception of what constituted acceptable Afrikaner culture. At the time it was a culture that expressed itself in anti-British sentiments, a certain rootedness in Afrikaner constructions of history and what was termed the *volkseie* (that which belonged to the *volk*).[51] It took various, but related forms: the near euphoric centenary celebrations of the Great Trek in 1938, the production of historical plays, the growth of Afrikaner youth movements, an outpouring of Afrikaner literature and the popularisation of *volkspele* (traditional folk dancing). Ultimately it involved the redefinition of Afrikanerdom along specific lines. Consequently, as far as leisure time was concerned, it was argued that "one cannot hope to educate a *volk* unless one is able to control and ensure that its entertainment is soundly based".[52]

The strategy of such entrepreneurs involved more than just promoting what they considered to be Afrikaner culture; it also implied that possible rival forms had to be countered. Dr H.F. Verwoerd

---

50 McKibbin: "Working Class Gambling in Britain", pp. 157–158 (emphasis in original).
51 See, for example, A. Grundlingh and H. Sapire: "From Feverish Festival to Repetitive Ritual? The Changing Fortunes of Great Trek Mythology in an Industrialising South Africa, 1938–1988", *South African Historical Journal*, 21 (1989), pp. 19–27.
52 University of the Free State Library, Archives of the Federasie van Afrikaanse Kultuurvereniginge, PV 202/iv/6/13/1/1/1, "Die Afrikaner se Vryetydsbesteding, 1942". (Translation)

The stylised "ideal" Afrikaner man. This cartoon appeared in *Die Transvaler* on 19 August 1938 under the caption "Back to the past". At the time many Afrikaners were under the spell of the 1938 Great Trek Centenary. Dog racing was clearly one of the pursuits to be avoided as it did not fit into a scenario predicated upon a specific reading of the past. *(Courtesy Willemien Froneman)*

who moved to Johannesburg in 1937 as an Afrikaans newspaper editor, viewed the matter seriously and argued that the threat to the Afrikaner was that "in urbanising he would undergo a process of proletarianisation in which he would lose all interest in Afrikaner culture and become merely an international worker".[53] In the process of constructing and homogenising Afrikaner nationalist culture, the popularity of dog racing with its army of impoverished Afrikaner supporters posed a problem. The British overtones and proletarian appeal of dog racing did not quite fit, nor could it be made to fit, the new cultural design in the making.

In the wider context of the powerful Afrikaner cultural drive during this period which in part contributed to victory at the polls in 1948, the very success and apparent unity of purpose, tend to obscure underlying fissures in the process of creating what was considered a suitable Afrikaner culture. Even during the 1938 Great Trek centenary celebrations which over time have come to assume iconic status as a prime example of Afrikaner unity, there were underlying tensions as to what should be considered suitable Afrikaner culture.

---

53 Quoted in G.D. Scholtz: *Hendrik Verwoerd*, (Perskor, Johannesburg, 1974), p. 90. (Translation)

The differences centred on *boeremusiek*, a musical genre later to be closely associated with Afrikanerdom, but at the time of the Great Trek commemorations was deemed by some of the middle-class Trek leaders as too frivolous and brash to match the solemnity of the occasion.[54]

In Johannesburg the Afrikaner poor did not necessarily share the same cultural concerns as their middle-class compatriots, and it was precisely this development that perturbed leaders such as Verwoerd. This concern linked up and found expression in the exponential growth of social work amongst the Afrikaner poor on the Rand.[55] Social work at the time, much heralded for its rehabilitative aims, was not ideological neutral and for Verwoerd, the founding father of the academic discipline at the University of Stellenbosch, it was an integral part of a larger political project.[56]

Politically a suburb like Vrededorp, one of the epicentres of the dog-racing culture, had a long and chequered history of entertaining Afrikaner nationalist politicians without being seduced by them. Writing on the period punctuated by strikes between 1906 and 1914, the historian Charles van Onselen has noted that in "their restless search for political direction the unskilled workers of Vrededorp demonstrated not only aggressive working-class consciousness but also considerable acumen..."[57] In succeeding years, identity politics in areas such as Vrededorp and other impoverished Afrikaner communities on the Reef continued to be shaped by the ebb of local conditions and the flow of wider nationalist forces.[58]

---

54 W. Froneman: "'Pleasure Beyond the Call of Duty.' Perspectives, Retrospectives and Speculations on Boeremusiek" (D.Phil thesis, Stellenbosch University, 2012), pp. 22–23. On these commemorations see also A. Grundlingh and H. Sapire: "From Feverish Festival to Repetitive Ritual? The Changing Fortunes of Great Trek Mythology in Industrialising South Africa", in *South African Historical Journal*, 21 (1989), pp. 19–27.
55 A.P. Smit: *Ons Kerk in die Goudstad, 1887–1947* (Nasionale Pers, Kaapstad), p. 471.
56 J.A. Tayler: "With her Shoulder to the Wheel: The Public Life of Erika Theron, 1900–1907" (D.Litt Phil thesis, University of South Africa, 2010), pp. 98–110.
57 C. van Onselen: *New Babylon, New Nineveh: Studies in the Social and Economic History of the Witwatersrand, 1886–1914*, vol. 2 (Longman, London, 1982), p. 161.
58 Compare L. Lange, "The Making of the White Working-Class: Class Experience and Class Identity in Johannesburg, 1890–1922" (D.Phil thesis, University of the Witwatersrand, 1998), pp.163–259.

The fluidity of these communities made it difficult for nationalists to establish stable moorings. Members of the Afrikaner middle classes were increasingly aware of a growing social divide between them and the working classes. In 1946 a church newspaper reported as a matter of concern that

> it is not easy to organise social interaction, exchange of ideas and unified action between the wealthier members of the *volk* and the poor. A fair measure of mutual trust between our social classes has already disappeared. We find among our lowly paid workers ... in the cities, doubts as to the intentions of their fellow Afrikaners when deliberate attempts are made to lend a helping hand.[59]

In this respect the Afrikaner poor displayed a pattern of behaviour which was fairly common among working classes elsewhere. As research on working-class culture and politics in London between 1870 and 1914 has reiterated, well-meaning interventions of the middle classes were not always received with deference and gratitude.[60]

Such class suspicions can be detected in responses to the cultural crusades of clergymen who opposed dog racing. Although first-hand Afrikaner working-class testimony is hard to find,[61] occasional signs of annoyance did surface. One man who had enough of what he regarded as the meddling of a social worker curtly told her that "he was fond of the dogs and it gave him pleasure".[62] The clergy in poorer areas also discovered that some members of their congregation were not too impressed by fire and brimstone sermons on the "evils" of dog racing. One minister of religion testified that if "they preached against dog racing too much there is the section which was inclined to disagree and they felt it was too much a matter of politics and they had to leave it entirely alone".[63]

---

59 *Die Kerkbode*, "Klasseskeiding in ons Volkslewe" (19 June 1946), pp. 797–798. (Translation)
60 A. August: "A Culture of Consolation? Rethinking Politics in Working-Class London, 1870–1914", *Historical Research*, 74, 184, (May 2001), p. 202.
61 Significantly in the more than 4000 pages of official inquiry into dog racing it was not deemed necessary to elicit the opinion of a single person from a working-class background. Clearly, it was seen as a matter which working-class people could not adjudicate.
62 TA, C.58, Dog Racing Commission, 1942, evidence of J. Terburgh, p. 1526.
63 TA, C.58, Dog Racing Commission, 1942, evidence of Rev. A.H. Swartz, p. 2836.

What was at issue here was a pointed rejection of the paternalism that often accompanied welfare and the way in which modes of cultural behaviour were prescribed. The very term "poor white" can in some ways be regarded as problematic in that it did not necessarily express the lived experience of those so categorised. Resentments to the term emerge in an Afrikaans play of the period where a woman described as "poor white" responded:

> I am no "blinking street woman" and also not a "poor white"... It is the "'charities'" and the "distress" and the "Mayor's Fund'" and all those people that want to make "poor whites" of us. My husband said that they are just like doctors who discovered a new illness and now wants everyone to have it.[64]

However, such sentiments did not translate into any organised attempts on the part of the poorer communities to defend their particular cultural pastime. The capacity to oppose the purveyors of all things good and nationalist in a meaningful way was simply absent. Nor perhaps would it have been in their best long-term interest to do so as the interventions of the Afrikaner middle classes can be seen to have had the effect of bringing poor whites back into the fold and positioning them to benefit from the success of the nationalist movement after 1948. But before the dawn of the new age, dog racing was one of those abominable elements that had to be extruded from the social life of working-class Afrikaners.

The demise of dog racing

There was a realisation amongst Afrikaner opponents of dog racing that it would be a long and possibly fruitless attempt to wean the poor off their favourite pastime. Hence, a far bolder strategy had to be followed; the temptation had to be removed completely. The first step in this direction was taken by lobbying for the establishment of a commission to look into the effects of dog racing. This commission held 91 sessions and 116 people testified, which mainly included representatives of various churches, social workers, school principals and members of the police force. As noted earlier, the minutes of the

---

64 Quoted and translated in J. van Wyk: "Nationalist Ideology and Social Concerns in Afrikaans Drama in the Period 1930–1940" (Unpublished paper, History Workshop, 1990), p. 7.

proceedings ran to more than 4000 pages. In its findings the commission steered away from taking a firm stand on the morality of gambling, but did recommend that in order to protect the gambler, stricter controls should be in place and the frequency of meetings should be curtailed, with no races taking place on Fridays when workers were being paid.[65]

The Dutch Reformed Church was not pleased with these recommendations. The recommendations, it argued, actually had the effect of stabilising the industry as more controls were instituted and they allowed dog-racing companies to carry on virtually unhindered with what the church regarded as nefarious practices.[66] Under the leadership of Revs William Nicol and A.M. Meiring the church made its views widely known in the press and also proceeded to gain support for the abolition of dog races from a number of organisations. Eventually the anti-dog-racing lobby consisted of 180 welfare bodies, 25 youth institutions, 10 youth bodies with 18 771 members, 100 school principals as well as the Welfare Department of the Johannesburg City Council.[67]

Significantly, English Protestant churches also joined forces with the Dutch Reformed Church. This co-operation strengthened the campaign considerably. It could now be claimed that churches which differed theologically and politically were prepared to settle their differences for what they regarded as the common good. The alliance alerted the provincial authorities of the breadth of opposition that cut across traditional divides.[68]

The movement against dog racing gained further momentum from a huge public meeting organised jointly by the churches in the Johannesburg City Hall on 4 March 1946. About a 1000 people attended the meeting and adopted a unanimous motion opposing the races. While representatives of the Afrikaans churches rehearsed their familiar arguments against the dogs, English church leaders placed less emphasis on the social ramifications and completely ignored ethnic dimensions. They sought, instead, to underline what they considered the "prevailing un-Christian attitude to life as a whole and more particularly to the stewardship of money and time". The atmosphere

---

65 TA, C.58, Final report of Dog Racing Commission, 1946.
66 *Die Transvaler*, 27 July 1946.
67 *Die Voorligter*, "Afskaffing van Hondewedrenne", July 1947.
68 *Die Voorligter*, "Afskaffing van Hondewedrenne", July 1947.

at the races was considered an ungodly one that reflected a more general malaise:

> The long waits between the races while people make their pathetic pilgrimage to and from the tote cubicles in the hope of collecting other people's money foolishly given in the same hope, the spectacle of thousands of God's children born in his image, yelling, shouting, booing and hissing as these dogs are made to run after a bundle of fur they are never intended to catch – is this not the anatomy of a melancholy 20th century?[69]

With the groundswell of public opinion behind them, a combined church deputation to the United Party administrator, J.J. Pienaar, sought to influence the views of the provincial administration on the matter. However, Pienaar showed some reluctance to act. Uppermost in his mind was a loss of 2% revenue accruing from betting on dog racing and also strong representations made by the dog-racing companies to continue with their operations.[70]

While disappointed with Pienaar's inertia, those opposed to dog racing kept up the pressure by lobbying individual members of the provincial council. Although the National Party was the first to oppose the dogs, increasingly the matter became one that transcended party politics. Within the United Party the question of dog racing was regarded as one that could be potentially damaging if the administration was seen as insensitive to an issue that had been elevated to the level of a pressing moral and social concern. The English-language press, generally supportive of the United Party, advocated that other sources of revenue should be found and that the provincial government should not by default associate itself with what could be regarded as an unsavoury business. The administration had to ask themselves:

> Is it ... any use a government maintaining the pleasant fiction that it is deeply concerned over the moral and social upliftment of the citizen when, all the time, it is casting lots with the other actors in the drama for the clothes of the unhappy victim?[71]

---

69 *The Star*, 11 May 1946.
70 *Die Transvaler*, 14 Mar. 1946; *Die Vaderland*, 16 May 1947; DRC Archives, Pretoria, "Ring van Johannesburg: Memorandum in Sake Hondewedrenne", 30 August 1946.
71 *The Star*, 7 January 1947.

Eventually it was a mix of such sensibilities and political pragmatism that prevailed. On 5 June 1947 the caucus of the United Party provincial council decided to abolish dog racing. A two-year period of grace was allowed for the companies to wound down their affairs, which meant that dog racing was only officially terminated in 1949.[72]

Conclusion

The demise of dog racing contains certain ironies. At one level it can be viewed as a cultural victory for the Afrikaner middle classes, but one that did not necessarily carry the blessing of those on whose behalf the struggle was won. Furthermore, although the dog racing companies undoubtedly exploited the poor, it was a form of exploitation which the working class for a particular set of reasons willingly participated in.

From the perspective of the environmentally conscious world of today, an additional irony emerges that during the long drawn-out campaign against dog racing a range of objections was proffered, but the question of cruelty to animals did not emerge once. The issue at the time was cultural identity and control over leisure time. In this contest the dogs themselves never featured. Ultimately, however, the role which the racing dogs played in human society emphasised certain hidden social dimensions.

Using dog racing as a prism has allowed one to access a particular manifestation of white working-class popular culture on the Witwatersrand. Glimpses of a vanished world appear, opening an aperture to reflect from a different angle on how some poor Afrikaners adapted to the urban environment and how cultural politics were conducted with a view to corral deviants into the nationalist fold.

This should not be seen in isolation. It was during this period that Hartenbos in the Southwestern Cape was to be established as an Afrikaner resort and in the attempts to infuse Afrikaner leisure time with what was considered suitable mores, much the same political and social concerns that helped to shape the dog-racing debate on the Rand became apparent, albeit with another outcome in mind.

---

72 Unisa, United Party Archives, Transvaal Provincial Council minutes of caucus meeting, 5 June 1947.

2
Holidays at Hartenbos: Sand, sea and sun in the construction of Afrikaner cultural nationalism, c 1930–c 1961

The representation of beaches, either in the media or by those who frequent them, can conjure up a number of related qualities. "A day at the English beach," it has been said, "is a particularly notable experience, full of rituals, symbolism, nostalgia and myths." These "special meanings" in turn "create experiences which have life-long echoes".[73] It is how these meanings are constructed that concerns us here. They may be completely private or they can have a wider significance.

In the case of South Africa, imaginings of Hartenbos beach resort on the Southwestern Cape coast were to be infused by a specific ethnic load. This chapter focuses on those processes that imbued Hartenbos with a sense of being an "Afrikaner resort". The enquiry proceeds from the assumption that cultural nationalism is essentially a social construct. This does not deny that it can have a "lived genuineness" with real-life consequences for many, but it still remains a product that needs to be manufactured and marketed before it can lay claims to presumed authenticity. There is a general consensus amongst theorists that cultural nationalism as a construction is most

---

73 S.M. Tunstall and E.C. Penning-Rowsell: "The English Beach: Experience and Values", *The Geographical Journal*, 164, 3 (November 1998), p. 319; see also J.K. Walton: *The English Seaside Resort: A Social History, 1750–1914* (Longman, London, 1983).

likely to emerge and can be at its most potent when collectivities experience fundamental ruptures over time and there is a perceived need to invent a new present and future by drawing inspiration from a selectively chosen and imaginatively deployed past.[74]

Within this broadly defined framework the following issues as they relate to Hartenbos are examined: the contextual conditions which gave birth to a beach resort that came to assume a specific Afrikaner character; the way in which the resort was developed; and the strategies through which meaning was assigned and implemented.

The genesis of an Afrikaner beach resort: The South African Railways and Afrikaner cultural assertion

For the origins of what in time was to become a prominent Afrikaner beach resort, one should look not to the pristine beaches of the Southwestern Cape where Hartenbos is located, but 1200 kilometres to the north, to the grim and grimy railway shunting yards such as Braamfontein in Johannesburg where from the early decades of the twentieth century an increasing number of Afrikaner wage earners congregated. As will become apparent, there was a direct causal relationship between Afrikaner railway workers and the establishment of Hartenbos in 1936.

Between 1910 and 1936, under the pressures of recurrent droughts, the economic depression of the early 1930s and increasingly capital-intensive farming, many Afrikaner families were driven from the land to the cities. Some of these newly arrived Afrikaner indigents in Johannesburg and other urban centres found employment in lowly capacities on the railways. The South African Railways as a government corporation were a huge employer of the burgeoning number of poor whites, yet not everyone could be accommodated; in the Transvaal alone there was a waiting list of 2000 men in 1910.[75] However, as the railway network expanded, these job seekers were

---

74 U. Özkirimli: *Theories of Nationalism: A Critical Introduction* (Palgrave, Hampshire, 2000), pp. 217–218.
75 G. Pirie: "White Railway Labour in South Africa, 1873–1924" in R. Morrrell (ed.), *White But Poor: Essays on the History of Poor Whites in Southern Africa, 1880–1940* (Unisa Press, Pretoria, 1993), p. 106.

gradually absorbed in the system. After the Anglo-Boer War (also known as the South African War) of 1899–1902 and during the subsequent reconstruction period, the Railways were under imperial sway and an essential cog in the imperialist machinery to modernise the country. An efficient transport system after 1910 helped to change an import-dependent economy into an export-oriented one and also played a major role in the rapid expansion of the economy during the First World War.[76]

During this period the railway personnel, particularly in the higher echelons, were predominantly recent British immigrants and with English as the sole language on the railways, a specific imperial railway ethos drawing upon metropolitan practices prevailed. High-ranking English-speaking officials, though, sought to portray the Railways as a neutral technocratic rational organisation in service of the white nation, bonding English speakers and Afrikaners in a new project which not only brought remote towns within relatively easy commutable distance of each other but also decreased the social distance between the two major white groups.[77] Whilst the growing physical reach of the railway infrastructure could hardly be gainsaid, its ideological reach was more problematic.

The view from Head Office was not necessarily the view from the shunting yards. Here many Afrikaners found themselves at the bottom rungs of the labour ladder. Hendrik Hoffmann from the Free State was one such recruit who, accustomed to a position of some authority on the farm, now found his position in the shunting yard humiliating. Fully immersed in the hierarchical black-white racial order of the time, he asked:

> "Do you know what work we did? We cleaned the carriages, the black railway carriages... The *bombellas* for the mineworkers. They came from the Transkei and the Portuguese territories. And the carriages smelt terrible, and then you had to go and clean them out. The windows also had to be washed and cleaned. It broke my heart."[78]

---

76 J. Forster: "'Land of Contrasts' or 'Home We Have Always Known'? The SAR&H and the Imaginary Geography of White South African Nationhood, 1915–1930", *Journal of Southern African Studies*, 29, 3 (September 2003), p. 661.
77 Forster: "The SAR&H", pp. 661–662.
78 Quoted in L. Callinicos: *A Place in the City* (Ravan Press Johannesburg, 1993), p. 11.

Not only the kind of work was offensive to some. Afrikaner recruits were also often treated with disdain by some established English-speaking workers who did not hesitate to swear at and bully newcomers whom they regarded as unwelcome intruders into their world.[79]

The material conditions under which they laboured and the condescending attitude of some English speaking co-workers had a stigmatising effect. Afrikaner railway workers employed to do manual labour were held in low esteem, at times also by some fellow Afrikaners in other occupations.[80] Feelings of inferiority were reinforced by the lowly accommodation provided by their employers in derelict camps, formerly inhabited by British soldiers and railwaymen during the South African War. These so-called "Tommy camps" added insult to injury as some Afrikaners smarted under the ignominy of being housed in the same camps that once accommodated their former foes.[81] Those who stayed in these camps on the outskirts of towns and cities were also regarded as the outcasts of white society and often labelled as "odd and peculiar".[82]

Despite this, the Afrikaner presence in the Railways increased steadily as is evident from the following table[83]:

Year	Percentage Afrikaans Speakers
1908	9,8
1915	27,8
1921	42,4
1925	49,1
1930	49,6
1935	54,3
1940	63
1945	71,8
1950	71,2

These figures indicate that the number of Afrikaans speakers as opposed to English speakers reached a tipping point in the early 1930s.

---

79 Pirie: "White Railway Labour in South Africa, 1873–1924", p. 107.
80 *Die Taalgenoot*, July 1938, "Die Afrikaner as Spoorwegman".
81 F.J. Kok: "Die Taak van Kultuurorganisasies in Minderheidsgroepe met Besondere Verwysing na die ATKV" (Unpublished D.Phil thesis, Stellenbosch University, 1992), p. 132.
82 *Die Taalgenoot*, November 1948, "Vervoerkultuur". (Translation)
83 *Die Taalgenoot*, September 1955, "Die Spoorwegman en Afrikaans".

As English speakers began to find more attractive career opportunities outside the Railways, their positions were taken by Afrikaners. The latter also gradually benefited by changes introduced by the Pact government, comprising the National Party and the Labour Party, which came to power in 1924. The Pact government was more sympathetic towards workers, especially Afrikaners, and in-service training in the Railways ensured that possibilities for upward mobility became a reality. At the same time the recognition of Afrikaans as an official language besides English also had the effect of slowly elevating the status of Afrikaners in the work environment. Although the number of Afrikaners in top positions were still disproportionate to the total numbers mired in the lower echelons, new opportunities to move through the ranks did open up and this meant that an enterprising individual was not restricted to remain a porter or sweeper for life.[84] While it is true that some were mentally just too incapacitated to move beyond menial work, others showed a dogged determination to carve out a better future.[85] Moreover, they also gradually became more assertive in challenging the criteria for promotion.[86]

These changes in the workplace and the firmer presence of the number of Afrikaners in the Railways combined to launch an initiative not only to maintain existing advances but also to move forward in securing and promoting wider Afrikaner interests on the Railways. As a result, the Spoorbond was formed to look after work-related matters and more important for our purposes, the Afrikaanse Taal- en Kultuurvereniging, Spoorweë en Hawens, abbreviated as the ATKV, was established in 1930. This organisation saw itself as the watchdog of Afrikaans language rights and cultural concerns on the Railways and sought to "promote the intellectual and cultural welfare of its members".[87] The organisation self-consciously realised that as rep-

---

84 *Die Taalgenoot*, July, August and September 1955, "Die Spoorwegman en Afrikaans".
85 J.A. Tayler: "With the Shoulder to the Wheel: The Public Life of Erika Theron" (Doctoral dissertation, University of South Africa, 2010), 121; C. van Jaarsveld: *Spoorwegkinders en die Depressie* (Fishwicks, George, 2010), pp. 4, 6, 11, 14.
86 R.H. Davies: *Capital State and White Labour in South Africa, 1900–1960: An Historical Materialist of Class Formation and Class Relations* (Harvester Press, Sussex, 1979), p. 298.
87 M.E. Botha: "Partikuliere Volksorg in die Afrikaanse Volkskultuur met Verwysing na die ATKV (SAS en H), 1930–1964" (Unpublished D.Phil thesis, Potchefstroom University, 1970), p. 187. (Translated)

resentatives of certain railwaymen they spoke on behalf of a specific class. The chairman Henning Klopper explained:

> We are not the intelligentsia of the *volk*, we are not the professors, doctors, advocates and teachers. No, we are the daily wage earners, the working class, the poor – and in some cases the outcasts of the *volk*. But thanks to God, it is these poor people, these daily wage earners, these rejects, yes it is they who had the fortitude, initiative and faith to become the cultural carriers of the *volk*."[88]

Railwaymen had to be more than ordinary railwaymen, they had to be Afrikaner railwaymen buying into a higher ideal of Afrikaner culture as expressed in Afrikaans language, Calvinist religion, Afrikaner historical traditions, customs and pastimes. The Railways were likened to a "spider web" and the threads comprised "one large family" united not only through their occupations, but also because they were members of a cultural organisation which was at the "core of a great Afrikaner idea".[89]

"ATKV powering 'Team Hartenbos'"
(Courtesy Hartenbos Museum)

An important impetus for the ATKV was to instill in Afrikaner railway workers a sense of pride in their work. However mundane the nature of their occupation might have been, workers were encouraged to think that their work was part of a bigger whole and hence there was no need to regard their contribution as inferior. The dis-

---

88   *Die Taalgenoot*, July 1937, "Hartenbos Presteer". (Translated)
89   *Die Taalgenoot*, July 1939, "Die ATKV". (Translated)

course was punctuated by the belief that labour in itself was an honourable activity and that it should not be seen in isolation, but served a greater purpose of enhancing the interests of the *volk*. The idea was not to create a docile workforce, but woven into this thinking was the central thread of promoting the human dignity and self-worth of Afrikaner railwaymen, putting them on par with English speakers through the elevation of Afrikaans to the same level as that of English. Hence, considerable attention was paid to finding the Afrikaans equivalents for English technical terms and a concerted attempt was made to use Afrikaans more consistently on the Railways. To dispel notions of inferiority, Afrikaner railwaymen had to be culturally the equal of their English-speaking counterparts. Much of the ideology of upliftment was disseminated through the official journal of the ATKV, "Die Taalgenoot" (The Language Companion), but also through formal and informal gatherings and networks of members.[90] It was not a case of merely informing railwaymen about Afrikaner culture, but culture had to serve a more exalted purpose. It was argued that the ATKV had to impart to railwaymen "a sense of their high cultural value" which would "take them beyond themselves" and allow them to "identify with a task much larger than their own person". The ideal was that every Afrikaner railway worker had to "identify with his work, with his team, with the railways service as a whole, with his country and his *volk* and with the Highest".[91]

The ATKV bore some resemblance with late nineteenth-century railway organisations in Britain, characterised by mutualism and so-called friendly societies in so far as it sought to provide benefits to its members, but it had a much more explicit political thrust.[92] During the 1930s, the ATKV was close to the crest of the rising tide of Afrikaner nationalism which had become such a salient political feature of the decade. Afrikaans literature and historical writing proliferated,

---

90 A.P.J. van Rensburg: "Op die Voorpos: die Verhaal van die Stigting, Strewe en Prestasies van die ATKV (SAS en H)" (Unpublished manuscript, Institute of Contemporary History, Bloemfontein, 1969), pp. 20–21; *Die Taalgenoot*, December 1950, "Die Adel van die Arbeid".
91 *Die Taalgenoot*, June 1962, "ATKV". (Translation)
92 For this development in Britain see S. Cordery: "Mutualism, Friendly Societies and the Genesis of Railway Trade Unions", *Labour History Review*, 67, 3 (December 2002), pp. 273–281.

casting an ideological net which included debating societies, drama associations, reading circles, coffee houses and certain schools, all keen to assign meaning to and shape the term "Afrikaner".[93] Perhaps the most visible of these enterprises were the 1938 Great Trek centenary celebrations. At the centre of this was the ATKV which was primarily responsible for its launch. The celebrations witnessed an unprecedented emotional outpouring in a huge symbolic spectacle with nine ox-wagons wending their way through the country from Cape Town to Pretoria and in every hamlet and village, nationalist sentiments reached fever pitch as the deeds of the Voortrekkers of a hundred years ago were translated into tales of heroism for a new generation with a new purpose.[94] The ATKV was clearly an organisation with a significant appeal and a finely honed sense of cultural nationalism.

As seen in the case of opposition to dog racing, one of the marked concerns of Afrikaner cultural entrepreneurs during this period was to patrol leisure time, especially activities which they deemed as demoralising and *volksvreemd* (alien to the nation).[95] The cities also gave rise to what was characterised as a "bohemian lifestyle" – pretentious artists who, it was claimed, was obsessed with smoking, drinking and "shameless" indulgence in sex. Such a dissolute disposition, it was argued, ran counter to sober Afrikaner mores and could easily lead to the development of a "poor white mentality".[96] How free time was spent had an important bearing on the spiritual welfare of the *volk* and it preferably had to conform to the totalising impulses of nationalism.[97] Even, and at times especially, on holiday one had to guard against lassitude and an idle existence outside the parameters of religion and the *volk*.[98]

---

93 I. Hofmeyr: "Building a Nation from Words: Afrikaans Language, Literature and Ethnic Identity, 1902–1924" in S. Marks and S. Trapido (eds), *The Politics of Race, Class and Nationalism* (1987), p. 110.
94 A. Grundlingh and H. Sapire: "From Feverish Festival to Repetitive Ritual?" *South African Historical Journal* (1989), pp. 19–38.
95 Chapter 1.
96 *Trek*, October 1940, "Daardie boheemse lewe: 'n woord van waarskuwing". (Translation)
97 University of the Free State Library, Archives of the Federasie van Afrikaanse Kultuurvereniginge, PV 202/iv/6/13/1/1/1, "Die Afrikaner se vryetydsbesteding".
98 *Die Taalgenoot*, April 1937, "Ontspanning". (Translation)

It was against this background that the issue of how railwaymen spent their holidays emerged. The ideal was to find a suitable holiday resort because, so it was claimed, Afrikaner railwaymen were not welcome in predominantly English-oriented resorts along the Natal coast. As a minority in these resorts, they were allegedly treated with disdain, partly because of the language they spoke but also because of the social stigma attached to ill-educated Afrikaner railway people. In order to remedy this situation, the ATKV executive council took a decision on 16 November 1936 to buy the Hartenbos estate, eight kilometres from the town of Mossel Bay, and to develop it as a beach resort for Afrikaner railwaymen.[99] With this decision, a sympathetic observer commented, it became possible for "people who could in the past only dream of a holiday at the coast and who often had to endure the insults of hotel doors being slammed in their faces as they were not welcome in other resorts, to become the owners of their own beach cottages." Therefore, Hartenbos was about to instill a "sense of equality to railwaymen".[100] It had to become a place where Afrikaners could find "inspiration" and "return invigorated and full of hope to their places of work in the cities where they struggle to make a living".[101]

In the beginning there was... *(Courtesy Hartenbos Museum)*

---

99 Botha: "Partikuliere Volksorg", p. 219.
100 Van Rensburg: "Op die Voorpos", p. 21. (Translation)
101 *Die Taalgenoot*. "Hartenbos in Vakansiegees". (Translation)

Developing Hartenbos

The Hartenbos project called for considerable planning and infrastructural development as rough and uneven farmland along the coast had to be converted to allow for the erection of elementary housing. It was a task undertaken with great enthusiasm. Hartenbos, it was reported in 1937, was a

> beehive of activity from early morning till late evening... Slowly but indisputably creative work is being done and in our mind's eye our dream is already a concrete reality which would be able to withstand any attacks. Rome was not build in a day and a complete beach resort cannot appear at the wave of a magician's wand... But we shall conquer![102]

Initially such idealism knew no bounds: in the long run a bustling Afrikaner city along the ocean was envisaged which would showcase the best Afrikanerdom could offer in all walks of life. "We look forward," was the visionary dream in 1936, "and we see a magnificent cultural city, with its monuments for the *volk*, its schools for the *volk*, its churches for the *volk* and other institutions for the *volk* in Hartenbosch."[103] However, as the enormity of the task set in, the sights were lowered and a modest yet comfortable resort town became the aim.[104]

Stands were made available on favourable terms, designed to suit the relatively limited financial means of the 30 000 members of the ATKV. The high level of membership and the fees that accrued accordingly meant that the organisation started off from a sound footing and was able to structure their finances to the benefit of the members. For those that could not afford stands and erect their own housing, other forms of rented accommodation were made available.[105] Hartenbos had to try and meet the needs of even the poorest of its members. "The eyes of our *volk*," it was said in 1939, "was on this little piece of land, and thank God no hopes have been dashed."[106]

---

102 *Die Taalgenoot*, November 1937, "Hartenbos". (Translation)
103 *Die Taalgenoot*, December 1936, "Ons eie vakansie-oord, Hartenbos". (Translation)
104 Van Rensburg: "Op die Voorpos", pp. 11–12.
105 *Die Taalgenoot*, Februarie 1939, "Erwe op Hartenbos"; *Die Taalgenoot*, June 1961, "Huisvesting op Hartenbos".
106 *Die Taalgenoot*, Maart 1939, "Hartenbosnuus". (Translation)

Initially, housing was very elementary, often reject split poles were used to provide the basic frame cladded with cheap asbestos.[107] For some the appearance of the houses was of far lesser importance than the joys of being able to spend a holiday at the beach. One Afrikaans author recalled his childhood days at Hartenbos during the late fifties as follows:

> As a child Hartenbos symbolised to me everything that was positive, attractive and pure in human kind. I did not notice the poverty and pain around me. The fact that my parents could not afford anything better than a very cramped asbestos house closest to the railway line, did not bother me.[108]

In time, though, the management committee became stricter in enforcing building regulations to prevent the appearance of a shantytown which would have reflected poorly on the aspirational aims of the ATKV.[109]

The first foundational years at Hartenbos were nevertheless marked by an overt sense of self-sufficency. Apart from an atttempt to cut costs in the initial development of the terrain, the project had to prove Afrikaner self-reliance. "We plough our own lands, milk our own cows, ... make our own bricks, manufacture our own chalk for marking purposes, saw our own wood and make our own furniture," the chairman reported in 1937.[110] Hartenbos, it was argued, had a "duty" to provide a suitable Afrikaner beach resort to Afrikaner railwaymen and their families.[111] It was clearly a purposefully driven project.

Whilst infectious enthusiasm helped to ease teething problems, it was not possible to sustain the endeavour by frenetic activity alone. From about 1939 to 1942 lack of detailed infrastructural planning and finely calculated financial budgets impacted negatively on activities. Personality clashes between top officials further added to the woes and for a while it appeared that the grand nationalistic project of Hartenbos was seriously imperilled. The issue was compounded

---

107 R. Kaljee: *Hartenbos bakens* (No publisher, Hartenbos, 1993), pp. 42, 56.
108 K. Kombuis: *Afrikaans my Darling* (Human and Rousseau, Cape Town, 2003), p. 135.
109 *Die Taalgenoot*, December 1961, "Hoe het Hartenbos as Dorp Ontwikkel".
110 Van Rensburg: "Op die Voorpos", p. 15. (Translation)
111 *Die Taalgenoot*, October 1937, "Hartenbos". (Translation)

by conditions during the Second World War which allowed only very limited building projects to be undertaken. Ultimately, however, the glue of nationalism held, wiser practical counsels prevailed, and combined with a number of strategic interventions, Hartenbos was able to move into a new phase of operations from 1943.[112]

The ATKV makes it happen. Hartenbos in the 1950s. *(Courtesy Hartenbos Museum)*

What further counted in Hartenbos's favour was that within a few short years of its existence, it had become a very popular destination for railwaymen. Demand regularly exceeded the accommodation available. The number of visitors increased exponentially as is clear from the following table:[113]

Year	Visitors to Hartenbos
1937/38	50
1943/46	1000
1950/51	9600
1960/61	20 111
1965/66	42 115

---

112 *Die Taalgenoot*, September 1951, "Uitbouing van Hartenbos"; *Die Taalgenoot*, December 1961, "Hartenbos se groeipyne"; Kaljee: *Hartenbos*, 36; Van Rensburg: "Op die Voorpos", p. 19.
113 Compiled from Van Rensburg: "Op die Voorpos", pp. 26, 27; *Die Taalgenoot*, May 1966, "Alles onder die Son by die See".

Underlying this growth in numbers was a number of interrelated factors. Hartenbos was situated on one of the main railway lines and therefore relatively easily accessible. Railwaymen were entitled to special travelling concessions which made the pilgrimage to Hartenbos less costly. Hartenbos also had a moderate climate with a relatively low rainfall and with a good swimming beach, warmed by the glistening Indian Ocean waves and adorned by white soft sand. Moreover, after the setbacks of the early 1940s, the undertaking was placed on a firmer business footing and staffed by committed officials, the facilities improved and accommodation became more readily available. Apart from these developments one also has to factor in that the number of Afrikaners in the Railways had grown. Moreover, in the 1950s and especially during the height of apartheid during the 1960s, the country experienced unprecedented economic prosperity. Afrikaners also benefited from having a greater say in government and started to fill top positions in the Railways more rapidly, while others also became more affluent as they branched into various sectors of the booming economy of the 1960s. A combination of these factors gave impetus to the development of Hartenbos and ensured its reputation as an attractive holiday destination.[114]

During the period of rapid expansion a central thread remained: Hartenbos self-consciously projected itself as first and foremost an Afrikaner resort. Subsequently, it was reported in the 1960s: "In spite of all the progress Hartenbos retained that 'something' – that character and blessed influence which is its hallmark and which makes it one of the cultural powerhouses of the republic. A holidaymaker arrives at Hartenbos and if he kneels on the ATKV estate, he can pick up a handful of soil and feel that it is *his*. He stays in one of the units and his neighbours are fellow Afrikaners, fellow members and no strangers. He is at home among friends and colleagues."[115] The processes that gave rise to this kind of proprietary claim and the way that a beach assumed a specific ethnic character through investing it with a particular set of meanings warrant our further attention.

---

114 *Die Taalgenoot*, December 1961, "Hartenbos se Toekoms as Vakansieoord"; *Die Taalgenoot*, September 1951, "Uitbouing van Hartenbos"; *Die Taalgenoot*, December 1939, "Hartenbos"; S. van Waart: *Mosselbaai: Seepoort van die Tuinroete* (Lapa, Pretoria, 2003), p. 217.

115 Van Rensburg: "Op die Voorpos", p. 40. (Translation; emphasis in original)

Imparting meaning

It is useful to approach the Afrikanerisation of Hartenbos as a kind of nationalist discursive formation – "a way of talking, thinking and apprehending the world that thereby lends its conceptual form and practical organisation".[116] Through a range of activities Hartenbos became a site where notions, images and understandings of Afrikaner nationalism were articulated and reworked in a leisure setting to be circulated and redistributed, ultimately adding to and feeding into the overall ethnic project.

One area where this kind of ideological work was particularly salient, was the interpretation of the natural environment in such a way that it became part of an emblematic Afrikanerdom. This was no unique kind of discourse. The literature on water, leisure and culture reveals that water is open to a variety of value-laden possibilities. As Susan Anderson has indicted in respect of Britain and Europe: "Differing geographic configurations, nationalist ideals, moral-religious beliefs and local conditions help account for dissimilar modes of representing coastal waters."[117]

In the case of Hartenbos, the general point of departure was that nature could not be disregarded, nor could its "glory" be fully described. Surrounded by a beautiful natural environment, Afrikaners were in a position where they could appropriate it as their "own Mecca" and more specifically for those employed on the Railways.[118]

A particular slant was to represent water and other elements of nature as a curative and restorative force in the life of Afrikanerdom: "It is a Mecca where we shall go to have refreshing waters poured over the tired and tormented soul of the *volk*." Afrikaners, it was predicted, would flock to Hartenbos to quench their thirst and they would thank God for the privilege to do so. At Hartenbos they would feel free: "Here," it was exclaimed in hyperbolic terms:

> I can stretch out my arms to fully inhale the clean fresh air in my shrunken lungs and nature in all its beauty, all its fullness can embrace

---

116 G. Day and A. Thompson: *Theorizing Nationalism* (Palgrave, London, 2005), p. 101.
117 S. Anderson: "Introduction: Pleasures of Taking the Waters" in S. Anderson and B.H. Tabb (eds), *Water Leisure and Culture: European Historical Perspectives* (Berg, Oxford, 2003), p. 3.
118 *Die Taalgenoot*, January 1946, "Hartenbos ons eie strandoord". (Translation)

me and weaken me with love for this earth. I nestle my tired body against her breast and drink from her milk, and strong like a son of the 'veld' I challenge this world with my foot firmly planted on my own piece of land. Who shall impede me in this holy place?[119]

Hartenbos and nature also had to serve as a counterpoint to the stresses and strains which Afrikaners were seen to endure in an uncompromising urban environment:

We had to have a little piece of land where we could express our deepest sensibilities and convictions without reservations, where we could retrieve our lost traditions and the spirituality of the *volk* without the restraints of the frenetical pace and whirlwind of so-called modernity which are all alien to the existence of our *volk*. As Afrikaners the soul-destroying, spiritually debilitating city life is alien to us... We are people who love nature ... there we feel at home ... free to interpret the beauty within us ... without fear of foreign interference or condescension.[120]

Nature became part of mutually reinforcing notions of a shared ethnicity, a unifying past and a common destiny. Hartenbos was a "panorama" of white sand and unruly waves on the one hand, and on the other the "jagged cliffs of the Outeniqua mountains which are etched like sentinels" against the blue sky. It was in this setting where "members gathered in a holiday spirit" and where the "brothership

"The sea air makes free". A prime spot at Hartenbos c. 1960. *(Courtesy Jeanne van Eeden)*

---

119 *Die Taalgenoot*, December 1937, "Die Hartenbos-onderneming". (Translation)
120 *Die Taalgenoot*, December 1937, "Die Hartenbos-onderneming". (Translation)

Holidays at Hartenbos

and sistership of our *volk* are expressed," where "we worked towards the realisation of our ideals," where "we guard over the rich heritage of the soul bequeathed to us by our fathers and the grief laden trails of blood along the path of this country of ours, this bountiful earth, this South Africa".[121] Moreover, the metaphoric linkages between Afrikanerdom and the sea were extended by comparing the sea to a purifying force which gets rid of flotsam and jetsam, in the same way Afrikaners were concerned about that which was "impure" and "foreign" to them.[122] Nature also loomed large in the memories that were generated during holidays and for those who returned regularly, recollections of an appealing sense of place were reinforced. One returning holidaymaker recalled: "Yes, Hartenbos beach... Oh how did I long for your dense bushes against the hillocks, your shady trees, your beautiful sandy shores and your safe beach. Would we ever forget our friends and the dear old beach?"[123]

Apart from personifying nature in Afrikaner terms, under the rubric of "cultural promotion", leisure was purposefully funnelled in directions that could enhance ethnic solidarity. Concerts, barbecues, sports meetings, debating societies, *volkspele* (folk dancing) and to some extent church services became mini cultural rallying points. Besides these events, the annual commemoration of the Day of the Covenant on 16 December which recalled the decisive Boer victory over the Zulu at Blood River (Ncome River) was particularly well attended as thousands gathered to hear a rehearsal of Afrikaner history which easily lent itself to nationalist mythmaking. These occasions were clear and potent markers on the social calendar of Hartenbos.[124]

Deliberate strategies were required to impart an almost all-pervasive Afrikaner dimension to these events. Along these lines, it was argued that Father Christmas, who during the annual Christmas Eve gathering handed out presents, was not in line with Afrikaner customs and that the venerable gentleman should be replaced by a more indigenous "Father Voortrekker".[125] Also in line with this mode

---

121 *Die Taalgenoot*, October 1937, "Hartenbos". (Translation)
122 *Die Taagenoot*, June 1939, "Die Branders van Hartenbos." (Translation)
123 *Die Taalgenoot*, March 1937, "'n Week van Genot". (Translation)
124 *Die Taalgenoot*, April 1960, "Plesier en Kultuur op Hartenbos".
125 Botha: "ATKV", p. 234. See also Grundlingh and Sapire: "From Feverish Festival to Repetitive Ritual?", p. 25.

of thinking a mini-gholf game, commonly known as putt-putt, was renamed *wapadspele* (wagon trail games) harking back to the Voortrekker and their ox-wagons. Popular pastimes were more than just leisure activities; *jukskei* (a traditional form of bowls) and *volkspele* were construed to be "the expression of the inner self, in perfect harmony with the built-in *volksgevoel* (a feeling of national spirit)"[126]. The "volksgevoel" knew no bounds and was even cast in classical terms; therefore a higher meaning was bestowed on the annual athletics meeting by investing it with the weight of antiquity through a comparison with the games in ancient Greece. "Is history not busy repeating itself at Hartenbos?" it was asked rhetorically.[127] Besides these events, other signifiers such as street names bore testimony to the attempt to remind holidaymakers of their history; names recalling Boer battles against the British and blacks, replete with potent symbolism, proliferated.[128] Moreover, through the ATKV the idea of the 1938 Great Trek centenary celebrations that evolved into unprecedented political and cultural drama can be traced back to Hartenbos where the notion of the Trek originated. Hartenbos, it was argued, provided the inspiration of how to be a *volk* and how to enjoy a festival, a celebration that will be retold from generations to generations and will instill love and pride for our little *volkie* (small nation)[129]. It was hard to escape the choreographed Afrikaner ambience that came to be associated with the beach resort.

What added to the appeal of social life in Hartenbos, was that ethnic rituals were cast in an almost carnivalesque form for all to enjoy. Everybody was invited to participate in a convivial atmosphere: "Greybeards, the youth, men and women, ugly young males and attractive young women." The scene was set "with women in flaring Voortrekker dresses and men in wide-rimmed hats, jolly children, ... cheerful dances, and songs in honour of the *volk*, flags waving, pleasant social interchanges and jests – an exuberant spirit prevailed." It was a spectacle to wax lyrically about: "At this Afrikaner resort you

---

126 *Die Taalgenoot*, February 1941, "Hartenbos in Vakansiegees".
127 *Die Taalgenoot*, December 1961, "Atletiek en Boeresport op Hartenbos". (Translation)
128 For the names see Van Rensburg: "Op die Voorpos", p. 26.
129 D. Mostert (ed.): *Gedenkboek van die Ossewaens op Pad van Suid-Afrika* (Nasionale Pers, Cape Town, 1940), p. 191.

cannot but be proud when you witness the soot-covered urban spirit transformed into a unique Afrikaans gem."[130]

The way Hartenbos was presented in the cultural imaginary of the *volk* created the impression that under the sway of a relaxed holiday atmosphere possible status differences amongst Afrikaners were dissolved. "There is no distinction," it was claimed, "between poor and rich, between labourer and departmental head – all are brothers, Afrikaners and members of an organisation in which ranks there are no differentiation."[131] Moreover, Hartenbos provided the opportunity for Afrikaners to express themselves free from what was termed "foreign elements". It was regarded as "one big factor which contributed to the popularity of Hartenbos ... that our members can holiday here without being restrained by a foreign element, everything belongs to us and feels like our own. And that creates a pleasant spirit of camaraderie and joint co-operation..."[132] Such representations of harmony can of course be overdrawn; in 1952 one individual did break out of the fold and in an apparent drunken state disrupted concert proceedings.[133] Very few such incidents were, however, recorded.

In assessing Hartenbos within the context of Afrikaner nationalism as a specific form of social construction as opposed to a presumed given, it is clear that the discourse functioned at various levels to embrace different elements of the holiday experience and imbue them with a heightened sense of ethnicity. Much of the cultural activities at Hartenbos were geared towards creating what Benedict Anderson in a celebrated phrase has called an "imagined community".[134] It will be misleading though to imply that those who went to Hartenbos were devoid of personal agency and mere unthinking recipients of nationalist ideology. There were sound reasons why being an Afrikaner, especially for railwaymen, made sense and why the cultural blandishments of Hartenbos were readily entertained. Besides a pre-configured sense of ethnicity that allowed for initial optimal

---

130 *Die Taalgenoot*, February 1941, "Hartenbos in Vakansiegees". (Translation)
131 *Die Taalgenoot*, February 1938, "Vakansiegees op Hartenbos". (Translation)
132 *Die Taalgenoot*, December 1939, "Hartenbos". (Translation)
133 Institute of Contemporary History, Bloemfontein, ATKV Papers, Verslag van Hartenbosbestuur, 1953.
134 B. Anderson: "Imagined Communities" in J. Hutchinson and A.D. Smith (eds), *Nationalism* (Oxford University Press, Oxford, 1995), pp. 89–96.

access to the social world of Hartenbos, once inside that world a number of perceived benefits accrued. These took the form of low-cost accommodation for many otherwise deprived of such a luxury, entertainment, conviviality and camaraderie, and an enhanced sense of self-worth that came from the realisation of being plugged into a larger community – suffused, saturated and submerged under the notion of Afrikanerdom. There is ample evidence of holidaymakers who expressed their satisfaction and at times gratitude for what they regarded as the privilege of being part of the Afrikaner experience at Hartenbos.[135]

Conclusion

The processes and strategies that gave Hartenbos its specific character were not unique. Writing on the general characteristics of cultural nationalists, John Hutchinson has pointed out:

> Typically cultural nationalists establish ... clusters of cultural societies and journals, designed to inspire a spontaneous love of community in its different members by educating them to their common heritage of splendour and suffering. They engage in naming rituals, celebrate national cultural uniqueness and reject foreign practices, in order to identify the community to itself, embed this identity in everyday life and differentiate it against other communities." [136]

Many of the endeavours outlined here had their corollaries at Hartenbos. Afrikaner history was rehearsed in a particular way, the natural environment was infused with redemptive and spiritual powers regarded as essential for sustaining a healthy community life, there was a subterranean animosity aimed at that which could be regarded as "foreign", and everyday existence during holidays was structured in such a way that it contributed to the dissemination of notions, images and understandings of what it meant to be an Afrikaner nationalist. This analysis also points to the need to look at developments and discourses at a local level and the way they create favourable conditions to buy into an overarching and wider form of nationalism.

---

135 *Die Taalgenoot*, June 1939, Letters page.
136 J. Hutchinson: "Cultural Nationalism and Moral Regeneration" in J. Hutchinson and A.B. Smith (eds), *Nationalism* (Oxford University Press, Oxford, 1995), p. 124 .

Although Afrikaner nationalism in its original form is all but a spent force today, Hartenbos has become a very popular holiday destination and still attracts mainly Afrikaans speakers. In this sense the foundations have been well laid. In 2013 a journalist observed that Hartenbos remained "a welcoming place" where "ordinary patriotic Afrikaners can feel at home and express themselves in their own terms and in keeping with their traditions".[137] But Hartenbos has also changed and in some respects become more commercialised. This is perhaps best illustrated by the permutations which marked the name changes of the main sea-facing restaurant: from nomenclatures reminiscent of Afrikaner ethnicity in its heyday, the erstwhile "Boeretroos Restaurant", "Koffiehuis" and later the "Mosselkraker" has today transmogrified into globalising American consumerism by becoming the "Tahoma Spur".

"A cup of culture", c. 1960. *(Courtesy Hartenbos Museum)*

---

137 J. van Wyk: *So Was Dit: Stories van Gister en Vandag* (Tafelberg, Kaapstad, 2013), p. 172.

3
Playing with purpose: Rugby and its wider significance in Afrikaner society, c 1900–c 1989

The phrases "rugby is more than a game" or "rugby is the soul sport of Afrikaners" are often heard in popular parlance. But if that is indeed the case, how can it be proven? Starting with an analysis of the growth of rugby in Afrikaner circles, this chapter examines the wider meaning of the game by exploring the possible connections between rugby and Afrikaner nationalism and the way in which perceptions associated with rugby have helped to shape male identity.

Dissemination of rugby among Afrikaners

The role of the University of Stellenbosch in the Western Cape is the key to understanding the historical connection between rugby, Afrikaner nationalism and the dissemination of the sport among the *volk*. For the best part of the twentieth century, Stellenbosch was considered the leading university in influential Afrikaner circles. It was to Afrikaners what the Oxbridge universities were to the national life of Britain and the Ivy League universities were to America.

Stellenbosch grew out of the Victoria College to become the first independent Afrikaans university in 1918. The University Council, representing the Afrikaans community, deliberately aimed to give the university a specific Afrikaner identity to counter that of the neighbouring and predominantly English-speaking University of Cape Town. "Stellenbosch", it was claimed later, was "born out of the need of the Afrikaner volk." As a true *volksuniversiteit*, it had to act as a steady light ... and beacon, illuminating the road of Afrikanerdom.[138] It was within this context that the game of rugby was played by the sons of the Afrikaner elite.

The first documented proof of a rugby club at Stellenbosch dates back to 1880, but the University Club was only officially founded in 1919. Rugby was already firmly established in Cape Town by the late nineteenth century, and its close proximity to Stellenbosch undoubtedly facilitated the development of rugby there. Stellenbosch had a head start over Afrikaner communities in the interior, particularly in the northern Boer Republics, where in some rural districts the game was completely unknown at the turn of the century.[139]

Stellenbosch was also the first and, for a while, the only institution where young, predominantly Afrikaner men were concentrated in one place for a reasonable period and where they had sufficient leisure to indulge in what has been called a game played "by young males in a state of hormonal pugnacity".[140] However, rugby at Stellenbosch was more than just an outlet for robust males in the prime of manhood. The game became part and parcel of Afrikaner student culture. One commentator regarded "the way in which students could transform their fun and play into a reverberating cultural act, as one of the salient features of student life in Stellenbosch".[141] With the rise of Afrikaner nationalism in the 1930s and 1940s, rugby became as much part of Afrikaner culture as *volkspele*, and celebrations like the 1938 centenary of the Great Trek.[142] The sport became part of a cluster of cultural symbols closely associated with resurgent Afrikanerdom.

Two outstanding personalities who virtually became rugby legends in their own lifetime, A.F. Markötter and later Danie Craven,

---

138 D. Kotze (ed.): *Professor H.B. Thom* (Universiteitsuitgewers, Stellenbosch, 1969), pp. 78–79. (Translation)

139 F.J.G. van der Merwe: "Sport and Games in the Boer Prisoner-of-War Camps during the Anglo-Boer War, 1899–1902", *International Journal of the History of Sport*, 9, 3 (December 1992), p. 442.

140 R. Archer and A. Bouillon: *The South African Game: Sport and Racism* (Zed Press, London, 1982), p. 69.

141 B. Booyens: "Studentelewe – die Jongste Tydperk", H.B. Thom (ed.), *Stellenbosch, 1866–1966: Honderd Jaar Hoër Onderwys* (Stellenbosch, 1966), p. 394. (Quotation translated)

142 Booysens: *Studentelewe*, p. 394.

did much to turn Stellenbosch into the Mecca of twentieth-century South African rugby. For Craven it was the "task of Stellenbosch to train and provide players for the club, Western Province, and South Africa. But it also had to do more. It had to train players for other clubs and provinces."[143] Stellenbosch Rugby Club regularly took the game further afield through annual tours to the Cape countryside, allowing people in "areas deprived of the opportunities enjoyed by students" to savour what was considered "sparkling student rugby".[144]

The process of strengthening the rugby fraternity and enhancing the reputation of Stellenbosch spawned its own subculture, in which enthusiasm for rugby as an Afrikaner male activity was equated with robust patriotism to the exclusion of other, perhaps more threatening, worldviews. Frederik van Zyl Slabbert, parliamentary leader of the white opposition in the mid-1980s, has graphically recalled how disillusioned he became with this subculture during his rugby-playing days at Stellenbosch in the 1960s:

> ... the post-mortems after the game with pot-bellied, beer-drinking "experts" from way back; the sight of players continually ingratiating themselves with sporting correspondents for some coverage; the pseudo-patriotic ethos that pervaded discussions on the importance of rugby in our national life; seeing successful farmers grovelling at the feet of arrogant second-year students simply because we were "Maties" [nickname for Stellenbosch students] on tour in their vicinity. Mentally it was not only escapist, it was a social narcotic to anything else going on in our society...[145]

The annual rugby tour was only one way of forging linkages between Stellenbosch and rugby on the platteland (countryside). More intensive and enduring was the role played by Afrikaans-speaking teachers and *predikante* (ministers of religion) in diffusing and popularising rugby on the platteland. Four years of teacher-training at Stellenbosch, and seven years of divinity studies for *predikante* at the Dutch Reformed Church seminary which was part of the university, not only equipped young male teachers and *predikante* with degrees, but

---

143 *Rugby*, June 1974, p. 39. (Quotation translated)
144 D. Craven: "'n Eeu van Sport" in Thom (ed.), *Stellenbosch*, p. 431. (Quotation translated)
145 F. van Zyl Slabbert: *The Last White Parliament* (Sidgwick & Jackson, Johannesburg, 1985), p. 20.

added a thorough knowledge of and unbridled enthusiasm for rugby to their educational and theological armoury. From Stellenbosch they sallied forth to towns in the platteland where, as local notables with considerable influence, they encouraged and strengthened the rugby-playing fraternity. In the Karoo town of De Aar, for example, it was a source of pride that in the 1950s the four local *predikante* not only involved themselves in the game, but that between them they had a sufficient number of sons to field a complete team.[146] More generally, one author claimed in 1956: "It is often said, with truth, that Stellenbosch-trained *predikante* and teachers have had the biggest share in making South Africa so rugby-conscious."[147] It was a two-way process. Many youngsters who had been exposed to and encouraged to play the game in the platteland came to Stellenbosch as students. For a considerable period the top players at the university hailed from the countryside.[148]

"Spreading the gospel." *(From D. Craven* et. al., Met die Maties op die Rugbyveld, 1880–1955, Stellenbosch *1955).*

---

146 *Vigor*, December 1955, p. 36.
147 A.C. Parker: *Giants of South African Rugby* (Cape Town, 1956), p. 57.
148 H.C. Marais: "Herkomspatrone van Stellenbosch se Toprugbyspelers" in *Geo-Stell*, 3 (1979), p. 48.

The dissemination of rugby among Afrikaners in the Transvaal followed a somewhat different trajectory. Until the bilingual Transvaal University College was transformed into the more purified Afrikaner and openly nationalistic University of Pretoria in the 1930s, there was no single institution in the north which, like Stellenbosch in the south, could attract a large number of young Afrikaner men. Although competitive rugby had been played at the Transvaal University College since 1909, the institution was less of a focal point for the diffusion of the game in Afrikaner ranks and its influence less pervasive than that of Stellenbosch.[149]

While Stellenbosch was an almost exclusively student town, Pretoria was the administrative capital of the country after unification in 1910, and the subsequent growth of the city was closely linked to the expansion of the civil service and related government agencies. The majority of young men, including Afrikaners, who moved to Pretoria in the early part of the century, came in a working capacity and had less time for leisure activities than students. Those who were interested in sport joined open clubs like Pretoria Rugby Club or Harlequins, but rugby to them was less of an all-consuming interest than it was for students. The popularity of the game fluctuated between 1910 and 1919. However, it survived and began to flourish in the 1920s with the provision of better playing surfaces and through the energetic efforts of administrators, officials and certain players – many of whom had learned their rugby at Stellenbosch before moving to Pretoria.[150]

With the increasing urbanisation of Afrikaners during this period, concerted efforts were made to reach out to young Afrikaners who came from the rural areas and found themselves in a new and strange environment, and to introduce them to rugby as a game which could instil discipline and confidence. It was argued at the time that "rugby is the best means of helping them to expend their energy that could otherwise steer them in a harmful direction".[151] The process at work

---

149 Compare D.H. Heydenrych: *Tukkie-Rugby, 75* (Pretoria, 1983), pp. 4–20.
150 F. J. Nöthling: "The Pioneering Years" in M.C. van Zyl (ed.), *Northern Transvaal Rugby 50* (Pretoria, 1988), 18, 22; I.P.W. Pretorius: "Senior Rugby in Pretoria, 1938–1989" (Unpublished MA dissertation, University of South Africa, 1989), p. 21.
151 Quoted in Nöthling: "The Pioneering Years" in Van Zyl (ed.), *Northern Transvaal Rugby*, p. 25.

here was not that dissimilar from what took place in the United Kingdom during the latter part of the nineteenth century when "muscular Christian" priests, many of them educated at public schools, took an active part in diffusing rugby among the working classes. The game was regarded as a

> means of moral and physical salvation, as activities which could help the denizens of the slums to become strong and physically healthy and to develop traits of character which would enable them to improve their miserable lot.[152]

By contrast, in neighbouring Johannesburg, the city of gold and commerce, little was done to draw the Afrikaner working class into the game. The rugby clubs in Johannesburg were predominantly English speaking and middle class. More so than in Pretoria, members of these clubs saw little reason to concern themselves with the recreational activities of working class Afrikaners. Although individual Afrikaners excelled at rugby in some of these clubs, on the whole, until about the 1930s, rugby did not have a great appeal for Afrikaners as a group in Johannesburg. Besides the fact that no real attempt was made by the clubs to popularise the game among Afrikaners in Johannesburg, working Afrikaners themselves had relatively little leisure time available to indulge in organised sport.[153] In addition, there was no Afrikaner educational or similar institution in Johannesburg at the time to promote the game.

However, this should not detract from the fact that even at this early stage, after the First World War, a number of Afrikaner players, mainly (though not exclusively) from the Western Province, rose to national prominence. After the war, sport in general experienced a revival and the visit of a New Zealand Imperial Services team in 1919 gave an added spark to the quickening of interest in rugby. This tour paved the way for the first South African rugby tour to Australia and New Zealand in 1921. Afrikaans-speaking players were well represented in Springbok ranks. Commenting on this, an Australian rugby critic was struck by the way in which

---

[152] E. Dunning: "The Development of Modern Football" in E. Dunning (ed.), *The Sociology of Sport: A Selection of Readings* (Frank Cass, London, 1971), p. 147.
[153] Compare J.J. Fourie: *Afrikaners in die Goudstad, 1886–1924* (Johannesburg, 1979), p. 166.

an essentially winter game can flourish in a hot country, and how it can attract men who have not a long heritage of British sport behind them... For the Dutch [Afrikaans] South Africans have taken to the rugby game as keenly as their English compatriots. In fact, they seem to outshine the English South Africans.[154]

During this period, though, rugby had not yet been invested with a narrow nationalistic Afrikaner ethos. The game was rather seen as an excellent way of promoting understanding between Afrikaans and English speakers and cementing a common bond between the "two white sections" which could foster the notion of a white "South Africanism", and could ultimately act in the interest of "the higher scheme of imperial unity".[155] Nevertheless, the fact that Afrikaners made their mark on the playing field in retrospect singled out the game as a sport with the potential to enhance the self-image of the Afrikaner.

Rugby and Afrikaner nationalism

Writing on the return of the rugby Springboks to the international fold in 1992 after 18 years of isolation, the British journalist, Frank Keating, reflected on the relationship between Afrikaner politics, nationalism and apartheid:

> Rugby is the mother's milk, the lifeblood, the elixir that fuels ... [Afrikaner] arrogance. And clothed in their vestments of green and gold, the Springboks are religious icons and totems to the faith.[156]

This is an oversimplification of a more complex set of evolving beliefs, but it does capture some of the essentials of the intimate relationship between rugby and the development of Afrikaner culture and nationalism. It is not, however, a straightforward relationship. The reasons why a marriage between rugby and Afrikaner nationalism took place at all call for an understanding of the historical dynamics of Afrikaner nationalism and the ethos of the game itself.

---

154 Quoted in P. Dobson: *Rugby in South Africa: A History, 1861–1988* (South African Rugby Board, Cape Town, 1989), p. 89.
155 *Who's Who in the Sporting World: Witwatersrand and Victoria: Rugby* (Johannesburg, 1933), pp. 2–3; South African Rugby Board Minutes, 1, Report on the 1912 tour to the United Kingdom, 6 February 1913.
156 *The Guardian Weekly*, 9–15 October 1992.

The 1930s and 1940s were important years. Afrikaner nationalism at this time can be interpreted as a broad social and political response to the different facets of the impact of capitalism on South African society, which left certain groups, including a large number of Afrikaners, stranded. It was within a context of increasing urbanisation and secondary industrialisation, as well as continuing British imperial influence in economic and cultural spheres, that Afrikaner nationalism made headway. Important ideological building blocks in this process – as we have seen in the development of Hartenbos and the demise of dog racing – were the promotion of a common language, the emphasis on what was perceived to be a common past, the unity of a common sense of religion, and the construction of what was considered a distinct and authentic Afrikaner culture.

A complex network of Afrikaner economic and cultural organisations was established and strengthened as a countervailing force to dominant British institutions and cultural practices. In the financial field, banks (such as Barclays Bank) and insurance companies (such as Old Mutual) with large British assets were opposed by Volkskas and Sanlam respectively, which concentrated on mobilising Afrikaner capital in the interest of the *volk*. At another level, youth movements like the Boy Scouts had their Afrikaner counterpart in the *Voortrekkers*.[157]

Representation of history played an important part in the construction of Afrikaner nationalism. The 1938 centenary celebrations of the Great Trek, with nine ox-wagons moving slowly from Cape Town to the northern provinces, turned out to be unprecedented political and cultural theatre. The centenary Trek, symbolically rooted in an ideal and heroic past, gave powerful expression to a desire for a more prosperous future, free from British domination. Pre-industrial "pure" Afrikaner culture was emphasised and reflected in dress, dance and *Voortrekkerkultuur* in general.[158] It also gave rise to a renewed inter-

---

157 For the nature of Afrikaner nationalism see D. Moodie: *The Rise of Afrikanerdom: Power, Apartheid and the Afrikaner Civil Religion* (University of California Press, Berkeley, 1975); H. Adam and H. Giliomee: *The Rise and Crisis of Afrikaner Power* (D. Philip, Cape Town, 1979); D. O'Meara: *Volkskapitalisme: Class, Capital and Ideology in the Development of Afrikaner Nationalism, 1934–1948* (Cambridge University Press, Cambridge, 1983).
158 For the 1938 centenary celebrations see A. Grundlingh and H. Sapire: "From Feverish Festival to Repetitive Ritual? The Changing Fortunes of Great Trek Mythology in an Industrialising South Africa, 1938–1989", *South African Historical Journal*, 21 (1989), pp. 19–27.

est in a sport like jukskei which had claims of being an original Voortrekker form of recreation. After 1938, jukskei gained some foothold in Afrikaner circles and was organised and played competitively,[159] but in terms of the overall sporting scene it remained very much a minority interest.

It was rugby that continued to capture the imagination of many Afrikaners. The gradual Afrikaner appropriation of the game was not without paradox: given that the main thrust of Afrikaner nationalism was often directed against the perceived hegemony of English culture, why then did Afrikaners show such a strong interest in a game that originated in England and epitomised the British upper middle-class value system?

Even if nationalist cultural entrepreneurs had hoped to establish a completely new and authentic all-Afrikaner culture, such a project was not always feasible or viable. To create a pure, hermetically sealed culture is not easily accomplished; it is often more practicable to adapt, reshape and mould whatever promising material is at hand. In the case of rugby, Afrikaners had already proved that they could excel at the game, and it made sense to proceed from the vantage point.

The nature of the game itself also appealed to the evolving self-image of nationalist Afrikaners. Implicit in rugby is a certain duality. On the one hand, it can be seen as a collective sport of combat which emphasises stamina, strength, speed and courage; symbolically, the rugged aspects of the game could easily be equated with a resurgent and rampant Afrikaner nationalism. On the other hand, despite being a rough affair, it was considered a gentlemen's game and an excellent way of inculcating moral discipline in future leaders. The ambiguous qualities of rugby fitted in well with the physical, psychological and ideological needs of nationalist Afrikaners at a specific historical juncture. It is with considerable justification therefore that authors Archer and Bouillon can claim that rugby was a sport

> ideally suited to ideological investment and the Afrikaners who considered themselves to be a civilising elite, a pioneer people conquering barbarism, recognised an image of their own ideology in its symbols.[160]

---
159 P.W. Grobbelaar (ed.): *Die Afrikaner en sy Kultuur: Ons Volksfeeste* (Cape Town, 1977), p. 219.
160 Archer and Bouillon: *The South African Game*, p. 66.

In time though, as Afrikaners stamped their authority on the game, certain shifts in values and attitudes took place. Rugby might have originated in England and subsequently been exported to the colonies. But in line with the wider Afrikaner quest for independent nationhood, the game came to be an integral part of the attempt to transform and transcend the imperial heritage by reformulating and modifying the values associated with it. Whereas the British might have projected the game as a training ground for the inculcation and encouragement of values such as sportsmanship, gentlemanly conduct and fair-mindedness, Afrikaners placed less emphasis on these and more on the game as an opportunity to demonstrate presumed Afrikaner qualities such as ruggedness, endurance, forcefulness and determination.

Moreover, while the British regarded rugby as part of the imperial sporting ethos, confirming relations between the different sporting families of the Commonwealth, Afrikaners viewed the game in explicitly nationalistic and ethnic terms. Indeed, as one commentator has noted in general, "the playing fields bequeathed by the Empire have become the symbolic sites of post-imperial struggles – for power, for identity, for the *style* of self-determination."[161] This was particularly true in South Africa. In other Commonwealth countries, such as New Zealand, the desire for national self-expression through sport was still moderated by a relatively strong sense of imperial kinship.[162] In South Africa, however, in Afrikaner ranks in the decades since the 1930s, Springbok rugby carried a thinly disguised anti-imperialistic message. Whilst such a transformation was obviously far-reaching in terms of class, some elements of the imperial ethos had residual remains in that rugby as a game was nurtured at elite institutions like universities.

In analysing the linkages between the discourses of rugby and nationalist ideology, it is possible, of course, to overstate the case. It can be argued that there is nothing particularly exceptional or significant in a group of people supporting their country's team in a specific sport. They do so for a variety of reasons which do not necessarily

---

161 Quoted in W. Roger: *Old Heroes: The 1956 Springbok tour and the Lives Beyond* (Hodder & Stoughton, London, 1991), p. 32.
162 R. Holt: *Sport and the British: A Modern History* (Oxford University Press, Oxford, 1989), pp. 228–229.

reflect a wider nationalistic ideology. J.G. Kellas has made the salutary point that

> the most popular form of nationalist behaviour in many countries is in sport, where masses of people become highly emotional in support of their national team. But the same people may display no obvious nationalism in politics, such as supporting a nationalist party or demanding home rule or national independence.[163]

However, the situation was somewhat different in South Africa. Support for the Springboks was much more closely aligned to the overall Afrikaner nationalist enterprise in its various cultural and political manifestations. English-speaking South Africans might also have supported the Springboks, but their support was more muted, tempered by notions of friendly rivalry between different commonwealth countries. For many Afrikaners, this was not the case; support for the Springboks was on the same continuum as membership of the National Party.

For Afrikaners who felt themselves oppressed and disadvantaged by the continuing British influence in South Africa, rugby created an opportunity to beat the English at their own game. It is no surprise that rivalry between Afrikaans and English speakers was particularly fierce on the playing fields. Clashes between Afrikaans and English schools, universities and clubs gave the lie to the cliché that rugby was "only a game". One 'participant-observer' at an intervarsity game between the University of the Witwatersrand and the University of Pretoria, after the latter had become an autonomous Afrikaner university in the 1930s, recalled:

> When Witwatersrand played Pretoria, it wasn't just rugby they were playing, there was an enmity and a bitterness and a hatred of each other. The overtones were quite clear. The major goal was to beat the other university not only in the game. I think the competition between two such universities was naturally bitter ... because it was the child of the hatred of the Afrikaans – or the English-speaking. It certainly didn't dissipate the tension.[164]

---

163 J.G. Kellas: *The Politics of Nationalism and Ethnicity* (Palgrave Macmillan, London, 1991), p. 21.
164 Quoted in Archer and Bouillon: *The South African Game*, p. 73.

Playing with purpose

"Father" of the white nation, Jan van Riebeeck, comes down from his pedestal to meet his brood of Springbok rugby "children" returning from a triumphant tour of Britain in 1952. This cartoon appeared in the *Cape Times* of 6 March 1952 at the time of the lead up to the tercentenary of Van Riebeeck's arrival in Cape Town. *(Courtesy Leslie Witz)*

Much the same could be said for the annual intervarsities between the Universities of Cape Town and Stellenbosch.[165] Furthermore, when South Africa competed internationally, the outcome of matches against British teams was of more than just sporting interest. The Springbok tour to Britain in 1951/52, which saw the South Africans winning 30 out of 31 games, was hailed as a major national triumph; by contrast, when the Springboks lost two test matches against the British Lions during the 1955 tour of South Africa, the result was met with stunned disbelief: "How could it happen that a *boer* has been defeated by an Englishman on the rugby field?"[166] Some players even received death threats from the public for bringing the "national game" into disrepute by losing against the British.[167]

---

165 Compare Booysens: "Studentelewe", p. 364.
166 B. Booyens: *Danie Craven* (Cape Town, 1975), pp. 152–160.
167 D. Craven: *Die Leeus Keil Ons Op* (Johannesburg, 1956), p. 62.

While Afrikaner-English rivalry was real enough, Afrikaners shared the middle-class character of the game with their English counterparts. The steady upward mobility of Afrikaners, particularly under a sympathetic government in power from 1948 onwards, was accompanied by the proliferation of Afrikaner educational institutions with rugby as the main winter game. The pool of potential rugby players from the burgeoning middle class constantly grew. Commenting on the 1956 Springbok tour to Australia and New Zealand, G. Hogg, chairman of the New Zealand Rugby Council, considered the Springboks to be "mostly the educated type, whilst the All Blacks are mostly workmen who were used to a hard life".[168] It was difficult for a player not comfortably employed or who did not have some means of private income or other form of assistance to play top-level rugby for an extended period. This prompted Martin Pelser, a prominent Springbok flank forward in the 1960s who had turned to paid professional rugby, to remark on the class nature of the union game:

> I cannot recount the many days of unpaid leave I had to take for the sake of amateur rugby... Amateur rugby, and especially Springbok rugby, is a game for the sons of rich men. I, and others like me, could no longer afford it.[169]

In the early 1970s, 51% of the provincial rugby players could be classified as white collar workers, 21% as professionals, 10% as students, 8% as farmers, and under 10% as blue collar workers.[170] While these statistics are revealing, it has to be borne in mind that in certain areas like Despatch and Uitenhage in the Eastern Cape, the game had a considerable following amongst the white working class employed in the motor manufacturing industry.

In general, soccer did not enjoy the same middle-class status as rugby among Afrikaners. Working class children of the 1920s and early 1930s, living in cities like Cape Town, often played soccer instead of rugby. This was mainly because, in the absence of grass playing fields or large suburban lawns, it was easier to kick a soccer ball in some dusty and stony backstreet than to play a hard, physical

---

168 South African Rugby Board Minutes, 4, Meeting with Mr G. Hogg, 10 April 1957.
169 *The Sportsman*, March 1966, p. 12.
170 J.G. Williams: "Sosiologiese Ondersoek na Bepaalde Aspekte van die Maatskaplike Milieu en Leefwyse van 'n Groep Provinsiale Rugbyspelers" (Unpublished MA dissertation, University of Pretoria, 1976), pp. 22–23.

game like rugby on an unyielding surface.¹⁷¹ With the rise of organised Afrikanerdom and an assertive middle class, soccer's working class origins were frowned upon. Moreover, the fact that soccer was a very popular sport among black people, gave it in an increasingly racially stratified society, the tag of being a "black man's game".¹⁷²

The middle class character of rugby facilitated its acceptance as a constituent part of the white, and especially Afrikaner, establishment. Many of the players came from more or less the same background, and shared the same values. To play rugby was a respectable pastime that met with the approval and conformation of wider society. "Mr Rugby" himself, Danie Craven, recalled that in his playing

Danie Craven: Seen here carrying a mascot on to the field at Newlands in a test against the British Lions in 1938; destined in the years to come to carry the aspirations of generations of rugby players. *(From C. Greyvenstein,* Springbok saga: a pictorial history from 1891, *Cape Town, 1977)*

---

171 W.G. le Roux: "Die Vermaaklikheid en Ontspanning van die Armblanke Kind in Kaapstad" (Unpublished MA dissertation, University of Stellenbosch, 1940), p. 82 and *passim.*
172 On soccer in South Africa see T. Couzens: "An Introduction to the History of Football in South Africa" in B. Bozzoli (ed.), *Town and Countryside in the Transvaal: Capitalist Penetration and Popular Response* (Johannesburg, 1983), pp. 198–214; F.J. Nöthling: "Soccer in South Africa: A Brief Outline", *Kleio* (1982), pp. 28–41; I. Jeffrey: "Street Rivalry and Patron-Managers: Football in Sharpeville, 1943–1985", *African Studies*, 15, 1 (1992), pp. 68–94; Archer and Bouillon: *The South African Game*, pp. 98–101, 195–198.

days in the 1930s, the word "rugby" was a name "to conjure" with, a magical word, and a rugby player was admired by all and sundry.[173] Admittedly, not all the spectators were middle class, but they were sufficiently ethnically integrated into Afrikaner society not to allow matters of class to affect their support of the game.

The way Afrikaner rugby meshed with the establishment fitted in with the general sociological pattern discernible in other rugby-playing countries. In 1974, Chris Laidlaw, a New Zealand scrumhalf and Oxford scholar, noted in no uncertain terms that:

> A central reason for rugby's international conformity is the fact that it is, universally, an establishment activity. Distressingly so. It is normally played and administered by conservative elements in society. The ... "rugger buggers" of today are far from radical; rugby's tradition would hardly have survived if they were. They are acquiring reputations as thundering bores with short hair and a suspicion of "lefties". Today's players are by and large tomorrow's Tories.[174]

Likewise, in the South African context, it has been claimed that players generally hold conservative world views, and that the nature of the game, with its particular traditions, seemed to attract "authoritarian personality types".[175] These corollaries are not without significance for Afrikaner nationalism; they reinforced values like respect for perceived tradition, rules and authority, integral to the nationalist movement, and at the same time encouraged a certain cultural conformity.

As a form of popular culture, rugby had considerable self-generating power, but it also needed to be recharged by outside currents in the form of touring teams. Such teams often received tumultuous welcomes and almost saturation media coverage. During the 1970 tour of New Zealand to South Africa, Laidlaw found that

> the All Blacks were pictured, pestered, pondered, prodded and praised until every man, woman and child knew that this player ate eggs for breakfast, that one ate spinach, this lock-forward visited the toilet twice a day, and that one twenty times.[176]

---

173 *Huisgenoot*, 27 May 1966, p. 30.
174 C. Laidlaw: *Mud in your Eye: A Worm's Eye View of the Changing World of Rugby* (Timmins, Cape Town, 1974), p. 6.
175 J.M. Coetzee in *Die Suid-Afrikaan*, August 1988, p. 4. See also Williams: "Sosiologiese ondersoek" p. 55, for views on race.
176 Laidlaw: *Mud in your Eye*, pp. 97–98.

Rugby tours by overseas countries provided a focal point for national interest, an opportunity to showcase a "sanitised" South Africa during the first decades of apartheid and, perhaps more importantly, to demonstrate that the Afrikaner could beat the best the world could offer. Cultural entrepreneurs explicitly stated that such events were important for promoting ethnic self-esteem.[177]

International sporting events can be likened to "exhibitionist events imbued with the authority to recreate or simulate the nation, offering a vigorous display of proxy body politic".[178] Prowess on the rugby field reinforced and fed into wider notions of the perceived attributes of the nation. Not for nothing are rugby internationals called "tests"; they act as barometers of the state of the nation in terms of power, bravery, determination and tactical acumen – all of which can not only reflect on the present and the past, but also constitute a portent of the future.[179] This kind of identification is clear from the fulsome way in which the Springboks on the demonstration ridden tour of the United Kingdom in 1969/70 were revered upon their return. They were severely tested on and off the field, but according to Gerhard Viviers, an Afrikaans radio journalist, they passed with flying colours: "We raise our hats high to these men," he wrote. "They were South Africa's best export products of recent years – brilliant ambassadors from a country which loves them dearly."[180]

Rugby's considerable spectator appeal – for example, the 1955 tour of the British Lions was watched by record-breaking crowds – further contributed to a common consciousness. Interest in rugby can be seen as one element contributing to the shaping of what Benedict Anderson, in a memorable phrase, has called "an imagined community".[181] One is hard-pressed to find a clearer expression of this sense of community and the fusion of the private and public worlds than in the official message of Danie Craven upon the oc-

---

177 For example J.R. Albertyn (et al.): *Kerk en Stad*, p. 262.
178 R. Nixon: "Apartheid on the Run: The South African Sports Boycott," *Transitions*, 58, 1992, p. 72.
179 Compare Nixon: "Apartheid on the Run", p. 72.
180 G. Viviers: *Rugby Agter Doringdraad* (J.P. van der Walt, Pretoria, 1970), p. 116. (Translation)
181 B. Anderson: *Imagined Communities: Reflections on the Origins and Spread of Nationalism* (Verso, London, 1983), p. 15.

casion of the 75th anniversary of the South African Rugby Board in 1964:

> South Africa, this is your celebration, your festival, for the game belongs to you... You have seen bright and dark days, smiles and tears; you have experienced tension and gaiety; certainty and uncertainty, but they have made you stronger and nobler. They have welded you together as nothing else in our history; and it has been this game which has provided you with a feeling of belongingness, of a oneness which so few people ever feel. It has taken you away from your own world into a larger world ... it has given you friends...[182]

Shared sporting enthusiasm holds out the strong possibility of sharing other wider interests as well. In this respect, Eric Hobsbawm has neatly outlined the role of sport in the formulation of a nationalistic consciousness:

> What has made sport so uniquely effective a medium for inculcating national feelings, at all events for males, is the ease with which even the least political or public individual can identify with the nation as symbolised by young persons excelling at what practically every man wants, or at one time in life has wanted, to be good at. The imagined community of millions seems more real as a team of eleven named people. The individual, even the one who only cheers, becomes a symbol of his nation himself.[183]

In South Africa, rugby performed precisely this function of merging and strengthening affinities. In this sense, the game can be seen as a powerful, if informal, disseminator of nationalist sentiment and a source of identification with the *volk* at large. Afrikaans newspapers played a significant part in this, realising early on that their readers were at least as interested in rugby as they were in politics.[184] For outside visitors to the country, the fit between nationalist politics and rugby as an integral element of Afrikaner popular culture was a distinct feature of the social landscape.[185] Given the game's prominence, it is not surprising to find that it was fully incorporated as part

---

182 R. Johnstone and C. Neville: *Rugby in South Africa* (Cape Town, 1964), p. i.
183 E.J. Hobsbawn: *Nations and Nationalism since 1780: Programme, Myth and Reality* (Cambridge University Press, Cambridge, 1990), p. 143.
184 L. Barnard and J-A Stemmet: *'n Lewe van sy Eie: Die Biografie van Volksblad*, Tafelberg, Cape Town, 2004, p. 126.
185 Roger: *Old Heroes*, pp. 32–33.

of the nationalist first five-year anniversary festivities of the Republic in 1966 when a Springbok team played against a team selected from the rest of South Africa.[186]

Rugby could also over time serve as a useful nationalist memory bank. In 1962 in a test against the British Lions, the Springbok centre Mannetjies Roux scored a remarkable solo try. The press at the time described the feat in almost euphoric terms: "While a host of defenders laid scattered in his wake or stood about with lowered heads, Roux – without a finger being laid on him – soared over the goal line."[187] It was a try that was destined to become engraved in the collective memory as an iconic moment. It echoed further than the stadium; symbolically it could be seen to represent a triumphalist nationalist movement moving into full swing with the banning of the African National Congress, an economy rapidly picking up steam and then to crown it all a brilliant try by Roux against the British. Years after the event the singer Laurika Rauch immortalised the moment in a popular nostalgic song with the refrain: "Do you still remember the try of Mannetjies Roux?" (*Onthou jy nog die drie van Mannetjies Roux?*)

Equally pertinent is the way in which an attempt was made to indigenise the culture surrounding rugby. One area in which this found expression was the widespread practice of assigning nicknames to prominent players. Nicknames in sport are, of course, not uncommon. They often serve the purpose of decreasing the psychological distance between the successful performer and the average spectator. It can be seen as a symbolic way of "cutting a player down to the size of ordinary people", and drawing the player into a private world of the familiar and the commonplace.[188] What is particularly notice-

---

186 W. Claassen: *Kaalvoetklong tot Rugbytoks* (Lapa Publishers, Pretoria, 2011), p. 88.
187 H. le Roux: *Sportpourri: Ervarings van 'n Joernalis* (Van Schaik, Pretoria, 1998), p. 42. (Translation)
188 Compare J.K. Skipper: "The Sociological Significance of Nicknames: The Case of Baseball Players" in *Journal of Sport Behaviour*, 7, 1 (February 1984), pp. 28–37; N. Petryszak: "Spectator Sports as an Aspect of Popular Culture – An Historical View", *Journal of Sport Behaviour*, 1, 1 (February 1978), pp. 14–27. For nicknames in the South African context see P. Pearson: "Function, Familiarity or Fun? Nicknames in Rehoboth, Namibia", African Studies Institute paper, University of the Witwatersrand, October 1988.

able about rugby nicknames in South Africa is the way in which they reflected an Afrikaner rural background. Approximately 60% of recorded nicknames had rural or related connotations: Jakkals (jackal) Keevy, Hasie (bunny) Versfeldt, Koei (cow) Brink, Skilpad (tortoise) Eloff, Padda (frog) Melville, Apie (monkey) Pretorius, Appels (apples) Odendaal, Wa (wagon) Lamprecht, and Boon (bean) Rautenbach were just a few of the names Afrikaner rugby enthusiasts affectionately bestowed on players.[189] The rural imagery evoked by these names correlate with a dimension of Afrikaner nationalism which had, as its representational theme, the notion of Afrikaners as solid, pioneering men of the soil, subsumed under the honorary title *boere*.[190] On the basis of this, it is not inconceivable that interlocking emblematic themes, drawing upon the familiar, acted as a further factor blending nationalism and rugby in the public mind. Significantly, as this element of Afrikaner nationalism gradually declined, nicknames with a rural connotation also decreased accordingly.[191]

Rugby politics: Intrawhite tensions and rugby as a *volksfees* (national festival)

Rugby politics was expressed in more than one way: in the boardroom and also more loosely, though equally significant, in the domain of popular culture as a spectacle with political undercurrents.

As far as the first dimension is concerned, there was a close link between nationalism and control over the game. The Second World War proved to be the catalyst for highlighting this interrelationship. The decision of the United Party government to participate in the Second World War in 1939 had a deeply divisive effect on the white community. A considerable number of nationalistic Afrikaners opposed South Africa's entry into the war, arguing that there was no need for South Africa to rush to the aid of the British, who from the days of the Anglo-Boer War of 1899–1902 were perceived by many Afrikaners as the traditional "enemy".

These antagonisms spilled over onto the playing fields and clubs when predominantly English-speaking and pro-war administrators

---

189 *Rugby*, February 1975, p. 38.
190 Compare Grundlingh and Sapire: "From Feverish Festival to Repetitive Ritual", p. 25.
191 For more recent names see *Die Burger*, 2 October 2010.

collected money for war funds during rugby fixtures and organised games with the specific aim of boosting the war coffers. The anti-war faction retaliated by organising games on behalf of the *Reddingsdaadbond*, an Afrikaner organisation which ostensibly collected funds for "poor white" Afrikaners. This added fuel to the fire, with some rugby unions – most notably the Eastern Province and the Western Province – being split right down the middle. Dissidents, incensed that rugby should be used to support the war effort, formed their own unions and arranged their own games. Rugby was now divided along pro-war and anti-war lines and the schism had a rough English-Afrikaans correlate.[192]

At the rugby-playing Mecca – the University of Stellenbosch – it was claimed that the club had no option but to break away because the Western Province Union had decided to introduce politics into sport. Conveniently ignoring that the establishment of their own union was equally political, the legendary and influential A.F. Markötter argued that rugby was of greater importance than any other possible concern. Upon leaving the Western Province Union, he exclaimed: "Mr Chairman, I have no religion. I have no politics. My religion and politics are rugby. You will not stop Stellenbosch from playing rugby."[193]

Although the divisions were serious enough at the time, once South Africa's involvement in the war had ended in 1945, it was possible in the less volatile post-war political atmosphere to work towards a reconciliation between the two factions. After patient negotiations, the breakaway clubs were eventually unconditionally admitted back into the fold.[194] To all intents and purposes, quiet had returned to the rugby front in 1945, but much of it was illusory since the thorny question of political control of the sport remained. Although Afrikaners had taken to rugby in large numbers, they had

---

192 F.J.G. van der Merwe: "Afrikaner Nationalism and Sport", *Canadian Journal of Sport*, 22, 2 (December 1991), pp. 40–42; G.B. Saaiman: "Sport en Politiek: Suid Afrika se Sportisolasie en die Invloed op die Binnelandse Politiek" (Unpublished MA dissertation, University of the Orange Free State, 1981), pp. 106–108; G. Kotze: *Sport en Politiek* (Pretoria, 1978), 11–20; Dobson: *Rugby in South Africa*, pp. 85–89.
193 Quoted in D.H. Craven: *Oubaas Mark* (Afrikaanse Pers-Boekhandel, Cape Town, 1959), p. 193.
194 Dobson: *Rugby in South Africa*, p. 92.

yet to capture the administration of the game and dictate its politics. Commenting on the emotions engendered by the divisions of the war years, A.J. Pienaar, President of the South African Rugby Board, noted:

> Dissident clubs should remember that rugby football was an English game, introduced by English pioneers, and fostered in this country by all sections of the community, English, Afrikaans, Jews, gentiles and coloured people, and that the dissident's views were not the only views that could be expressed or respected.[195]

Although unintended, implicit in this was an important message for Afrikaners: unless they had full control of the various bodies involved in rugby, they would be unable to influence the wider social and political dimensions of the sport in South Africa.

Afrikanerisation of the rugby establishment was a slow process. In the Transvaal it took at least 20 years for Afrikaners to gain ultimate control of the union. Attempts had already been made in the mid-1940s to oust English speakers from the administration of the union, but it was only in 1965 that J. le Roux was able to wrest the reins from the long-serving H.J. Sanderson, as the first Afrikaner president of the Transvaal Rugby Union. Le Roux's election was preceded by an intensive campaign to influence various clubs and to ensure that members with Afrikaner sympathies were well placed in the organisational structure of the union. Le Roux's victory did not come as a bolt from the blue; it was carefully orchestrated and meticulously planned. Nothing was left to chance: on the eve of the election, arrangements were even made with the employer of a "doubtful" member who, it was suspected, might vote against the Afrikaner faction, to send him out of town on "business" on the crucial day to ensure that he would not be able to cast his vote.[196]

In the Cape Province the South African Rugby Board was for much of its history under the sway of English speakers or anglicised Afrikaners and conducted its business in a time-honoured clubbish fashion. There was a distinct disjuncture between an English-oriented board and the great preponderance of Afrikaans-speaking rugby players. Gradually, however, particularly after the Second World War and the National Party ascent to power in 1948, more Afrikan-

---

195 South African Rugby Board Minutes, 2, 17 May 1943.
196 Kotze: *Sport en Politiek*, pp. 11–28.

ers found their way into top administrative positions and in 1956 Danie Craven as an Afrikaans speaker was elected as president of the board.[197]

Of undoubted importance in bringing about Afrikaner control of the rugby administration was the Afrikaner Broederbond (the Brotherhood). The Broederbond was a secret, cultural organisation consisting of elite Afrikaners. Its actual influence on state policy and high-ranking National Party politicians is probably often exaggerated, but its cultural sway cannot be dismissed. As rugby was considered the "national" game of the Afrikaner, it is not surprising to find that, over the years, the Broederbond gained significant influence in the rugby unions.[198]

What is surprising, however, is that Danie Craven, chairman of the board and destined to occupy that position for successive decades, was not a member of the Broederbond. Why was such an important position entrusted to a *non-Broeder*? Part of the answer is that even though the Broederbond was powerful, it was not omnipotent. Craven, through his long association with rugby in South Africa and his overseas contacts, and by virtue of his forceful personality, managed to attract support from *Broeder* and *non-Broeder* alike. Ousting Craven and installing a *Broeder* would have called for an exceptional effort and a unique candidate to match Craven's credentials. It seems, too, that in broad ideological terms, the Broederbond was able to live with Craven. While he was more pragmatic and less purist than most *Broeders*, the division between Craven and the Broederbond was not unbridgeable. Craven had grown used to dealing with *Broeders* at the University of Stellenbosch, and the rugby world was no different. Although he was a supporter of the United Party, he was of the opinion that there were also "good people" in the *Bond*.[199] This did not imply that the two parties trusted each other wholeheartedly. Craven made it clear that he would not tolerate undue interference in rugby affairs by the Broederbond. In turn, at the time of the South African tour to New Zealand in 1956 with Craven as manager, there were widespread rumours that the Broederbond had seen to it that Dan

---

197 H. Gerber: *Craven* (Tafelberg, Cape Town, 1982), pp. 174–178.
198 I. Wilkins and H. Strydom: *The Super-Afrikaners* (Jonathan Ball, Johannesburg, 1978), p. 245.
199 G. Gerber: *Dok Craven: Agter die Kap van die Byl* (US Press, Stellenbosch, 2000), p. 75. (Translation)

de Villiers, a *Broeder*, was appointed as assistant manager with the deliberate intention that he should keep a watchful eye on Craven.[200]

While Afrikaner control over the administration of rugby was well established in the 1960s, changes in the social composition of Afrikanerdom began to affect the popularity of rugby as the main, and often only, sporting pursuit of young Afrikaner men. These changes were related to a booming economy and the increasing embourgeoisement of Afrikaners. The South African economy registered a real growth rate of 8,1% in 1963, 6,7% in 1964 and 6,6% in 1965. More and more Afrikaners had come to excel at business and in leading professions, and along with their domination of the civil service as an almost exclusive preserve, they gained in confidence and social self-expression. They no longer felt inferior to English speakers. With greater wealth at their disposal and a modified self-image, it was possible to embrace more varied leisure-time interests. Sports such as swimming, cricket, golf and tennis slowly began to compete with rugby.[201] It was with some unease that the rugby establishment commented upon these trends. The youth, it was claimed in 1968, was becoming "soft" and King Rugby ran the risk of becoming a third-rate sport in South Africa.[202] It was an unduly pessimistic view. Although social developments did affect rugby, the game had over the years built up too much support among Afrikaners to be seriously threatened. The linkages between Afrikaner nationalism and rugby might have become slightly more tenuous, but they were not in any danger of being severed. Rugby's real challenge in the late 1960s was not to come from changing social patterns among Afrikaners, but from an Afrikaner government intent on the rigid application of apartheid regulations.

Apartheid was more than a system of legally entrenched racial

---

200 T. Patridge: *A Life in Rugby* (Southern Book Publishers, Johannesburg, 1991), pp. 70–73; Roger: *Old Heroes*, 90; Kotze: *Sport en Politiek*, p. 121; P. Dobson: *Doc: The Life of Danie Craven* (Cape Town, 1994), pp. 133–135.
201 D. Welsh: "Urbanisation and the Solidarity of Afrikaner Nationalism", *Journal of Modern African Studies*, 7, 2 (1969), pp. 265–276; W. Beinart: *South Africa in the 20th Century* (Oxford University Press, Oxford, 1994), p. 178.
202 South African Rugby Board, 4, President's report, 1968. See also *Die Huisgenoot*, 27 May 1966 and Q. van Rooyen: *Springbok-triomf* (Tafelberg, Cape Town, 1972), pp. 106–107.

discrimination; it also completely skewed the distribution of access to resources. Facilities for whites were far superior to those of blacks. This belied the often quoted claim that apartheid provided "separate but equal" opportunities. Having made rugby its "national" game, the Afrikaner establishment until the 1970s had little concern for the rugby being played by other population groups. Although black rugby had a long history in the Eastern Cape (where missionary influence coupled with the zeal of new rugby converts carried the ball from the late nineteenth century through to the 1960s), its unions functioned separately from the white ones.[203] The inequality between white and black rugby was graphically reflected in the contrasting conditions in which the game was played. Mono Badela, a well-known figure in Eastern Cape black rugby circles, highlighted these:

> Talk South African rugby, and the images which spring to mind are fairly obvious. Sweaty white men in green jerseys, Springbok badges on their chests. Titanic battles on the plush green grass of Ellis Park, Loftus Versfeldt or Newlands. Currie Cup fever, tours to Australia, France and England... The pictures are vivid and clear ... but there is another side to South African rugby – the game played in the dusty Eastern Cape townships of New Brighton, Mdantsane, Kwazakhele and Zwidi. There, the images are of dilapidated stadiums which look more like cross-country courses than playing fields. Scenes of African and coloured working class people, scrumming down on a dusty stony surface, car headlights illuminating a cold winter's night.[204]

The differences in playing conditions were to be an enduring theme in the overall history of rugby in South Africa. It also spawned, as will be discussed later, different political responses and sporting boycotts.[205]

What is of interest at this point is how rugby emerged during turbulent political times as an effervescent form of public culture,

---

[203] For a history of black rugby see J.B. Peires: "*Facta non verba*: Towards a History of Black Rugby in the Eastern Cape" (Unpublished paper, History Workshop, University of the Witwatersrand, 1981); Dobson: *Rugby in South Africa* pp. 167–227; A. Odendaal, "The Thing that is not Round: The Untold Story of Black Rugby in South Africa" in A. Grundlingh, A. Odendaal and B. Spies: *Beyond the Tryline: Rugby and South African Society* (Ravan Press, Johannesburg, 1995), pp. 24–63.
[204] M. Badela: "Scrumming down", *Leadership*, 12 (5) 1993, p. 117.
[205] See chapter 4.

assuming a new importance. Indeed, it can be argued that from 1970 to 1989 rugby as a cultural activity started to displace traditional and formalised Afrikaner culture such as *volksfeeste*. These festivals were usually associated with the "sacred history" of Afrikanerdom's inexorable march to a supposed apartheid heaven on earth. The Day of the Covenant, celebrated annually on 16 December, glorifying the nineteenth-century Great Trek as bringing "light" and "civilisation" to the interior, was of particular significance. From the 1930s until well into the 1960s the celebrations of the Day of the Covenant were important and well-attended occasions. In many ways these *volksfeeste* represented the high point of stylised public Afrikaner culture, characterised by an ideological blending of past achievements and current challenges.

However, in the 1970s and 1980s, as Afrikanerdom became increasingly divided politically and as the country lurched from one crisis to the other, these celebrations started to lose whatever binding force they might have had. In the face of external sanctions, a declining economy and internal black insurrections, the past that had earlier made perfect ideological sense and that had projected Afrikaners as the "natural" rulers of South Africa, now no longer seemed appropriate. Formalised Afrikaner popular culture started to lose its appeal.[206]

Furthermore, interest in traditional festivities also declined as different leisure patterns, fuelled by consumerism, emerged. Eugene Terreblanche, leader of the Afrikanerweerstandsbeweging (AWB), who in his fiery oratory made much of the "sacred history" of Afrikanerdom, found that what he called the "Coca-Cola culture" muffled the sound of his ethnic drum in places like the Eastern Transvaal Highveld coal-producing areas. Commenting on this, a journalist noted:

> Coca-Cola, Lion Lager, colour televisions, microwave ovens, videos, fast cars and caravans – these are what concern the volk here much more than political ideologies or AWB rallies. Far from being traditionalists who reject the modern world, the Afrikaners here rush to acquire every latest bauble of modernity.[207]

---

206 Grundlingh and Sapire: From "Feverish Festival to Repetitive Ritual?", pp. 19–37.
207 *Frontline*, April 1988.

Whereas *volksfeeste* had become decidedly anachronistic for large sections of Afrikanerdom, rugby as a cultural phenomenon maintained its enduring attraction. Rugby provided entertainment in an almost carnivalesque form: it did not carry an overt political message – at a time when many Afrikaners welcomed a respite from unrelenting political pressure – and it provided an opportunity for predominantly male camaraderie and time-honoured ritualistic social behaviour. In short it was a *volksbyeenkoms*, a closing of the ranks, but without agonising political soul-searching and sombre overtones.

Writing on sport as popular culture, an American author has observed that the "sports carnival is, in a sense, a celebration, an escape into a fantasy and revelry, a brief relief from the mundane, often routine affairs and constraints of everyday living and working".[208] Rugby as a cultural carnival in South Africa was no different. This was particularly noticeable during the "rebel" New Zealand tour under the name of the Cavaliers in 1986. Afrikanerdom might have been politically divided, the country gripped in a state of psychosis as black people forcibly challenged the structures of apartheid and the tour itself highly controversial and "illegitimate". But all of this merely heightened the need of embattled whites for a momentary escape from the harsh realities of South Africa. A columnist in the Afrikaans press went to the heart of the matter when he reflected on the "rebel" tour:

> Whites certainly have a right to enjoy that which is *lekker* [particularly pleasing]. Must we all sit in sackcloth and ashes and hypocritically mourn all the ills of this old world, all the lies and deceit, just because we live in South Africa? And do we have to keep ourselves from all the joys of life until the day that the supposed utopia … of a non-racial South Africa will arrive, when whites will have to cede all the rights to a radical black clique? If the New Zealand tour can be a moral injection for this country – even if it's only for whites – it would be a good thing. South African now needs every bit of positivism [sic] it can find.[209]

Another journalist wrote with heartfelt emotion and more than just a touch of nostalgia on the eve of the test between the Cavaliers and the Springboks at Newlands, Cape Town:

---

208 L. Kutcher: "The American Sport Event as Carnival: An Emergent Norm Approach to Crowd Behavior" in *Journal of Popular Culture*, 16, 1982, p. 39
209 *Oosterlig*, 25 April 1986. (Translation)

Along the touch line, thousands will get gooseflesh when the Springboks and All Blacks as elite inheritors of the long-standing rugby friendship, run onto the green turf of Newlands under the shadows of Table Mountain. There may be yellow stripes on the black jerseys of the All Blacks and the sponsors' logo next to our beloved bokkie on the chests of the Springboks, but that does not matter. Sports fans will be saying: "Long live rugby between the Springboks and these All Blacks!"[210]

Rapport reports on a rugby test with a telling banner headline, *(Rapport, 16 August 1992)*

It was the near obsession with rugby, to the exclusion of much else, that worried someone like Morné du Plessis, destined to be manager of the South African squad for the World Cup. Du Plessis, a noted Springbok captain of the 1970s, who had run into trouble with the establishment for his anti-apartheid views, was of the opinion in the mid-1980s that white people, and particularly Afrikaners, made far too much of rugby. Rugby, he said, had become "a symbol of our way of life", and the game was in danger of becoming associated with "white dominance and arrogance".[211]

The significance of rugby in a beleaguered society was underlined by the involvement of the South African Defence Force in the game. The Defence Force with a huge bi-annual intake of national conscripts did much to promote the game. Part of the reasoning was that rugby, as a disciplined team game, could help in the moulding of young men into soldiers. "You can take a rugby player and within

---
210 *Die Burger*, 10 May 1986. (Translation)
211 *Die Suid-Afrikaan*, December 1988–January 1989.

half an hour make a soldier of him," was the opinion of Magnus Malan, head of the Defence Force.[212] In the early 1980s, the Defence Force produced eight players for the Springbok team. Although this might have been a matter of pride for the Defence Force, for anti-apartheid political activists who viewed the Force solely as an army in the service of an illegitimate government, it provided ample proof of the close interrelationship between the game and the ruling establishment.

Rugby and masculinity

It has been said that much of Afrikaner historiography dealing with the history of the *volk* has been predominantly "conceived of in terms of male actors who create and sustain the nation by military and constitutional or political struggles from which women were by definition excluded".[213] While tentative attempts have recently been made to address the situation, on the whole this neglect has skewed historical understanding on at least two levels: it rendered women historically invisible, and as a natural corollary it contained no conception of gender relations with the result that the notion of masculinity remains unproblematised. In the conceptual literature on these issues it has now become almost axiomatic that "masculinities are fluid and should not be considered as belonging in a fixed way to any one group of men".[214] What concerns us in this context is the way in which rugby helped to shape a particular male identity and how this became manifest.

Rugby, in part at least because of the rough, physical nature of the game, has acquired a reputation of being pre-eminently "a man's game". It has been described as the "ultimate man-maker", inculcating values such as "courage, self-control and stamina". All of these, it is claimed, are the products of the "man-to-man" element in rugby, for to "play rugger well, you must play it fiercely, and at the

---

212 Quoted in Roger: *Old Heroes*, p. 203.
213 D. Gaitskell, J. Kimble and E. Unterhalter: "Historiography in the 1970s: A feminist perspective", *Southern African Studies: retrospect and prospect* (Centre of African Studies, University of Edinburgh, 1983), p. 164.
214 R. Morrell: "The Times of Change: Men and Masculinity in South Africa" in R. Morrell (ed.), *Changing Men in Southern Africa* (Natal University Press, Durban 2001), p. 7.

same time, and all the time, remember while doing so that you are a gentleman".[215] In colonial Natal rugby not only had a clear upper middle-class connotation but also provided the opportunity for male bonding. As Rob Morrell has explained: "For the men ... in those moments when there was no war to fight, black labour to discipline, flooded rivers to ford, transport wagons to drive, women-in-distress to rescue ... rugby remained as a reliable place where they could enjoy the company of friends." [216]

From a very young age, boys in rugby-playing countries have been socialised into a world where rugby is an important element in the construction of male identity. Although some boys might have spurned the narrow basis upon which male identity was defined, the culture of the sport, imbued with a strong sense of tradition, encouraged conformity. "If you did not play rugby," was the less than subtle assumption, "there must be something wrong with you, *boetie* (lad)."[217] The presumed connection between rugby and manliness was often woven into father-son relationships. An evocative illustration of this ritual transmission is to be found in many photographs of primary school rugby: "A real lineout on a full-size field of little boys with bewildered expressions, knobbly knees, and spindly arms, all in real uniforms and short hair. Savage-looking parents patrol the sideline."[218]

One arena in which a rough and ready frontier-type masculinity played itself out, is to be found in the rivalry between South Africa and New Zealand rugby teams. The All Blacks were seen to come from farming stock – excellent species of manhood, strong and hardened by manual labour in a harsh climate – and much the same characteristics were assigned to their Afrikaner opponents in the Springbok team. Such perceptions did not necessarily accurately

---

215 E.H.D. Sewell: *Rugger – The Man's Game* (Hollis & Carter, London, 1950), p. 22.
216 R. Morrell: "Forging a Changing Race: Rugby and White Masculinity in Colonial Natal, c 1870–1910" in J. Nauright and T.J.L. Chandler: *Making Men: Rugby and Masculine Identity* (Frank Cass, London, 1996), 115.
217 *Rapport*, 19 August 2013. (Translation)
218 M.N. Pearson: "Heads in the Sand: The 1956 Springbok tour to New Zealand in Perspective" in R. Cashman and M. McKernan (eds), *Sport in History: The Making of Modern Sporting History* (University of Queensland, Sydney, 1979), p. 282.

reflect the vocational background of the players, but it came to constitute an emblematic theme, projecting and encompassing the nature of the contest between the two countries. Although both societies were rather small and isolated, through rugby their men could demonstrate their prowess and indulge in a self-constructed battle for world supremacy in a sport that is not played in many countries. Each tour served the ritual affirmation, celebrating at the same time their distinctiveness as different colonial societies as well as a shared identity which foregrounded white males as player-heroes and a supporting cast of near delirious spectators.[219]

A particular tour that stands out as an epic in this regard is the 1956 Springbok tour to New Zealand. A ready chord, playing on the notion of frontier masculinity, was struck with the depiction of the Springboks as the "descendants of the rugged Voortrekkers who pioneered South Africa for white civilisation and ... impressed with their manliness..."[220] In the press the scene for a gigantic clash of masculinities was set even before the tour started. On the Australian leg of the tour, reporting on the Springboks emphasised the physical appearance of the South African tourists, sounding an early warning to the New Zealand rugby fraternity. Much was made of the "clean-cut cast of countenance and athletic looks" of the players and in forthright terms some were described as the "embodiment of virile manhood". There were, so it seemed, almost no limits to the masculine traits of some Springboks, even to the ludicrous extent that the facial stubble of one player was reported "as almost twice life sized". Although the way in which the male body was depicted was exaggerated, it was not out of place given the rough nature of the game in which the size of the body, particularly for those who played in certain positions, was an important consideration for success on the field. The way in which bodies were built and the way they were to be used was an important element for defining masculinity. A corol-

---

219 J. Nauright and D. Black: "'Hitting Them Where it Hurts': Springbok – All Black Rugby, Masculine National Identity and Counter-Hegemonic Struggle, 1959–1992" in J. Nauright and T. Chandler (eds), *Making Men: Rugby and Masculine Identity* (Frank Cass, London, 1996), p. 206.
220 F. Andrewes: "'Demonstrable Virility': Images of Masculinity in the 1956 Springbok Rugby Tour of New Zealand", in G. Ryan (ed.), *Tackling Rugby Myths: Rugby and New Zealand Society* (University of Otago Press, Dunedin, 2005), p. 123.

lary of this was that a male build which deviated from the ideal rugby type was seen as an aberration. Those players who were of smaller stature, despite their skills and speed on the field, were not deemed to be in the same masculine league. Therefore, Tommy Gentles, the diminutive and bespectacled but talented university-educated scrum-half of the 1956 Springbok team, was described as "looking like a pedant escaped from a university library" or as a "fourth-form swot who has been put into long pants too soon."[221]

A hallmark of the 1956 tour was the particular physical nature of the contest – it was a tour where the respective teams literally put their bodies on the line for what was seen as the greater glory of their countries. "Test rugby", it was reported in South Africa, "is war on the playing field, from that we cannot escape. Where rough men square up to one another and the sporting achievements of their respective countries are at stake, the spectator cannot expect parlour games."[222] The test matches turned out to be an exhibition of the punishment the male body could mete out and absorb on the field. There was an almost mutually agreed but never fully expressed assumption that within the controlled space of the rugby field a certain level of violence, particular in the scrums, rucks and mauls, was to be expected and such behaviour shaped the contours of idealised masculine behaviour on the field. The conduct of a player who indulged in fisticuffs without the referee noticing was not necessarily regarded as transgressing the rules of the game; his actions were tacitly condoned as what was expected of him as a man. During the 1956 tour, the New Zealand selectors even drafted in a former heavyweight boxer to "sort out" what was considered a "troublesome" Springbok front row. The construction of masculinity revolved around the controlled use of boots, fists, elbows and knees: male violence on the field was sanctioned in its context in very much the same way as killing during warfare is licensed by its context.[223] However, one should be careful not to overstate the case; the game still had to be fair and therefore unbridled brutality could not be countenanced. In part this notion had its origins of the sport as a "gentlemen's" game,

---

221 Andrewes: "Images of Masculinity", pp. 123–124.
222 Addendum to *Die Huisgenoot*, 5 November 1956, "Skinner – Bokser of Voorryman". (Translated)
223 Andrewes: "Images of Masculinity", pp. 122–123.

played by men who knew how to be hard and fair at the same time. In international rugby where ethnic pride was at stake and the dominant form of masculinity was seen to be put to the supreme test, the line between what was acceptable expressions of violence and what not, became very fine indeed. At one point Danie Craven, manager of the 1956 Springbok team, thought that that line had been crossed and considered calling off the tour. The likely repercussions of such a step and the aspersions that it would cast on his men, made him decide otherwise though.[224]

The association between rugby and manliness was often carried over from youth to adulthood, and it was also reinforced off the playing field through the practices and rituals which became part of the rugby-playing community. One such South African practice worth recounting is that of *borselling*: the team lifts one of the members chest-high and beats him on the backside with bare hands.[225] For some it was meant to be a form of initiation; for others who had transgressed the rules of a touring party it was a form of punishment. But there is also a sense in which this act can be seen as promoting team cohesion and therefore, implicitly, firmer male bonding.

Apart from the players whose "maleness" could find forceful expression on rugby tours, the game also offered male spectators an opportunity to celebrate, however briefly, a collective camaraderie. A journalist once recalled the importance that watching rugby at Newlands in Cape Town had for her father in the 1950s and early 1960s:

> For him it was a vicarious pleasure, a dream of camaraderie and manhood that assured him an escape into a world of physical splendour that was reasonably cheerful and brotherly, a sort of war with rules, and oranges to suck at half-time.[226]

Since the game was such an overpowering male activity, where "maleness" mattered above all else, it is not surprising that because of inadequate contact with the members of the opposite sex some rugby men were inclined to stereotype women. Therefore, Danie

---

224 P. Dobson: *Doc: The Life of Danie Craven* (Human & Rousseau, Cape Town, 1994), p. 117.
225 Pearson: "Heads in the Sand", 285. See also Roger: *Old Heroes*, 91; J. Robbie: *The Game of my Life* (Pelham, London, 1989), p. 125.
226 L. Sampson: "Yesterday's Heroes", in Anon, *Laughing through the Turmoil* (Johannesburg, 1990), p. 49.

Craven's view of women was that they "should be soft, soft by nature, soft by word of mouth. If they are not soft, they simply do not have influence over a man". Craven, and probably a host of other young sportsmen of his generation, also tended to shy away from casual affairs. "I got to know women late," he told a journalist in the mid-1980s.

> Do you know, my dear, I went on four overseas tours and never had a woman. I now think I was a bloody fool. But do you know that my rugby meant so much to me that I thought in those days that if I had a woman it would affect my game, that it would be unfair to my country.[227]

While Craven's views reflect an outlook usually associated with perceived Victorian values of an earlier era, changing social and sexual mores of later decades brought about corresponding changes in the attitudes of rugby players towards women. Writing approximately 32 years after Craven's playing days, Chris Laidlaw, who came to South Africa with the All Blacks in 1970, had this to say:

> Unlike beer, women on tour are not compulsory. Sometimes taken, sometimes left, they are a commodity to be utilised only if instantly available and free, which they usually are, in considerable plentitude. The sex scene on rugby tours is a woman's liberationist's nightmare.[228]

Besides the attitude and behaviour of some rugby players on tour, it is also instructive to look at the conduct of some rugby enthusiasts. An incident which took place in the mid-1960s is particularly revealing since it incorporates and reflects upon a range of attitudes. A journalist has recounted that on the morning before a test match to be played at Ellis Park in Johannesburg, crowds of white men were queuing for standing room. Many of them had had a fair amount of alcohol, and they started pelting black passersby with *naartjies* (tangerines). To the great merriment of the crowd, the blacks dropped whatever they had with them and quickly retreated in the opposite direction – all of them, that is, but a solitary black woman.

She was fashionably attired with high-heeled shoes, make-up and a wig. She summed up the situation, clutched her handbag and strut-

---
227 Sampson: "Yesterday's Heroes", p. 50.
228 Laidlaw: *Mud in your Eye*, p. 58. See also Roger: *Old Heroes*, p. 90.

ted past the men. Incensed by such defiance, the men grabbed fistfuls of *naartjies* and bombarded her. One *naartjie* dislodged her wig to reveal a cleanly shaven head. The men fell about in paroxysms of laughter. But without any outward show of emotion, she picked up the wig, dusted it, reached into her handbag to find a vanity mirror, and calmly and coolly replaced and adjusted the wig. Proudly and apparently unperturbed, she went on her way.[229]

This incident demonstrates attitudes deeply rooted in class, race and gender antagonisms. The fact that the woman was smartly dressed, in clothes that were probably more expensive than many white women could afford, was one reason why the ire of the crowd was aroused. In her dress she conveyed an upper middle-class image which made the men suspect she had ideas above her station. Even more visible, and perhaps more important, was the issue of race. At the height of apartheid in the mid-1960s, the dignity of many blacks had been stripped away along with their citizenship. Some whites were inclined to interpret assertive behaviour on the part of black people as deliberately provocative. For a black person to challenge white supremacist notions in everyday life, especially at Ellis Park and at such a moment, was to open the floodgates of racism. On top of this, the fact that it was a woman who was daring to breach the barricades of a demarcated male public space aroused even greater indignation. Symbolically then, what the woman represented was anathema to an inebriated male crowd.

In analysing the way gender was refracted through rugby, one also has to note how certain practices such as female cheerleaders or champagne girls can slot women into purely decorative roles, subordinate to more important proceedings on the field and often the object of lewd male responses. Nelle Dreyer, a champagne girl from Stellenbosch University in 1969 for the annual intervarsity against University of Cape Town has recalled that she found the behaviour of male students appalling. Part of her "duties" was to visit male residences before intervarsity:

> It was no fun to be the only girl amongst a horde of men in a huge dining hall where rude jokes were made when you appear. It was even less fun if the men started to pound the tables with spoons as soon as you

---

[229] *Vrye Weekblad*, 4–10 October 1991.

start to talk after they had commanded you – not asked – to climb on the table when addressing them while their only intention was to look at your legs.[230]

After this experience Dreyer refused to accept further invitations. She left university to pursue a successful career as a professional model, but the way she had been objectified within the context of the rugby subculture remained a sore point.

The practice of female cheerleaders has over time remained remarkably intact as is evident in the current preening and prancing

"We shall defy any gender red card – now and in the future".

---

230 N. Dreyer: *Voorbladnooi: Van Pleinstraat tot Parys* (Protea Boekhuis, Pretoria, 2011), pp. 168–169. (Translation)

performances of young women at Varsity Cup competitions. This has happened despite strides towards greater female equality in university settings. It would appear that the possibility of shining in the reflected glory of male rugby players is a powerful inducement for some women, uncoupled from other gender advances on campus.[231]

Of course, many women attended rugby matches as enthusiastic ordinary spectators. For Afrikaner women at Stellenbosch in the 1930s and 1940s, rugby on Saturdays was a major social occasion.[232] In later years, the importance of having women spectators at rugby matches was officially endorsed by the South African Rugby Board. "The school girl of today is a spectator of tomorrow," it was said in 1968:

> They will have their families, and if they are rugby ... women, their children will be also... We who attend mixed [co-educational] schools know what an important role girls played in our rugby lives and how important rugby was to them too.[233]

It is not difficult to detect the male assumptions in the position outlined by the South African Rugby Board. Women were welcomed into the fold because it served the interest of men and of the sport in general. This is not to deny that some women might have had a genuine interest in the game, and in all likelihood male rugby heroes were also their heroes. Structurally, however, because rugby was such a dominantly male activity, entry into that world, wittingly or unwittingly, could only be on terms predetermined by men. This situation was similar to the place of women in the political mobilisation of Afrikanerdom in the 1930s and 1940s; the ideal of the *volksmoeder* (mother of the nation) at the time meant that women could only gain social recognition as participants in the lives of their husbands and children.[234]

---

231 M. Mordaunt-Bexiga: "Rugby, Gender and Capitalism: 'Sportocracy' up for sale", *Agenda*, 25,4, 2011, p. 72.
232 E. Theron: *Sonder Hoed of Handskoen* (Tafelberg Uitgewers, Kaapstad, 1983), p. 83. Interview with Ms B. Sieberhagen, a student at Stellenbosch during the 1930s and 1940s, 6 January 1994.
233 South African Rugby Board, 4, President's report, 1968.
234 E. Brink: "Man-made Women: Gender, Class and Ideology of the 'Volksmoeder'", in C. Walker (ed.) *Woman and Gender in Southern Africa to 1945* (David Philip Publishers, Cape Town, 1990), p. 288.

The creation of male space and the allotment of time to that phenomenon went beyond the duration of the game. Equally if not more important than the game was the *braai* afterwards. It presented an opportunity for a further expression of what it meant to be a male rugby supporter. The informal culture and interconnectedness between rugby, *braaiing* (barbecuing) and the construction of masculinity are well captured in the following journalistic depiction:

> *Braais* and rugby (and beer and Klippies [brandy] and Coke of course) are synonymous. Where there is rugby, there is bound to be plenty of *braaiing*... It is unthinkable that the day could end after the match. From the thrills of rugby, inevitably, it is on to the thrills of *braaiing* – the sound of crackling *wingerdstompies* [wood], the wonderful smell of smoke and sizzling steaks and *boerewors*. What better place for the *manne* to gather round? The fire, of course, is the centre of the gathering. Have you seen the men, one hand in the pocket, the other clutching a cold beer, staring into the flames each caught up in his own thoughts? And then one of them comes up with some wise crack or dirty joke.[235]

Although rugby was a game that took Afrikaner men out of their houses and into male public spaces, it can be argued that there seems to have been a residual and subconscious hankering to personalise and domesticate what took place on the field and to bridge the divide between the public and the personal. Is this perhaps why a predominantly female space – the kitchen – and the language of Afrikaner rugby enthusiasts became replete with terms associated with that perception of domesticity? The terms in question are:

> If a centre knocked on, someone would shout: "He has butter fingers" or "he had porridge in his hands." If he took a gap, "he cut through like a knife through butter". The tired forwards *"het aangesuiker gekom"* ["sugared" along, meaning to arrive slowly]. The ball was an "egg" ... the scrum was the "oven". A good game is *"kookwater"* [boiling water]. The forwards *"kou harde bene"* [chewing on hard bones]. The defenders *"smeer"* [to spread like butter] opponents on the grass. The wing *"pypkan"* [dummies] the fullback. He is a *"vetgesmeerde blits"* [greased lightening]. The fighter is sent to the *"koelkas"* [fridge].[236]

The expression of masculinity through rugby in Afrikaner circles might well have not been unique – it can be argued that "rugby men"

---

235 *SA Rugby*, Desember 1997.
236 H. Pienaar: "The Boere and the Egg-Shaped Ball", *Sidelines* (Spring 1996), p. 15.

elsewhere behaved broadly in much the same way – but it did carry its own imprint in terms of particular discourses and practices that emerged.

Besides the manifestations of these linkages, the point must be made that masculinity in rugby is not necessarily static. The journalist Liz McGregor who has spent a great deal of time interviewing professional or semi-professional players has recently rightly cautioned:

> Contrary to the stereotypes of brutish rugby players, I found them highly emotional and frequently sensitive. The deep bonds they develop with each other seem to augur well for their capacity for rich emotional relationships in other areas of their lives. I thought rugby provided a space in which they could be openly and intensely vulnerable.[237]

This view accords with studies relating to rugby players in the United Kingdom which found that the notion of "hard rugby men" has become more eroded along with earlier homophobic ideas. Consequently what it means to be a "man" in rugby has also shifted.[238]

Conclusion

In 1989 Tommy Bedford, one of the few English-speaking Springbok captains since 1960, commented critically on the rugby establishment and claimed that over a period of 25 years, it had worked "mainly to promote the Afrikaner, his Church, his Party, his Government and the Broederbond, but all of it was to the detriment of rugby, sport and South Africa".[239] This situation, somewhat bluntly described by Bedford, was the outcome of a more complex historical process.

The dynamics of this development, it has been suggested, are to be found in the important role played by the University of Stellenbosch, the coupling of rugby symbolism, ethnic nationalism and anti-imperialism, the middle-class character of the sport, the spectator appeal of rugby and its ramifications – including gender implica-

---

237 L. McGregor: *Touch, Pause, Engage: Exploring the Heart of South African Rugby* (Jonathan Ball, Johannesburg, 2011), p. 271.
238 E. Anderson and R. McGuire: "Inclusive Masculinity Theory and the Gendered Politics of Men's Rugby," *Journal of Gender Studies*, 19, 3 (2010), p. 259.
239 *Die Suid-Afrikaan*, December 1988–January 1989.

tions – and for the greater part the reinforcement of particular notions of masculinity, and ultimately effective political control of the game. These factors combined to elevate rugby into the Afrikaners' "national sport". Even so, the conversion was not complete. In respect of the middle-class character of the game, some of the older imperial ethos was retained and in the area of gender relations, the question of continuity in the transmission and appropriation of a sporting culture manifested itself most pertinently.

Ultimately this demonstrates that the transformation of a sporting culture is seldom in all respects comprehensive – traces and elements of the old will be incorporated into the new. It also points to the complexities of interpretation in dealing with the issue of sport in a colonial setting. The intriguing question is: "Where does the promoting hand of the colonial master stop and where does the adapting and assimilating indigenous tradition start?"[240] Although no sport is ideological *per se*, the values and norms invested in and associated with rugby, or any other sport, can and often do make it ideological. Afrikaner appropriation of the game in South Africa, which coincided with general Afrikaner nationalistic political ascendancy, was in the final analysis a way of demonstrating and representing a specific brand of ideological power. This course set it apart from what went before. It also, because of its alignment with apartheid, was bound to come under pressure from opposing political forces after 1969.

---

240 R. Cashman: "Cricket and Colonialism: Colonial Hegemony and Indigenous Subversion?" in J.A. Mangan, *Pleasure, Profit, Proselytism: British Culture and Sport at Home and Abroad*, 1700–1914 (Frank Cass, London, 1988), p. 261.

4
From international isolation to inclusion: The quest for rugby respectability, 1969–1994

A marked feature of the growing international anti-apartheid movement was the way in which sport was targeted as part of a strategy to sway the National Party government. How the anti-apartheid movement abroad gained support and managed to exert pressure in ensuring South Africa's isolation, deserves a separate study; what concerns us here is how white South African society responded to its exclusion from the international rugby fraternity and how it over time sought to position the game in such a way that the doors of international participation could be opened and rugby could regain its former respectability.

The sporting boycott: responses and impact

In the 1960s, rugby, like almost everything else in South Africa, was strictly segregated. No "mixed" teams and no matches between black and white teams were allowed. Prime Minister Hendrik Verwoerd, whose name has become synonymous with the period of high apartheid, was not prepared to grant any concessions on this score – even if it involved jeopardising the chances of international tours to South Africa. His announcement to this effect in 1965 effectively scuttled the 1967 All Black tour of South Africa, which would have included some Maoris.

After Verwoerd's assassination in 1966, his successor, B.J. Vorster, relented somewhat. Vorster, himself having been active in rugby administration in the Eastern Cape during the war years, was sensitive to the importance of rugby as a flag bearer of Afrikaner nationalism in the international arena. Even so, his decision to allow so-called "non-whites" in foreign teams to play in South Africa met with opposition from within and contributed to the breakaway of a few National Party members of parliament to form the *Herstigte* (Reformed) National Party in 1969. While Vorster had opened the way for the 1970 All Black tour to South Africa, which contained three Maoris and one Samoan, his "largesse" did not extend to cricket, and an English cricket team with a former South African coloured player, Basil D'Oliviera, was not allowed to play in South Africa.

Vorster argued, rather unconvincingly, that D'Oliviera's selection was not based on merit and that he had been deliberately chosen to embarrass the South African government.[241] What is revealing is that Vorster seems to have been more concerned about the international stature of rugby, the premier Afrikaner sport, than that of cricket, a game played mainly by English speakers and one at which few Afrikaners excelled at international level at the time. Narrow ethnic considerations seem to have been a factor in permitting concessions for rugby, but not for cricket. It is also likely that, at a time of increasing political pressure from those opposed to "mixed" tours, Vorster was keen to placate such elements and willing to sacrifice cricket (but not rugby) in the process. There might well have been substance in the remark of Norman Middleton, president of the non-racial South African Council of Sport that "rugby of all sports has a mystical significance and importance" and that isolation in other sporting codes could still be tolerated but in the case of rugby it was far less palatable."[242]

The end of the 1960s was a turning point as far as South African rugby relations were concerned. Nothing made this clearer than

---

[241] R.E. Lapchick: "The Politics of Race and International Sport: the Case of South Africa" (D.Phil. thesis, University of Denver, 1973), pp. 147–150, 179–184, 247, 252–253; G. Kotze: *Sport en Politiek* (Pretoria, 1978), pp. 51–79; R. Archer and A. Bouillon: *The South African Game: Sport and Racism* (Zed Press, London, 1982), p. 74; R. Thompson: *Retreat from apartheid: New Zealand's sporting contacts with South Africa* (Oxford University Press, Wellington, 1975), pp. 35–42.

[242] Quoted in J. Nauright and D. Black: "'Hitting Them Where it Hurts': Springbok-All Black Rugby, Masculine National Identity and Counter-Hegemonic Struggle", *Making Men: Rugby and Masculine Identity* (1996), p. 212.

the 1969/70 tour to Great Britain. Under the guidance of Peter Hain (who had been to school in South Africa and whose family had left the country after harassment by the Security Police in the 1960s) an assortment of anti-apartheid organisations launched large-scale demonstrations against the tour. Through various disruptive tactics they came close to forcing the South African management to disband the tour. In South Africa the conduct of the demonstrators was met with stunned indignation. It was unheard of that the cream of South African rugby should be humiliated and insulted by demonstrators whom the Afrikaans press often described as "long-haired, unwashed, drug-taking, communist agitators". Under these circumstances, nothing gave the Afrikaner rugby public more pleasure than when none other than Mannetjies Roux, a backline replacement, impetuously and unceremoniously kicked a demonstrator in the pants during a pitch invasion at Coventry – an act which immediately elevated the already popular Roux to the ranks of an even greater folk hero.[243]

"Yellowcarded": Peter Hain, leading anti-apartheid activist during the 1969/70 Springbok tour to Britain. *(From P. Hain,* Outside In, *London, 2012)*

---

243 Lapchick: "The Politics of Race", pp. 304–318; Kotze: *Sport en Politiek*, pp. 125–131; P. Dobson: *Rugby in South Africa* (South African Rugby Board, 1989), p. 132; *Beeld*, 9 November 1969. (Quotations translated from the latter source)

This incident, however, was the exception to the rule. The players had strict instructions not to retaliate. Often the politics of the protestors were beyond the understanding of men who had in the first place thought they came to play rugby. Piet Greyling, a flank forward, was astonished when a demonstrator ran onto the field and spat him in the face. "As Springboks we thought we were quite important," he said. "We were heroes at home, and we thought we were doing a great job. Now this guy was spitting in my face and I could just not imagine why. It seemed so strange. I was more amazed than angry."[244] Others became depressed and Dawie de Villiers, the captain, had his work cut out to hold the team together. He faced unprecedented difficulties and with tact and determination did his best to prevent the tour from completely unravelling.[245]

Between 1970 and 1989, as international opposition against apartheid rapidly gained ground, at least nine official rugby tours involving South Africa were cancelled. Apartheid sport in the 1980s, one analyst remarked, almost became as "sealed off as a faulty nuclear reactor encased in a concrete sarcophagus."[246] To rugby supporters it was an exasperating experience. When the Springboks did manage to venture overseas, they were given a torrid time by demonstrators in Australia in 1971 and even more so in New Zealand in 1981. What was particularly galling was that this happened in New Zealand; the All Blacks were after all a longstanding "honourable foe" and New Zealand and South Africa traditionally had strong rugby ties. It was the first time since the introduction of television in 1975, that white South Africans could actually witness the chaos caused by that ill-fated tour of New Zealand in 1981. Bleary-eyed rugby supporters in South Africa, getting up early in the morning (due to the time difference) to watch their favourite game, were often greeted with scenes of clashes between police, pro-tour and anti-tour supporters, and pitch invasions by demonstrators. In the last test an anti-tour protester even made several low-flying sorties over the field at Eden Park, dropping flour bombs, smoke bombs and pamphlets on

---

244 Quoted in E. Griffiths: *The Captains* (Jonathan Ball, Johannesburg, 2001), p. 219.
245 Griffiths: *Captains*, pp. 219, 224, 237.
246 R. Nixon: "Apartheid on the Run", p. 79.

the field.[247] Reflecting on the tour twenty years later, Johan Claassen, who was the beleaguered manager, had his regrets: "It was not worth it. We were in an impossible situation at the time but, if I look back, I have to say no rugby tour is so important that it is worth that kind of conflict."[248]

At the time though, the sports boycotts did not lead to a change of political heart among white rugby supporters. On the contrary, right from the start of the demonstration era such tactics provoked general condemnation. Anti-apartheid protesters were seen as an ill-informed and manipulating minority. During the 1969/70 tour of the United Kingdom, Gerhard Viviers, the popular Afrikaans rugby commentator, described demonstrators as the scum of British society who were sick in mind and body, "pink British sewerage rats, whose protest should be summarily dismissed by all civilized people".[249] Danie Craven likewise weighed in:

> We despise the conduct of the demonstrators, the way in which rugby matches were turned into chaos, the childishness and banalities of the demonstrators. We would like to put it clearly and openly that if these people think that they can influence us or that we shall change our way of life because of demonstrations, they are making a grave error.[250]

In 1973 he was still of the same opinion and regarded the boycott of South African rugby as symptomatic of a "sick world". He continued:

> What the pressure groups are after, not even they know. Behind all the demonstrations and shouting, primitive ways of expressing feelings there must be motives which exclude sport altogether.[251]

Events during the 1969/70 tour had a further sequel which went beyond mere public condemnation of the demonstrators. Peter Hain was privately prosecuted in England and charged with criminal con-

---

247 Several books and articles have appeared on the New Zealand tour. For a South African angle see W. Claassen: *More Than Just Rugby* (H. Strydom, Johannesburg, 1985) and R. Louw: *For the Love of Rugby* (Johannesburg, 1987).
248 Quoted in Griffiths: *Captains*, p. 315.
249 Viviers: *Rugby Agter Doringdraad*, p. 101. (Translation)
250 Quoted in Booyens: *Craven*, p. 183. (Translation)
251 South African Rugby Board Minutes, Microfilm 11, Craven's presidential report, 1973.

spiracy. The vindictive intent of this prosecution was clear from the less than subtle slogan of the campaign to have the leading demonstrator incarcerated: "Pain for Hain." Part of the funding for the prosecution came from a concerted fundraising drive in South Africa which saw numerous businesses, rugby clubs and individuals enthusiastically and often generously contributing. The charges, however, did not stand up in court and Hain was acquitted.[252]

There was perhaps, in retrospect, given the background of administrators and supporters in South Africa who were first and foremost "rugby men", an understandable blind spot as far as the linkages between sport and politics were concerned. But such views also reflected just how isolated South Africa had become from worldwide movements. Whereas in the rest of the world the 1960s were pre-eminently an era of social protest – expressed in student uprisings in France, Germany and America, and in the anti-Vietnam war demonstrations in America, as well as in cultural forms through anti-establishment music – in South Africa the entrenchment of rigid apartheid laws had become the major feature of society.

Despite this, it was hoped that South Africa's prowess on the rugby field would ensure that sporting relations would be maintained. The 1970 All Black tour to South Africa was a case in point. A series victory over the All Blacks was regarded as of paramount interest in order to prove to the sporting world at large that by excluding a champion team such as the Springboks from the international arena the game had much to lose.[253] There was also a general feeling at the time, an Afrikaans columnist noted in 2013, that during the years of the sport boycott rugby was a way in which white people could demonstrate to the outside word that they were on the right track politically and were able to stand their ground.[254]

This offensive also found expression on the diplomatic front. For example, one of South Africa's most senior diplomats, P.H. Phillips, was dispatched to New Zealand as Consul-General in 1969. He actively dispensed much pro-government information, including mate-

---

252 P. Hain: *Outside In* (Biteback Publishing, London, 2012), pp. 81–92; SARB Archives, Box File, Hain Prosecution Fund.
253 N. Steyn: *Weer Wêreldkampioene: Die 1970 All Blacks in Suid-Afrika* (J.P. van der Walt Publishers, Pretoria, 1970), p. 12.
254 *Die Burger*, 15 February 2013. The journalist was Dana Snyman.

rial on sport, to New Zealanders who were deemed to be influential in political circles. His mission created the impression that although South Africa had very little trade or strategic relations with New Zealand, Vorster had thought it wise for South Africa to maintain a high profile in New Zealand because of historical rugby ties. It was seen as a way of not only buttressing white support at home, but also as an effort to stave off growing threats of sporting sanctions.[255]

However, these hopes were dashed. After the cancellation of a proposed Springbok tour to New Zealand in 1973, it gradually dawned on South African rugby supporters that the antagonism against racially selected sport teams from South Africa was much greater than they had anticipated. They also felt that rugby in particular was targeted for demonstrations. There was indeed some justification for this assumption as anti-apartheid activists associated rugby exclusively with Afrikaners and apartheid, as is clear from the way in which a journalist conflated the issue:

> Apartheid carried an extra emotional charge when it came to the culture of The Game. It became the totem of white power, implicitly celebrated every time a whites-only team ran out in South Africa's name. It symbolised racial exclusiveness as a natural order of things – another dream of purity through sport.[256]

It was the realisation that the anti-apartheid movement in sport was not going to disappear overnight that prompted the National Party government to modify its rigid sports policy. During the 1970s a complicated and convoluted re-formulation of National Party policy took place. Outwardly the impressions of racially integrated sport had to be created. Yet this had to be done without actually sacrificing apartheid principles. As past masters in Orwellian "new speak", National Party policymakers devised the notion of "multi-national" sport. "Multi-national" sport was confined to a few special events at top levels only, leaving intact the apartheid pattern of sport lower down the scale; it entailed competition between the four main racial

---

255 D. Black and J. Nauright: *Rugby and the South African Nation: Sport, Cultures, Politics and Power in the Old and New South Africas* (Manchester University Press, Manchester, 1998), p. 84.
256 Quoted in W. Roger: *Old Heroes: The 1956 Springbok Tour and the Lives Beyond* (Hodder and Stoughton, London, 1991), p. 34.

groups (white, African, coloured and Indian) representing separate "nations", or between international teams from abroad and each of these groups individually. On the surface it could be seen as multi-racial sport, whites playing against coloureds for instance, but it was not multi-racial sport in the sense of people of many races freely participating together. Nor was it in any way non-racial sport organised without reference to racial origins. Therefore, "multi-national" sport, although it could be mistaken for multi-racial sport, was in fact a re-articulation of apartheid ideology. Indeed, as one observer commented at the time: "To enter the realm of South African sport is to enter a crazy world where race shapes and distorts everything."[257]

By and large in the early 1970s the organisation of rugby at the top level did not differ much from the government's "multi-national" policy. Some coloured people played for the South African Rugby Federation (the team was called the Proteas) and African people for the South African Rugby Association (called the Leopards). On occasions these teams also went on separate overseas tours – the Proteas to England in 1971 and the Leopards to Italy in 1974. With these tours the South African Rugby Board sought to demonstrate that not only white, but also African and coloured people were sent on overseas tours. To those ignorant of the intricacies of South African society, these might have appeared as worthy attempts to promote African and coloured rugby, but in reality they perpetuated apartheid's racial divisions in sport.

On tour, it was reported, South African authorities also tried to shield coloureds from too much contact with "liberal" Englishmen. In addition to this, the Proteas, coming from apartheid South Africa and many of them being abroad for the first time, were socially ill-at-ease. An English coach assigned to them, found that "they were subdued, overawed in the clubhouse. They were like dogs, cowering in the corners of their kennels."[258] The tour manager, Cuthbert Loriston, nevertheless claimed that the tour was worthwhile as it gave coloured players opportunities of broadening their outlook and gaining experience in a way that was not possible in South Africa in

---

257 J. Brickhill: *Race against Race: South Africa's "Multi-national" Sports Fraud* (International Defence and Aid Fund, London, 1976), p. 4.
258 Quoted in C. Laidlaw: *Mud in your Eye: A Worm's Eye View of the Changing World of Rugby* (Timmins, Cape Town, 1974), p. 189.

the early 1970s.²⁵⁹ But that was precisely the essential political point that Loriston had missed – what the Proteas were experiencing in England was what they were legally and otherwise prohibited from doing in their own country.

On their return, some of the Proteas were ostracised by their communities for going on the tour. As a result of such pressures, some Federation clubs also shifted their allegiance to the South African Rugby Union (SARU), with its unambiguous and uncompromising anti-apartheid stand. In the ensuing years the predicament of certain coloured rugby players, caught between opposing forces, remained much the same. Errol Tobias, an artisan from Caledon in the Western Cape and the first coloured Springbok rugby test player, found on the tour of New Zealand in 1981 that some members of the tour management discriminated against him, while at home his wife received threatening letters because he had gone on what was considered a racist tour. He had to be persuaded to stay on tour.²⁶⁰ Tobias would have preferred not to be drawn into the political cauldron of South African rugby. His view was simple but sincere: he wanted to play for his country and prove to "coloured" youngsters that they can also play international rugby.²⁶¹

Already by the mid-1970s it had become clear that the "multinational" sports policy of the government was not having the desired effect of countering the sports boycott. Craven's influential friends in the International Rugby Board, such as Albert Ferasse, president of the French Rugby Board, had impressed upon him the need to field a mixed team against the touring French in 1975. He took the advice to heart. Despite initial rebuffs from Prime Minister Vorster and the Minister of Sport, Piet Koornhof, Craven managed to obtain permission for a mixed team to oppose the French at Newlands.

In 1977 Craven also extracted government concessions for mixed national trials. On an organisational level the SARB, SARA and SARF amalgamated in 1978, though the white SARB tended

---

259 P. Dobson: *Rugby in South Africa: A History, 1861–1988* (Cape Town, 1989), p. 184.
260 Laidlaw: *Mud in your Eye*, p. 189; Dobson: *Rugby*, p. 184; Louw: *Rugby*, pp. 147–148; G. Gerber: *Dok Craven: Agter die Kap van die Byl* (US Drukkery, Stellenbosch, 2000), p. 141.
261 *Die Burger*, 16 June 2011. See also Gerber: *Craven*, p. 269.

to dominate in this arrangement. Craven, who had a good personal relationship with Abdullah Abass of SARU, also made overtures to this organisation in order to bring about unity. Abass (despite being rudely treated by Koornhof when he and Craven had earlier gone to see the minister in connection with mixed trials) carefully considered the possibility of such a merger. However, SARU delegates voted twelve against nine against further negotiations. Such discussions, they argued, should only take place once all apartheid laws had been repealed.[262]

It is possible that Craven's initiatives on this front at least in part had to do with an earlier secret meeting he had with none other than Peter Hain in London. Craven had contacted Hain and met him in the latter's apartment in early 1977. Initially both parties were understandably apprehensive, but gradually relations thawed and Hain later reflected that underneath Craven's "gruff Afrikaner assertiveness was a traditional, well-mannered gentleman. I rather liked him and sensed that the feeling was mutual."[263] Indeed, and on his part Craven did not find Hain the ogre that he had imagined.[264] Hain presented Craven with a list of reforms as a starting point for considering the lifting of the sporting boycott. Satisfied that Hain was not actually anti-sport or anti-rugby as such, Craven took heart from the meeting without perhaps fully appreciating the enormity of the political challenge.

Craven can certainly not be accused of a lack of trying in his efforts to bring about greater racial integration in South African rugby. In part he was hampered by a government which was slow to initiate change. But he was also overtaken by events. Particularly after the Soweto uprising of 1976, which in retrospect can be seen as the beginning of the end of apartheid, black demands for full political rights had gained momentum. Although Craven publicly took an anti-apartheid stand, he was in certain respects essentially conservative. He readily acknowledged the wrongs of apartheid, but as far as politics was concerned, as late as 1987 he was only prepared to sup-

---

[262] T. Partridge: *A Life in Rugby* (Southern Book Publishers, Cape Town, 1991), 100; P. Dobson: *Doc: The Life of Danie Craven* (Human & Rousseau, Cape Town, 1994), pp. 176–178.
[263] Hain: *Outside In*, p. 74.
[264] G. Gerber: *Craven*, Tafelberg, Cape Town, 1982, p. 264.

port a qualified franchise for black people[265] – an option which the Progressive Federal Party, as the white opposition in parliament for the greater part of the 1980s, had already abandoned in 1978.

Craven's position on the vote indicates that he was out of touch with the dynamics of South African society during the 1980s as the country went through a period of dramatic and often traumatic upheavals. Support for a qualified franchise, amidst these circumstances, showed a limited understanding of the nature of black aspirations and the process of transformation that was underway. Indeed, in a biography of Craven, P. Dobson, in an otherwise flattering portrayal, is not far off the mark in describing Craven's political outlook as naive.[266] At times Craven's suspect judgement of broader political issues meant that he was prone to antagonise sports activists. Therefore, in the case of the Watson brothers of Port Elizabeth who were the first white rugby players to join the non-racial SARU in 1976, Craven – partly through a lack of understanding of the significance of this step – strongly opposed the move. As a result and although he might not have meant it to be construed in such a way, his position was taken as proof of racism.[267]

Craven was very active in the organisation of rugby clinics across the country. Between 1982 and 1991 more than 314 clinics had been held and these were attended by over 88 000 players. These clinics involved children from all races and also led to senior feeder teams, mainly from the platteland, comprising white as well as African and coloured players. Dobson is convinced that "Craven's enthusiasm for the clinics became a mission and was not related to tours from overseas".[268] These clinics might indeed have assumed a life and ethos of their own, but it remains a moot point whether they would have started off at all had there been no international pressure on South African rugby authorities. The possibility exists that if Springbok rugby had not been threatened, there would not have been an incentive to embark on such a venture. In the 1950s and 1960s, before international pressures started to take its toll, little effort was made to promote the game to people other than whites.

---

265 *Sunday Times*, 4 January 1987.
266 Dobson: *Doc*, p. 135. See also p. 181.
267 *Vrye Weekblad*, 28 July 1989; Dobson: *Doc*, p. 135; *Cape Times*, 16 October 1976.
268 Dobson: *Doc*, p. 222.

Perhaps Laidlaw's view, in a general comment on Craven's attempts to draw all races into the game, provides a more rounded assessment. "Danie Craven," he wrote, "who, although his basic motive is the preservation of South African Rugby on the international scene, has been a strong advocate of multi-racial sports in the Republic and ... is a sensitive, humane and extremely idealistic man beneath his dictatorial facade."[269]

A related question involves the impact of these efforts on race relations. One view is that sporting activities, as organised by Craven, helped to break down racial barriers.[270] The nature of the clinics, with youngsters from various races playing together without undue friction, might have created the impression of racial harmony. In a highly stratified society the importance of establishing areas of common interests cannot be summarily dismissed. Yet, under apartheid conditions and in the absence of meaningful social and political reform, sport could only have a limited impact. The structural constraints imposed by apartheid remained intact and were not threatened by sporting activities: Africans, coloureds and whites could play together, perhaps enjoy a beer together, but that was where it ended; they had to return home in their racially segregated trains, sleep in their racially defined suburbs and townships, and the following morning go to their places of work where their positions were also largely determined by race.[271] On the surface mixed rugby created the impression of equality, while in all other areas inequality was deeply entrenched. Rugby was powerless to change this, nor could it realistically be expected to do so.

Craven was prepared to go to great lengths to get South Africa back into international rugby. In August 1983 he was instrumental in arranging a huge press conference, lasting two weeks and involving 55 media people from different overseas countries in order to showcase the level of integration (for example, the clinics) that had been attained in South African rugby. The visitors criss-crossed the country in an expensive exercise totalling R750 000, but "the rewards were well hidden, if they existed at all".[272]

---

269 Laidlaw: *Mud in your Eye*, p. 192.
270 Dobson: *Doc*, p. 222.
271 Compare Partridge: *A Life in Rugby*, p. 103.
272 Dobson: *Doc*, p. 233.

As black protest started to mount in the 1980s and South Africa moved into the spotlight of world media attention, it became increasingly difficult for the Springboks to compete internationally. Rugby administrators had to resort to all kinds of subterfuges: the Argentinians, for example, generally known as the Pumas, came out as the Jaguars in 1982 and 1984, supposedly representing South America.[273]

The greatest outcry was caused by the New Zealand "rebel" tour of 1986. This took place in the wake of the cancellation of the official 1985 All Black tour which, to the great disappointment of the white South African rugby public, had been stopped at the last moment. For Craven, this was akin to a national disaster:

> I knew people who actually cried openly – grown men... It was a sad moment, and only when a country has actually experienced that kind of monumental disappointment can they appreciate just how South Africans generally and the SARB in particular felt that day.[274]

White South Africa felt it had deserved the tour. So did Louis Luyt, businessman and rugby administrator destined to become president of SARFU. He was the driving force behind the 1986 tour which was arranged without informing the New Zealand or South African Rugby Boards or the International Rugby Board. The company who ran the Yellow Pages telephone directory was the main sponsor of the tour.

The tour temporarily eased the rugby hunger of white South Africans, but also reflected the tensions in South Africa at the time. The New Zealanders, travelling as the Cavaliers, were, with one or two exceptions, a full All Black side. They had a punishing schedule, crammed with tough matches, and adding to the pressure was constant police surveillance as fears existed that the tour might be violently disrupted. The captain, Andy Dalton, remarked that the demands of the tour had been so heavy that unlike other rugby tours, there has been little time for levity, to the extent that the coach, Colin Meads, advised the team to "drink more beer" – an exhortation that Dalton wryly noted, "must have been a rugby first".[275]

The tour took place at a time when black townships had become

---

273 Dobson: *Doc*, p. 172.
274 Quoted in Partridge: *A Life in Rugby*, p. 114.
275 *The Star*, 27 May 1986. See also *New Nation*, 6 May 1986.

increasingly ungovernable as many residents refused to bow to apartheid laws and regulations. Shortly after the tour, the government imposed a suffocating national state of emergency which allowed for little political expression. Given these circumstances, it is not surprising that the tour, which took place in defiance of the international boycott, evoked strong reactions in black quarters. Ebrahim Patel of SARU condemned the "deceit and secrecy" with which the tour was arranged and the "callous disregard" it showed for the "feelings and political realities of the oppressed people in South Africa".[276] Sam Ramsamy of SANROC in London was equally scathing about the tour, but also made a wider political point that the tour had revealed the rugby establishment as desperate to obtain international tours. This was seen as a measure of the success achieved by the anti-apartheid sports movement abroad.[277] Although no large-scale protest movements against the tour were organised in the country, some incidents did occur. In Cape Town opposition to the tour flared up, literally, as 700 pupils from township high schools took to the streets and set fire to a mound of directories of Yellow Pages, the chief sponsors.[278] Away from the streets, but fully informed about the tensions in South Africa, a Commonwealth Eminent Persons Group on a general fact-finding mission to South Africa at the same time as the rebel tour, regarded the rugby extravaganza as an emotional outlet for the white community.[279]

The tour had certain repercussions. Although Craven was sidelined in the organisation of the tour, once the New Zealanders were in South Africa, he gave the venture his full support. Craven was in London, attending an International Rugby Board meeting, when news of the tour broke. He was caught off guard, but ignored a request from the International Board that the players should be sent back to New Zealand. Craven argued that South Africa had deserved a tour by New Zealand and although he did not approve of the secretive way in which it had been organised, he regarded it as poetic justice after all the other tours that had been cancelled as a result

---

276 *Cape Times*, 1 May 1986.
277 *Post Natal*, 26 April 1986.
278 *The Star*, 17 May 1986.
279 S. Ramphal (ed.): *Mission to South Africa: the Commonwealth Report*, Penguin, London, 1986, p. 44.

of anti-apartheid pressure. Craven's stance on this issue severely strained his relations with the IRB – a body which he had always held in high esteem.[280] In addition, there were strong and persistent rumours that the New Zealanders were paid to tour South Africa. It was most likely the case, though it did not become public knowledge. In another instance – that of the rebel tour by the South Pacific Barbarians in 1987 – there was clear-cut evidence of money being an incentive to tour.[281] If one had to reason by analogy, it would be safe to assume that the New Zealanders were also compensated for their efforts.

These rebel tours were expedient, short-term opportunistic affairs and ultimately counterproductive, as they turned Craven's friends at the IRB against the SARB. In some ways rugby under the SARB was in a worse position after the tours than they were before the arrival of the Cavaliers. The deteriorating situation had a negative effect on preparations for the centenary celebrations of the Board in 1989 which were to include a World Invitation XV.

In their quest for international acceptance, leading rugby administrators, in particular Danie Craven and Louis Luyt, now realised that they had to explore other hitherto closed avenues. It was under these circumstances that a series of meetings with the African National Congress in exile was arranged in, amongst other places, Harare. The ANC wielded considerable influence in the anti-apartheid sports movement, and Craven argued at the time that the route of South Africa's re-admission to international rugby was through Africa. This was a departure from the earlier policy of relying on "friends" in the IRB.

It could not have been easy for Craven to come to this decision. At the time white public opinion was inflamed as a result of a bomb explosion at Ellispark stadium on 2 July 1988 towards the end of a Currie Cup game. Two people died and the incident – arguably the most explicitly violent case to be associated with the history of sport in South Africa – was attributed to the ANC.[282] Craven nevertheless pressed ahead.

---

280 Partridge: *A Life in Rugby*, 114–115; Dobson: *Doc*, 144–145; *The Star*, 8 June 1986.
281 Dobson: *Doc*, pp. 145–146, 148; Partridge: *A Life in Rugby*, p. 114.
282 *Die Burger*, 4 Julie 1988.

His contact with the ANC not only raised the ire of some members of the National Party government (somewhat ironically because less than two years later the same government was to embark on full-scale negotiations with the ANC) but that of some Rugby Board members as well. The media, as was to be expected, made much of the meetings with the ANC, but in the end the discussions yielded little of substance. However, the mere fact that top administrators were willing to talk to the ANC had a beneficial effect on the opinion of overseas rugby people. At the time of organising the World XV for the Board's centenary, a prominent British rugby official was reported as saying: "You should thank Dr Danie Craven and Dr Louis Luyt for the positive mood towards South Africa. The talks Dr Craven and Dr Luyt held with the ANC in Harare last year made all the difference."[283] The contact with the ANC can also be seen as a harbinger of developments that were to pave the way for rugby unity after 1990.

There is no clear-cut assessment of the efficacy of sport sanctions, especially as far as rugby is concerned, in promoting change in South African society and politics. One commentator argued that "isolation prompted moves towards integration in the sports most affected by boycotts and that by the 1980s the principle of racial integration in sport was widely accepted".[284] As a general statement this is probably accurate, but it needs to be qualified. Attitudinal surveys have revealed that although the idea of integrated national rugby teams chosen on merit was favourably received, support for mixed teams at club and school level was much weaker.[285] The country's exclusion from international sport can then be seen to have had a differential impact on white attitudes. At a national level, mixed sport could be

---

283 Quoted in Dobson: *Doc*, p. 181. For the contact with the ANC see also Partridge: *A Life in Rugby*, 130–144; *Beeld*, 5 September 1988; *Rapport*, 11 September 1988; *Vrye Weekblad*, 28 April 1989; *Die Suid-Afrikaan*, December 1988/January 1989; A. Guelke: "Sport and the End of Apartheid" in L. Allison (ed.), *The Changing Politics of Sport* (Manchester University Press, Manchester, 1993), p. 168.
284 Guelke: "Sport and the End of Apartheid" p. 168.
285 Human Sciences Research Council, *Sport in the RSA* (Pretoria, 1982) p. 37. See also G.J.L. Scholtz and J.L. Olivier: "Attitudes of Urban South Africans Towards Non-racial Sport and Their Expectations of Future Race Relations – A Comparative Study" in *International Review for Sociology of Sport*, p. 19, (1984), pp. 131, 139.

tolerated because it was an important showcase to the outside world, but racial mixing lower down the order was seen as another matter.

Equally problematical is the relative importance of sport sanctions, and rugby in particular, in moving the National Party government away from apartheid and ultimately abandoning the system altogether. There is a range of opinions on the matter. Adrian Smith, a historian from Southampton University who as a youngster participated in the demonstrations, was of the opinion in 2006 that the effect of sport isolation made South Africans feel like pariahs and together with the "inevitable drop in the standards of rugby, was a key force for change."[286] Other academics like John Nauright and David Black, aware that the importance of the effect of the sports boycott can easily be overstated, would not assign the sport boycot pride of place, but still regarded it as a consideration. In 1993, they argued that:

> It is our contention that the generally unexpected decision of the De Klerk government to launch the current process of change cannot be understood without an appreciation of the corrosive societal and psychological effects of steadily expanding cultural sanctions. And of these, the loss of international rugby links, above all with New Zealand, were the most potent.[287]

There were of course also other more pressing concerns. As analyst Adrian Guelke, has explained:

> Economic pressures, especially after the passage of the Comprehensive Anti-Apartheid Act by the United States in 1986, loomed much larger [than sport sanctions] in both the thinking of whites and the calculations of the government. Thus an explicit objective of the reforms embraced by... De Klerk was to meet the conditions laid down in the American legislation for the lifting of sanctions.[288]

The role of sport in facilitating change in South Africa therefore has to be put in perspective. In the mid-1960s, when a New Zealand tour to South Africa was in jeopardy because of the possible inclusion of

---

286 *The Telegraph*, 20 September 2006.
287 J. Nauright and D. Black: "Much More Than a Game: Springbok-All Black Rugby, Sanctions and Change in South Africa, 1959–1992" (Unpublished paper, 1993), pp. 30–31.
288 Guelke: "Sport and the End of Apartheid", p. 168.

Maoris, Jan De Klerk, father of F.W. de Klerk, and Minister of Home Affairs at the time, told Craven that "rugby was the least of his problems..."[289] It would be surprising if his son, some 25 years later, had regarded rugby in a different light.

Overall a number of factors impacted on the South African situation in the late 1980s. International sanctions had debilitated the economy and restricted room for maneuvering on the part of the state; internal insurrections placed further strain on the state as a recurring cycle of repression and resistance shaped the contours of South African society; armed attacks by the ANC, though never seriously extending the military, added to increased instability; and the international order had changed with the collapse of communism in Eastern Europe, impressing upon the state that it could no longer play the West off against the East. Dawie de Villiers, a prominent member of the De Klerk government and well known as a Springbok rugby captain from 1965 to 1970, considered the boycott as having a cumulative effect of frustration among rugby supporters, but as having little effect on actual deliberations by the power brokers.[290] At best it can be claimed that rugby sanctions, perhaps more so than other sporting codes with less of an Afrikaner appeal, had over time an indirect and ancillary impact inasmuch as they helped to contribute to an overall sense of exclusion from international affairs.[291]

With South Africa being buffeted from all sides, State President F.W. de Klerk made what was probably the most important speech of any white South African leader in parliament on 2 February 1990: he formally unbanned the African National Congress (ANC) and other proscribed organisations. This effectively ended 30 years of exile for the country's major black political organisations.

The rocky road of rugby reconciliation

De Klerk's speech signalled the end of apartheid as official state policy. Although the negative social and economic effects of a discriminatory policy which had been entrenched for decades could not be erased by decree overnight, the fact that apartheid measures were to

---

289 Quoted in Dobson: *Doc*, p. 166.
290 Personal discussion with Dr Dawie de Villiers, 3 April 2013.
291 Nauright and Black: *Rugby and the South African Nation*, p. 92.

be scrapped from the statue books did open up the way for a fundamental restructuring of society. It also meant that the long-standing international sports boycott of South Africa could be reassessed.

Rugby administrators welcomed De Klerk's announcement. Danie Craven, president of the SARB, described it as a "wonderfully encouraging move" which would facilitate South Africa's re-entry into international sport. Jan Pickard of the Western Province Rugby Board was even more optimistic and wasted no time in informing the public that "they would be surprised to see which teams would come and tour without further ado in 1990".[292] Other observers were more cautious and warned that the political influence of the National and Olympic Sports Congress (NOSC), affiliated to the ANC, should not be underestimated; until the various establishment and anti-apartheid sporting bodies were united under one banner and until it was clear that the dismantling of apartheid had become an irreversible process, the chances of foreign tours to South Africa were slim.[293]

However, this is not the way Craven saw the situation in February 1990. He had an imperfect grasp of the magnitude of the change required in South Africa and this had a bearing on his failure to understand the precise linkages between rugby and politics. For Craven, the abolishment of apartheid primarily involved the scrapping of social and economic discriminatory practices. It did not entail a universal franchise, majority rule and a totally new political dispensation. Publicly, Craven made it clear that the "government had to be very careful about the vote. There is one thing that the government must never do, and that is to give everybody an equal vote."[294] He could see no reason why South Africa could not return to rugby as usual; apartheid, as far as he was concerned, was officially abolished and international tours could be resumed.[295] The fact that a new political order still had to be negotiated and that the transitional process was fraught with pitfalls and possible reversals was immaterial to him.

Sports people in anti-apartheid organisations had to take such political realities into account; sport has been an important weapon in their arsenal and to surrender it without being able to show tangi-

---

292 *Die Burger*, 5 February 1990. (Translation)
293 *Rugby 15*, May 1990.
294 *Die Burger*, 5 February 1990. (Translation)
295 *City Press*, 2 December 1990.

ble gains would have been politically unacceptable. Therefore, the NOSC resolved that establishment sporting bodies like the SARB should support the moratorium on sports tours and work together with anti-apartheid forces in eliminating all discrimination in sport before seeking fresh international ties. The SARB had to show its commitment to change. "This is the time", it was argued, "for the SARB to display its sincerity, to catch the moment".[296]

The moment, however, meant different things for different people. Craven was in full agreement that one controlling body should be established – he had already had a discussion as early as 1977 on this issue with the anti-apartheid SARU and had also met the ANC in Harare in the late 1980s – but he baulked at the idea of a moratorium. Patel of SARU, on the other hand, maintained that a condition for the unity talks between his organisation and the SARB was that the moratorium should be supported. SARU was deeply suspicious that the SARB was only interested in unity talks for the sake of expediency. The Rev. Arnold Stofile, junior vice-president of SARU in 1990, warned that anti-apartheid sports people and administrators had to be "vigilant not to be used as tools by the racists, as window dressing for international tours, or to be blackmailed into entrenching international tours."[297] Stofile's call echoed a wider concern in the ANC during this period, namely, that in dealing and negotiating with the National Party government, the movement added greatly to the credibility of the government at home and abroad.[298] More than likely this stiffened SARU's resolve not to accede to international tours prematurely.

For the greater part of 1990 and well into 1991 a series of acrimonious exchanges between Craven and Patel followed. Exploratory talks between the two organisations grounded to a halt amidst accusations and counter-accusations of intransigence, insensitivity and opportunism. Whilst other sporting codes managed to merge with relative ease, rugby remained the odd one out. "Perhaps it is the aggressive nature of the game that causes rugby officials to fight," one

---

296 *Sunday Star*, 18 February 1990.
297 *New Nation*, 8 November 1990.
298 T. Lodge: "The African National Congress in the 1990s" in G. Moss and I. Obery (eds), *South African Review 6: From "Red" Friday to Codesa* (Ravan, Johannesburg 1992), p. 70.

journalist observed wryly.²⁹⁹ But central to the impasse were two almost diametrically opposed perceptions of the role of sport in society. Craven tended to deny the social significance of rugby and consistently argued against what he considered to be outside interference in rugby matters. For the NOSC and SARU there was not such a stark dividing line between sport and society. Sport was seen as "interlinked with the total social formation" and had to "reflect society".³⁰⁰

It had by that stage become clear that the "warring bodies" were unable to establish common ground. In March 1991 Steve Tshwete, ANC sport spokesperson and later to become South African Minister of Sport and Recreation, entered the fray. Tshwete was a keen rugby enthusiast and had played representative rugby in the Border area during the early 1960s. Apart from his sporting credentials, he had spent fifteen years on Robben Island as a political prisoner and another eleven years in exile. While on Robben Island he had been involved in organising rugby competitions amongst his fellow prisoners.

Tshwete had gained a reputation as "Mr Fix It" for his part in brokering talks between other sporting codes, most notably cricket. He regarded the establishment of one controlling body as being paramount in countering sectionalism and of empowering previously disadvantaged sections of the population. It was therefore essential, he argued, for SARU and the SARB to "get together so that they influence each other in a way that any hardened attitudes can be broken down". Tshwete was also concerned about the perceived negative spin-offs which the rugby war had on wider South African politics. "It is a delicate process," he said, "where the rugby talks are bound to influence the political process in the country and vice versa, so that whatever is done, we should operate under this new body." This was also the message he tried to convey to Craven, whom he found more "attentive and not insensitive to the demands of the occasion".³⁰¹

There is also evidence that Craven had become increasingly aware that without the blessing of an organisation like the ANC as well as SARU, the SARB would find it difficult to organise an in-

---

299 *Business Day*, 28 January 1991.
300 *New Nation*, 8 November 1990.
301 *Weekly Mail*, 8 March 1991.

ternational tour without it being disrupted by demonstrations and violence. The rebel English cricket tour of 1989-90, which had to be aborted midway because of mass demonstrations, was a stark reminder to Craven that the same could happen to rugby.[302] Craven was averse to being dictated to, but he was pragmatic enough to realise that, without some strategic repositioning, South African rugby would not get back into the international fold.

Tshwete played a continuing part in steering the talks towards unity. Pressure was exerted on both Patel and Craven. A meeting was even arranged between Nelson Mandela, ANC president at the time, and Craven. This apparently further helped to smooth the way. In December 1991 it was announced that a new unified sporting body, the South African Rugby Football Union (SARFU), would be launched early in 1992. The new body committed itself to the development of rugby across the board and in particular in disadvantaged areas; at the same time the go-ahead was given for international tours in 1992.[303] In the process SARU had to drop the moratorium on tours, but for the first time in its history of more than a hundred years, the SARB had to take the opinions and influence of people other than whites seriously and, moreover, act upon them.

While the SARB had coloured and black affiliates in the past, they had never exerted the same pressure as Patel and SARU.[304] Now rugby administrators faced up to each other as equals. An interim constitution, designed to underpin the unity process, ensured 50/50 representation for the SARB and SARU. Craven was to be joint president with Ebrahim Patel, the latter to take over in 1993. Despite the apparent equitable 50/50 agreement, it was an uneasy unity; both parties were driven to it by circumstances rather than conviction.

Establishing a sense of unity in the boardroom, however shaky, was one issue; ensuring that the policy was accepted and implemented lower down the ranks was another. In certain areas in the platteland and in the Western Province, pressure had to be applied to bring recalcitrant white subunions into line. Incidents on the field underlined the difficulties of the merger. It was with considerable

---

302 Compare *Sunday Times*, 27 January 1991.
303 *Pretoria News*, 9 December 1991; *Die Burger*, 15 February 1992; P. Dobson, *Doc: The Life of Danie Craven* (Cape Town 1994), pp. 182, 187.
304 *Beeld*, 6 April 1989.

trepidation that some clubs from predominantly white areas ventured into often volatile African or coloured townships to fulfil their league fixtures.

Although such fears were often without foundation, a few matches were indeed marred by unruly crowd behaviour and racial animosity. In the Karoo town of Graaff-Reinet, for instance, a game between a white team from De Aar and the local coloured team had to be abandoned before the end of the first half as 80 angry spectators stormed onto the field, disagreeing with a decision from the referee and threatening to attack the white team. "Kill them, kill them," the spectators were reported to have shouted. "Today we will be looking through the ribcages of the boers! We are going to necklace them. Close the entrance gates so that we can show them who is the boss!"[305] The referee sprinted to his car and the players rapidly retreated to the change rooms. Similar incidents occurred in the Eastern Cape and on occasion the police had to disperse the crowd with teargas.[306] In "ordinary" rugby games players are often given free rein to needle the opposition; it was too much to expect no flare-ups and racial baiting between players from communities which had long histories of antagonism.

An agreement that rugby would be promoted amongst the disadvantaged communities of South Africa was a key element in the process that led to unification. SARFU officially launched such a programme in March 1993. A sum of R13 million was spent in the first year and a great deal of activity marked the programme: more than 116 000 young, predominantly African and coloured rugby players attended clinics and coaching courses, and 6000 coaches, 650 referees, and 1772 administrators from all over the country were involved in organising and supervising proceedings.[307]

With all the frenetic activity, the programme outwardly appeared to be off to a very satisfactory start. But appearances proved to be deceptive. Certain development efforts bordered on fiascos as a result of poor organisation. While some of this chaos can be attrib-

---

305 *Rapport*, 19 July 1992 (translation). See also *Volksblad*, 13 July 1992.
306 *Eastern Province Herald*, 18 July 1994; *Eastern Province Herald*, 22 July 1994; *Die Burger*, 21 July 1992.
307 *The Star*, 16 August 1994.

uted to teething problems, international bickering and jockeying for lucrative executive positions on the development committees were problems of a different order. "Little men with nary a constructive thought, have to see to their livelihood – not latent talents," was one caustic verdict.[308]

The development programme faced enormous challenges. As a result of years of apartheid-induced neglect, rugby had to start from scratch in many townships. Extremely poor facilities were major obstacles. In certain areas people with as little conception of the game as the boys they were supposed to coach were appointed as coaches.[309] Furthermore, there was some political undercurrent of resistance to rugby as a game associated with the police and apartheid.[310] The enormity of these problems raised the possibility that SARFU might lose heart and that the programme might backslide after the first flurry of activity.

Indeed, in 1993 some observers were of the opinion that with the World Cup in the offing, the development programme had lost much of its former urgency. Administrators, it was reported, viewed "development as a necessary evil, and at best tolerated as with a naughty child. You know it's yours, but for heaven's sake, keep it at bay."[311]

The programme nevertheless did appear to have some successes. The press was keen to give publicity to black youngsters who showed rugby promise, and it was almost as if the media was half-relieved at being able to report in a positive vein.[312] Perhaps more important than the number of black boys excelling at the game was the way in which the programme raised questions about the place of rugby in South African society as a whole. One journalist pointedly remarked:

> It is hard to write about back row moves immediately after returning from a township like Nyanga [close to Cape Town]. The gut-wrenching impact of squalor and day-to-day desperation to which many of our fellow South Africans are subjected, tends to put a test match at Newlands into perspective.[313]

---

308 *Rugby 15*, October/November 1993.
309 *Cape Argus*, 3 June 1994; *Sunday Times*, 7 January 1994.
310 *Sunday Times*, 16 August 1992.
311 *Rugby 15*, October/November 1993.
312 Compare *Die Burger*, 12 June 1992; *Volksblad*, 30 May 1994.
313 *Sunday Star*, 23 August 1992.

For an organisation like the South African Council of Sport (SACOS), which had adopted a position of doctrinal purity and had stayed outside the unification process, it was precisely the contrast between lush, well-manicured sporting fields in white areas, and the sheer struggle for survival in nearby dusty black townships that added a grotesque dimension to the spectacle of establishment sport and vindicated their position of "no normal sport in an abnormal society". SACOS argued that sport played on this basis was not truly nonracial, that the unity that was achieved was a "scam-unity", and that despite the political changes in the country, the existing social and political disparities were perpetuated in the new order. The reconstruction of South African society, and with it South African sport, was far more important for SACOS than playing international sport.[314]

Steve Tshwete adopted a more pragmatic view. He fully acknowledged the discrepancies, but nevertheless argued that sport could act as a "healer" in a country torn by race, cultural and other differences. For this to happen, it was necessary to move away from the notion that rugby was mainly an Afrikaner game and soccer mainly a black game in South Africa.[315] Patel saw this as a long-term process. Although he had his reservations about some aspects of the development programme, he realised that a situation which had developed over years could not be turned around overnight. Nevertheless, he regarded the unification process as an important breakthrough which has ensured that "SARFU belongs to the future children of South Africa". It was therefore, he claimed, "unreasonable" for those who had "planted the tree of unification to expect to immediately reap the fruits of the tree".[316]

As a result of adopting such flexible positions before the advent of majority rule, South Africa was readmitted to international sport. Whether the unification process and sport in general could add significantly to dissolving racial tensions, and whether a game like rugby could realistically be expected to play a part in easing the burdens of those in the townships, remained a moot point.

---

314 *City Press*, 7 June 1992.
315 *Weekend Argus*, 5 March 1994.
316 *Rugby 15*, August 1993. See also *Weekly Mail and Guardian*, 13 May 1993.

Rugby as usual?

The first international rugby teams to visit South Africa after 1990 were the All Blacks from New Zealand, the traditional rivals of South African rugby; and the Wallabies from Australia, the World Cup champions at the time. These teams came out in August 1992. Although they visited the "new" South Africa, many of the tensions of the old order remained unresolved. Before and during their visit the politics of transition often spilled over into the sporting arena.

It was with great anticipation that the South African rugby public awaited the contests with New Zealand and Australia. But not all rugby supporters realised that the tours were only possible because of political processes which were under way in the country and that the position adopted by the ANC was crucial in allowing international sport to take place. Some of the rugby fanatics in the platteland were therefore able to tell an Australian journalist: "Ja, ... Mandela is a terrorist and must die," and in the same breath ask, "but do you think Naas [Botha] is up to the All Black and Wallaby flyhalves?"[317]

While popular misconceptions and prejudices on the platteland and elsewhere were not likely to be dislodged by an appeal to reason, SARFU as the highest rugby authority in the country had to show itself supportive of the process which had made the tours possible in the first place. This necessitated a reassessment of the significance of sporting symbols of an earlier era, such as rugby's supreme symbol – the Springbok.

With the establishment of a new rugby union and South African rugby on the brink of emerging from apartheid isolation, symbols of an earlier era were seen as inappropriate by some. Mluleki George, formerly of SARU and a committee member of the newly formed SARFU, argued that the Springbok emblem represented the hurtful years of apartheid and white supremacy. In the new era, it had to be replaced by a more representative symbol. Such views caused an outcry amongst rugby traditionalists for whom South Africa's rugby history was intimately tied up with the Springbok emblem. What is more, they did not regard the Springbok as a symbol of apartheid.

---

317 *Weekly Mail and Guardian*, 13 August 1992.

It was officially approved as an emblem of the SARB in 1903 and first used on an overseas tour in 1906/07, therefore preceding the apartheid period under National Party rule. But white supremacy went back much further than the beginnings of National Party rule in 1948, and for the general public the Springbok was undoubtedly a sectional symbol, representing whites and predominantly Afrikaners. Before the arrival of the touring teams, a compromise was reached: the Springbok from the SARB was retained, but combined with four proteas and a rugby ball from SARU. However, they promised that after the World Cup of 1995, the Springbok emblem would be reviewed again.[318]

Rugby administrators not only had to come to an agreement on the Springbok emblem; they also had to adopt positions on the continuing violence in the country, which at one point threatened to scuttle the impending tours. In the two years between 1990 and the end of 1991, over 6000 people had lost their lives in politically motivated violence.[319] In general terms, a variety of pressures contributed to the violence: rapid urbanisation of black people once the earlier restrictions and restraints of apartheid had fallen away; growing class differentiation and competition over scarce resources; and intense political rivalry and jockeying, often assuming an outwardly ethnic form.[320] The question of violence had reached crisis proportions in mid-1992, especially after a particularly vicious slaying in the township of Boipatong in the Vaal Triangle where 44 people, amongst them several women and children, were hacked to death. Although many South Africans had already become desensitised by continuing mayhem in the townships, the sheer brutality of these killings shocked anew. Allegations of a "third force" and possible police complicity in the massacre at Boipatong compounded matters further. These events, tragic as they were, were at times used by certain groupings to gain political mileage, and dramatically underscored the need for the immediate termination of violence as a national priority.

---

318 Compare *Evening Post*, 15 June 1992; *Die Burger*, 22 June 1992; *Volksblad*, 27 July 1992; *Rugby 15*, September 1993, *Beeld*, 4 June 1994.
319 South African Institute of Race Relations, *Race Relations Survey*, 1991/92 (Johannesburg 1992) p. xiii.
320 M. Morris and D Hindson: "The Disintegration of Apartheid: From Violence to Reconstruction" in Moss and Obery (eds), *South African Review 6*, p. 157.

In ANC quarters, it was strongly felt that it would have been insensitive for national sporting events to carry on as usual. Referring to Boipatong, Steve Tshwete argued that South Africans "could not afford to behave as a normal nation, as if nothing has happened. The feeling is that we want to come together as South Africans during this period of mourning."[321] Tshwete was also concerned about allegations that the police were connected to the violence; if that was the case, he argued, players from the police and security forces should be purged from top teams because they belonged in the camp of the "enemy" and associated themselves with violence.[322]

Tshwete's assumptions about a common South African nationhood might have been premature and his condemnation of the security forces overhasty. But the ANC did not really need watertight arguments – they had more than sufficient influence and leverage. As one commentator observed at the time: "It is a simple fact that, currently, the ANC's huge standing overseas means no game can be played, no race run, no tour hosted without its approval."[323] Rather than risking possible cancellation of the tours, SARFU negotiated with the ANC and came to an agreement that suitable respect would be shown at all test matches to the victims of violence.[324]

However, this was not to be. On the day of the test against the All Blacks (15 August 1992), the crowd was in a defiant mood. They had their beloved rugby back; the celebrated green and gold-jerseyed Springboks were about to tackle the mighty All Blacks. It was an historic return to the international arena after years of isolation; an occasion brimful of nostalgia and tradition for predominantly Afrikaner male rugby fanatics who vividly recalled test matches which they had attended in the "old" South Africa. It was not an occasion where they were going to comply meekly with ANC demands – an organisation which little more than two years previously they had regarded as a band of "terrorists".

Large sections of the crowd were intent on ignoring the agreement between the ANC and SARFU that the National Anthem (*Die*

---

321 *Pretoria News*, 24 June 1992.
322 *The Star*, 23 June 1992.
323 *Sunday Times*, 5 July 1992.
324 *Beeld*, 10 July 1992.

Stem) would not be sung officially at the test, that the existing South African flag would not be hoisted, and that a minute's silence for those who had died at Boipatong would be observed. The ANC regarded this as a reasonable position and a reflection that the country had as yet no credible national symbols and that many were dying in the townships.[325] Such compromises might have saved the tour, but they also demonstrated a certain naivety as far as crowd behaviour is concerned. There was a vast gulf between seemingly rational boardroom decisions and the attitude of exuberant, if not inflamed, rugby supporters convinced that the decisions were taken to humiliate them as a community.

"Into extra time...": a farewell flutter of the flag. (Rapport, *16 August 1992*)

Early on there were signs of trouble. Encouraged by the Afrikaans press, amongst other institutions, thousands of fans arrived at Ellis Park with the national flag symbolising white South Africa and plenty more were on sale at the stadium. This was unusual. For a crowd to make so much of the national flag at test matches had never

---

325 *Weekly Mail and Guardian*, 27 August 1994.

been part of South African rugby culture or tradition under apartheid. Spectators had not previously shown any real interest in the flag. But now, as the crowd wished to make a political point in an orchestrated fashion, the popularity of the flag soared to unprecedented heights. To discern the political message was not difficult as some inebriated fans waved their flags and chanted in unison: "*F... die ANC, f... die ANC*". Inside the stadium notes were being passed around, urging the crowd to sing *Die Stem*, come what may.[326]

The showdown came when, just before the main game, the crowd was asked for a few moments' silence. Immediately close on 70 000 white people responded with a heartfelt rendition of *Die Stem*. One observer vividly recalled the occasion:

> For that moment inside the concrete bowl, it seemed like a besieged tribe had gathered to take strength in their numbers and to send a message of defiance to their perceived persecutors. It felt like being in a bull-ring, and it was not certain whose blood was more passionately desired: that of the foe on the field or of the millions outside who knew nothing of the ancient ritual but were believed to be threatening it.[327]

What added to this defiant performance was that the anthem, contrary to the previous agreement, but with the blessing of Louis Luyt from SARFU, was played on the public address system. On the field South Africa did rather well, losing only by a narrow margin, but off the field the behaviour of the crowd elicited strong negative opinion. Black commentators regarded the singing of *Die Stem* – an anthem closely associated with apartheid – as deliberately provocative and the very antithesis of the spirit of change. Tshwete also came under fire for allowing himself, or so it seemed, to be used by the white rugby community:

> White South Africa thanked him in a very special way ... the way only white South Africa can ... They cocked their snook at him and made it plain that now he had marvellously played his part of the useful idiot, he should kindly "voertsek" [clear off] and leave them to their "traditional ways of life" and pastimes. Poor man.[328]

---

326 *The Star*, 17 August 1994.
327 *The Star*, 17 August 1994.
328 *The Sunday Star*, 23 August 1992.

Tshwete himself said that given the agitation before the time, the display of the "apartheid flag" was to be expected and there was little that could be done about it. But he was very annoyed that the minute's silence was not observed and that the anthem was being played officially:

> The signal they wanted to send was "to hell with the blacks and Boipatong". It was a refusal with contempt, to identify with the plight of their compatriots who are on the receiving end of violence.[329]

For a while the real possibility existed that the following week's test against the Wallabies at Newlands, Cape Town, would be cancelled. Australian Rugby Union president, Joe French, said that the team was ready to go home, should the ANC demand it. However, SARFU apologised for the incident and distanced itself from the order to play *Die Stem*.[330] With this, the match was saved.

Symbolically the behaviour of the crowd can be seen as the last convulsions of a dying order – it was an act of nationalistic cultural defiance by people who knew that politically the South Africa they had known and supported had all but vanished. Almost in desperation they challenged the ANC, saying: "Here is my anthem, here is my flag. Here I stand today and I sing: '*Ons sal lewe, ons sal sterwe! Ons vir jou Suid-Afrika!*'"[331] But emotionally gratifying as such a stance might have been, it had no wider political purchase because the world outside the stadium had changed irreversibly. It was also a one-off act; although a fair number of flags were in evidence at Newlands the following week, the minute's silence was observed and the crowd refrained from singing the national anthem en masse.[332] All in all it was a far less brazen display of Afrikaner nationalism at Newlands than at Ellis Park.

Under a democratically elected government, the new South African flag – representing the spirit of the "small miracle" of the country's relatively successful formal political transition – had made some headway amongst rugby supporters. As if to make the point, miniatures of the flag were also sewn onto the shorts of national team members.

---

329 *The Star*, 22 August 1992.
330 *Sowetan*, 18 August 1992.
331 *Beeld*, 17 August 1992 (translation). See also *Rapport*, 16 August 1992.
332 *Cape Times*, 24 August 1992; *Business Day*, 24 August 1992.

The Luyt show

South African rugby lurched from crisis to crisis in the post-isolation period. On the field, despite a promising start against the All Blacks in August 1992, the Springboks had yet to win a series against the top rugby-playing countries after two years. The selectors kept on bringing the changes – a record number of players became Springboks – but found it difficult to find a winning combination.

Off the field, matters were not much better as various controversies dogged SARFU. Central to much of the drama was the larger-than-life Louis Luyt, president of SARFU in 1994. Luyt had succeeded Patel, the latter having taken over the reins after the death of long-serving rugby supremo, Danie Craven. Patel had declared himself unavailable for re-election in 1994 and this left the door open for Luyt to be elected unopposed as president. The circumstances surrounding Patel's resignation were not clear. He claimed that his work as headmaster of Lenasia Muslim School (close to Johannesburg) precluded further involvement with rugby, but whether this can be taken as a full explanation is open to question.

It does, however, appear that a number of board members did not regard Patel as suitable for the position of president. He was described as

> an extremely ... nice-to-know person ... [but] has not in any way proven – apart from his historical importance in so far as unification is concerned – that he has the "guts and thunder" bona fides of what is expected from a national rugby president.[333]

In Louis Luyt, SARFU certainly found a "guts and thunder" president. At times he created the impression that he actively sought confrontation. "You name it, Louis Luyt has fought over it," was the way one journalist summarised it:

> Shamateurism, provincialism, provincial poaching, dinner invitations, selection policies, team discipline, world cup venues, the bad manners of other people, the absence of due deference to his own eminence.[334]

Luyt's decision to allow *Die Stem* to be played at Ellis Park, his arguments with the International Rugby Board, and his unseemly public

---

333 *Rugby 15*, April 1994.
334 *The Star*, 19 August 1994.

wrangles with Jannie Engelbrecht, Springbok manager of the 1994 tour to New Zealand, caused a considerable outcry. At one point, amidst the fight with Engelbrecht, Luyt even briefly resigned from the presidency. Luyt's track record and his tendency to ride roughshod over opponents called forth the unflattering comment that he was a man with "less sensitivity and fewer principles than a rugby ball".[335] His outbursts were also seen as damaging to the image of South African rugby administration, giving the impression to the outside world that local administrators were "a clamorous rat pack of barefoot yokels squabbling in the dust of a distant country".[336]

Such criticisms need perspective. Luyt's background was not that of the usual solidly middle-class rugby administrator. His was a rags-to-riches story. Luyt was born in 1932 and went to school in the barren Karoo village of Hanover. During the depression years of the early 1930s, his father worked as a farm labourer, earning a paltry wage. As the son of a "poor white", Luyt put himself through university at Bloemfontein. His first major business, a fertiliser company, Triomf, grew from humble beginnings as a one-man door-to-door selling operation into a multimillion rand concern. However, with the crash on the Johannesburg Stock Exchange in the 1980s, his company collapsed. Critics claimed that Luyt had taken his money out in advance, but he denies this. Be that as it may, Luyt as a businessman was far from finished. He had a hand in several businesses; from his Cape farms alone he expected to earn R20 million in exports within three years. He also owned a private jet, and it was rumoured that on board the supersonic aircraft, surrounded by executive splendour, officials from the former non-establishment unions, not used to being entertained in such luxury, have been inclined to shift their political positions.

Not all of Luyt's enterprises were equally well-considered. In the late 1970s he was embroiled in a national scandal for acting as a front man in a government bid to run a sympathetic pro-apartheid newspaper with taxpayers' money. He claimed he was deliberately misled.[337]

---

335 *Weekly Mail and Guardian*, 27 August 1992.
336 *Weekly Mail and Guardian*, 27 August 1992.
337 *The Star*, 19 August 1994; *Natal on Saturday*, 27 August 1994; *Sowetan*, 18 July 1992.

In the world of rugby administration, Luyt's undoubted business acumen stood him in good stead. He turned losses incurred from the giant Ellis Park stadium into profits by adding 50 private suites for rental, and renting the stadium out for international soccer matches and other entertainment. He also raised the sponsorship of rugby in South Africa from R35 million to R85 million.[338] Although critics found it hard to fault his financial achievements, he was accused of running rugby affairs like a personal fiefdom, to the extent of involving close family members in arrangements for the World Cup. He responded by claiming that his family did not benefit financially from their involvement.[339]

For Luyt himself, there was a close connection between his aggressive style and the route that he had to travel to get to the top. "I've tried to psycho-analyse myself," he said, "Why am I like I am? I think it's because I've always had to fight for myself. I had to fight for eight years before I went to varsity, and even then, I had to work at night to support myself. That could be the problem with my life. I had to fight for everything I ever got ... I wasn't a favourite. I wasn't a *Broeder*, didn't belong to any organisations. That's bullshit. I have always been my own master."[340]

At times Luyt's blunt, pragmatic and goal-oriented approach showed little appreciation for wider political matters. Hence, when rising levels of pre-election violence in 1994 threatened to derail plans for the World Cup, Luyt argued in racial terms that it was a "black" and not a "white" problem, and that as far as the World Cup was concerned, supporters could easily be isolated from what was going on in the rest of the country. "Most of the violence has been outside Johannesburg," he said. "It has been black-on-black violence, not black-on-white. We will certainly make sure that everybody visiting South Africa is booked into the right places."[341]

Post-1990 politics in South Africa was even more of a minefield than before and Luyt, almost without fail, triggered several explosions. Along with the Ellis Park anthem debacle, he gained a reputa-

---

338 *Rugby 15*, July 1993; *The Sunday Star*, 12 July 1992; *Weekly Mail and Guardian*, 12 August 1994.
339 *Beeld*, November 1994.
340 *The Star*, 19 August 1994.
341 *The Citizen*, 31 March 1994.

tion in certain quarters "as an archetypal worst of old-style white South Africans – brash and arrogant, proud of his lack of concern for his fellow citizens..."[342]

It would be misleading, though, to view Louis Luyt only in the light in which certain sections of the media have chosen to portray him. In a wider context, Luyt represented more than an abrasive and offensive personality. In terms of rugby management and structures, he symbolised the passing of an amateur "gentlemen" era and the beginning of a new, more overtly professional period with concomitant competitive managerial styles. The 1995 World Cup was to provide him with a world stage.

Conclusion

In retrospect the only realistic chance of Springbok rugby to have regained international recognition hinged on wider political changes in the country. However, at the time few administrators could foresee that re-entry into the family of world sport would call for a substantial reversal of the reigning political order and that piecemeal adjustments were of little significance. It turned out to be a long and winding road to reach the point where international tours could recommence. In ways that were unimaginable in the 1980s, given the fact that South Africa was in the throes of successive states of emergencies and an international outcast, the world opened up in the early 1990s. In 1995 the holy grail of rugby – the Rugby World Cup – appeared within grasp.

---

342 *Weekly Mail and Guardian*, 27 August 1992.

5

Explaining euphoria: The 1995 Springbok Rugby World Cup victory and its impact

The 1995 Springbok Rugby World Cup victory over their traditional foes, the All Blacks, has drawn the attention of a large number of scribes over the years. While much of this writing provides useful information, it lacks a central thrust in trying to explain why events on the field and their subsequent reverberations beyond the stadium assumed a specific form and content. For an understanding of this, one needs to look at the nature of support for the victorious Springbok team which in a rare historical moment seemed to have transcended race divisions and at how contextual influences helped to shape the outcome. Likewise the significance of subsequent rugby developments which appeared to contradict the sense of unity generated during the tournament is of interest.

Repackaging rugby

Saturday 24 June 1995 was indeed a red-letter day in South Africa. Before a capacity crowd at Ellispark stadium in Johannesburg and with millions watching the finals of the Rugby World Cup on television, the Springbok team narrowly managed to beat the much vaunted New Zealand All Black team in extra time through a drop goal by the fly half, Joel Stransky. South Africa was the new rugby champion of the world. On hand to present the Cup to the victorious captain, Francois Pienaar, was South Africa's most celebrated prisoner-turned-president, Nelson Mandela, decked out in Pienaar's spare number 6 jersey – in an unmistakable show of identification and support. It was the perfect climax to a tournament which saw South Africa taking pride of place in the rugby world after the international sports isolation of the apartheid years.

Unprecedented scenes of mass euphoria followed the Springbok victory, unleashing a celebration of exhilarating excess of hugs and hurrahs, of merriment and madness. From the usually staid tree-lined, predominantly white suburbs to dusty black township streets, black and white South Africans seemed to have discovered a sense of common unity as the victory was toasted across the land. For a country with a long and painful history of division and conflict, and in the sporting arena where rugby in particular was being perceived as the game of the Afrikaner oppressors, such celebrations were thrillingly extraordinary.[343] Six years after the event, a journalist could still enthuse: "In spirit, in mansions and shacks, in every nook and cranny of a vast land, Francois Pienaar, the world champion Springbok, will never die."[344]

Not only the revellers in the street, but also normally reserved and taciturn academics had outspoken opinions. Wilmot James, a sociologist at the time, expressed what he regarded as the significance of the Springbok victory as follows:

> South African sport teams have excelled beyond expectations and in doing so have elevated the concept of national unity in a way that 1000 lecturers and community workshops could not have begun to achieve. President Nelson Mandela, too, is a major party to the lifting of the national spirit... Some people wonder aloud how deeply athletic excellence can penetrate the spirit. However, it is a mistake of the intelligence to think that prowess on the sports field evokes merely a momentary sentimentality for the masses. It sets an unmistakable example, involves millions of people in collective forms and celebrations, and is in fact a powerful example of spontaneous ideology.[345]

Whilst the notion of "spontaneous ideology" is unlikely to be included in social science handbooks as an established frame of reference, it certainly captured the mood at the time.

---

343 There is no shortage of reports on the euphoria which accompanied South Africa's Rugby World Cup victory. All the newspapers carried banner headlines and extensive commentary. I found the reports in the Afrikaans Sunday newspaper *Rapport* (25 June 1995) to be the most graphic.
344 Griffiths: *Captains*, p. 455.
345 *Democracy in Action* (March. 1996), p. 3.

If dry-as-dust academics could sense something exceptional, it is not surprising that professional purveyors of sentimentalism and sensationalism in the media world would latch onto it. This happened with the 2009 Hollywood release of *Invictus*, produced by none other than Clint Eastwood with Morgan Freeman cast as Nelson Mandela and Matt Damon as Francois Pienaar. Based on a one-dimensional book by John Carlin with the title, *Playing the Enemy: Nelson Mandela and the game that made a nation* (2008), the film exploits the dramatic elements of the event and revels in imparting a "feel good" quality. A critic has pointed out that *Invictus* "bears the marks of a movie tailored by and for a predominantly American standpoint", in which American predilections and narrative structures prevail. Ultimately, the film's "aesthetic Manicheanism yields binaries that leave its moralising message and triumphant ending unencumbered by historical complexity or nuance." [346]

Besides filmic representations of the event, it also resided in popular Afrikaner historical memory. Shortly after the victory, the outcome was interpreted in virtually sacrosanct, near religious terms. In the Afrikaans press it was editorialised:

> Nobody would argue that the Springboks became the carriers of something almost mystical. Something of the soul of the *volk* perhaps? Spectators at the Ellispark stadium said that they will never forget the experience. They felt they were purified. The Springboks indeed became elements of the soul.[347]

Even fourteen years after the event and despite the fact that the notion of South Africa as a rainbow nation – which was peddled under the seemingly benign Mandela – all but disappeared under his successor, the more Africanist inclined Thabo Mbeki, the memory of an event which held out the promise of reconciliation still maintained its grip. In 2009 the popular Afrikaans magazine *Huisgenoot* invited readers to submit letters recalling their experiences of that day. It was flooded with literally hundreds of letters which spoke in the most vivid way of the positive energy radiated at the time. These were, it was reported, "wonderful memories, full of the pride of the nation

---

346 S. Robolin: "Of Colour and Blindness in *Invictus*", *Safundi: The Journal of South African and American studies*, 13, 1–2 (2012), p. 122.
347 *Volksblad*, 29 July 1995. (Translated)

and hope for the future".[348] The event had clearly become an historical marker in Afrikaner popular memory. It has also set a benchmark for judging all future World Cups.[349] Additionally, it was probably one of the few strands of remembrance in Afrikaner society, albeit of an informal kind, that incorporated more than a purely ethnic element and had an inclusive dimension to it insofar as a sense of unity with other South Africans was part of the historical recall.[350]

However, there is always a gap between historical reality and historical memory. This calls for an analysis of the underlying circumstances that contributed to shaping the euphoria of the day. For a fuller understanding it is helpful to begin with attempts to re-model the Springbok rugby ethos along appropriate post-apartheid lines.

Springbok rugby, as we have seen, has long been associated with the Afrikaner and apartheid. The unification process between anti-apartheid rugby organisations and mainly white establishment organisations, which followed in the wake of political changes after 1990, was painful and slow. Given these perceptions and the generally volatile political situation in the country, some World Cup Organising Committee members had reservations about whether the tournament should be staged in South Africa at all. The directors of the World Cup had only come to the decision in January 1993 once they had been given adequate assurances by the ANC and the government. Even so they realised that they had to keep a close watch on the situation.[351]

The South African rugby hierarchy was alive to the problems and the real possibility that the tournament could be disrupted by dissent and conflict. Louis Luyt was not a man who tolerated failure easily. For all his bluster and at times bombastic behaviour, he fully understood the need to work in a different political environment after the outcome of the 1994 elections.[352] What is more, he had a personal

---

348 *Huisgenoot*, 31 December 2009, "Daai dag in 1995" pp. 22–25. (Translated)
349 G.J. Botma: "Lightning strikes twice: The 2007 Rugby World Cup and memories of a South African Rainbow Nation", *Communicato: South African Journal for Communication Theory and Research*, 36, 1, 2010, pp. 1–19.
350 Compare *Huisgenoot*, 31 December 2009, "Daai dag in 1995". Testimonies reflecting mutual celebrations with black people.
351 *Cape Times*, 20 January 1993.
352 *New Nation*, 23 June 1995. See also E. Griffiths: *One Team, One Country: The Greatest Year of Springbok Rugby* (Viking, Johannesburg, 1996), p. 5.

disdain of the ethos and tradition of the International Rugby Board (IRB) and thought that South Africa could present a much more polished show. He regarded the cosy and clubbish world of the IRB as completely out of step with the modern world of sport:

> I saw the last World Cup in England and it was laughable. There is a great problem with the five unions... They were fighting over who would wear World Cup blazers. They'd spent bloody hours discussing petty matters and who would go to dinners and who could sit nearest to the queen. It was all very petty.[353]

Confidently Luyt could proclaim in September 1994 that as far as organisation for the World Cup was concerned: "We are up to date. We are waiting ... for the World Cup directors to catch up with us now. We've got everything under control. We do it professionally."[354]

For the World Cup to be a success, one of the prerequisites was that rugby had to project a more positive image of embracing the new order in South Africa, which after all, made it possible for the tournament to be held in the country. "Rugby," it was reported, "is known to be keen to improve its poor image and portray itself as a catalyst for change..."[355] To this end a new management structure had to be deployed; the perceived stodgy Afrikaner functionaries of the old order had to be replaced with more progressive officials. As the wording of the advertisement for a Chief Executive Officer (CEO) made clear, they were now looking for someone who was capable of taking the union "into a new phase of its operations".[356]

Out of 1000 applications, Edward Griffiths, a noted sports journalist, was appointed to the position of CEO. It was a significantly different type of appointment. Usually such positions were reserved for Afrikaans speakers from the inner circle of rugby administrators with years of service to the game. Griffiths was English speaking and at 32 relatively young with little direct experience of rugby administration. He was born of British parents in what is today Zimbabwe, and was educated at Charterhouse and New Castle University. In 1985 he moved to South Africa. Griffiths quickly familiarised himself with the nature of the South African sporting ethos and subtly

---

353 *Sunday Times*, 23 October 1994.
354 *Rugby 15*, September 1994.
355 *Sunday Times*, 12 February 1995.
356 *Sunday Times*, 12 February 1995.

infused his knowledge of local sport with the fresh perspectives of an outsider. From this vantage point he wrote critical yet constructive articles on South African rugby. This brought him to the attention of SARFU and in 1994 he was appointed as media liaison officer for the Springbok tour of Wales, Scotland and Ireland. Wise to the ways of the media, a confident and articulate Griffiths wore the mantle of "spin-doctor" with distinction. Louis Luyt, so often in the centre of public relations disasters, was impressed; in Griffiths he saw the ideal person to refashion the image of South African rugby during the forthcoming World Cup tournament.[357] With the not inconsiderable weight of the President of SARFU behind him, Griffiths was virtually assured of the position.

Another significant appointment to the management team was that of Morné du Plessis as manager. Du Plessis, a Springbok rugby captain from 1975 to 1980, was one of the few Springboks of the apartheid era who was sensitive to the iniquities of the system and

Some of the men who made it happen on and off the field: Keith Christie (coach), Francois Pienaar (captain), Morné du Plessis (manager) and Joel Stransky (of drop-kick fame). *(From E. Griffiths,* Kitch: Triumph of a decent man, *Johannesburg, 1997)*

---

357 The information on Griffiths is drawn from the *Cape Times*, 27 June 1995 and the *Sunday Times*, 12 February 1995.

the rationale behind the sporting boycott. Although he was careful in not making overt political statements, his decision in 1981, at the height of his sporting powers, to decline the captaincy of the boycott-breaking and, as it turned out, demonstration-ridden and divisive tour of New Zealand, spoke volumes for his wider insights. Subsequently, he was wooed by the Progressive Federal Party – the white parliamentary opposition to apartheid – as a possible candidate. In 1994 rumours had it that he was also approached by the African National Congress (ANC) to stand as a candidate in the country's first democratic election. Du Plessis steered clear from direct political involvement, but his sympathies were fairly widely known. Former anti-apartheid sporting activists regarded him as an ideal choice as manager because of the almost unique combination of sporting and "progressive" political credentials.[358] Appointing someone of Du Plessis's calibre was a further important step in the effort to enhance the image of Springbok rugby in a new political environment. It also helped that he did his job very effectively. The coach, Kitch Christie recalled: "I can't remember being so immediately impressed by anyone in my entire life as I was by Morné... From my point of view as a coach, he was the perfect manager." [359]

Equally important was the marketing potential of someone like Francois Pienaar, the 1995 Springbok captain. Pienaar, a friendly, accessible and articulate individual, who during the World Cup tournament was to enjoy a good relationship with President Nelson Mandela, was well aware of the wider ramifications of his role.

With the key personnel in place, the rugby show was about to embark on what Griffiths later described as "an exemplary public relations campaign".[360] Griffiths considered the Springboks to be in the "entertainment industry", but their responsibility extended "far beyond the rugby field".[361] In the world of public relations where perceptions tend to determine reality, the Springboks had to project an image of being "humble, excited and unashamedly proud of

---

358 The paragraph on Du Plessis is based on Griffiths: *One Team*, 46–50; *Die Suid-Afrikaan*, May–June 1995.
359 E Griffiths: *Kitch: Truimph of a decent man* (CAB publishers, Johannesburg, 1997), p. 88.
360 Griffiths: *One Team*, p. 114.
361 *Sunday Times*, 19 November 1995.

their new democracy", and this had to be repeated at "infinite press conferences and public appearances".[362] Whatever some Springboks might have thought privately, in public they certainly played their roles well. A British journalist was impressed: "The 1995 Springboks are politically correct, user-friendly, polite and accessible, they offer daily photo opportunities, attend regular press conferences that provide stage-managed sound-bites." Yet he was not completely convinced and added pointedly: "But doubts exist as to whether they really represent reality."[363]

Amongst other reasons, such doubts were bound to persist in the absence of any attempt to add, even at a symbolic level, a distinctive African dimension to South African rugby. The tournament, after all, was taking place in a "new" *African* country. A good starting point to begin addressing this was to ensure that the Springboks knew the words of the "new" part of the national anthem, "Nkosi Sikelel' iAfrica", as well as the "old" part, "Die Stem", which many South Africans associated with the apartheid order. Television close-ups zooming in on the facial expressions of players before test kick-offs, at times embarrassingly revealed that some players regarded "Nkosi" at best as superfluous or at worst with disdain. Morné du Plessis was determined to change this. He even obtained the services of an African languages lecturer from the University of Stellenbosch to coach the players in the pronunciation of the Xhosa anthem. "Most of the guys can't even remember the words of pop songs", he said, "but they will know the words of the anthem."[364]

In a further bid to lend more African colour to the team, an African workers' chain-gang song "Shosholoza" (literally meaning "pushing" or "running" together) was adopted as a theme song. It was not without a certain irony that a traditional mineworkers' song which was sung by workers from neighbouring countries on their way to the mines where they ran a risk of an early death through disease and accidents, became a cultural element in the representation of a supposed "new" South Africa.[365] Other similar initiatives

---

362 Griffiths: *One Team*, p. 114.
363 Quoted in *Eastern Province Herald*, 24 June 1995.
364 *Economist*, 27 May 1995; see also Griffiths: *One Team*, p. 49.
365 J. Nauright: "Global Games: Culture, Political Economy and Sport in the Globalised World of the 21st Century", *Third World Quarterly*, 25, 7 (2004), p. 1327.

which foregrounded African concerns followed. It was widely publicised that the Springboks supported a community-driven campaign, Masakhane ("let us build together"), in the black townships.[366] The "Africanisation" drive received an unexpected fillip when a black newspaper, *The Sowetan*, coined the term Amabokoboko for the Springboks. This African derivative rapidly gained currency. The degree of cultural fusion implicit in this term helped to contribute to the subsequent retention, amidst some controversy, of the springbok as an official emblem, despite its earlier apartheid associations, of South African rugby.[367] Dovetailing with these developments, the Springboks also had to be seen as standard bearers of national unity; hence the official slogan of "One Team: One Country". All these various strands neatly tied together in the notion of South Africa as a "rainbow nation" – a metaphor for ethnic diversity and much pedalled by one of South Africa's Nobel Prize winners, the often theatrical Archbishop Desmond Tutu.[368]

While the refashioning of the symbolic imagery of South African rugby was meant to showcase the changes in internal emphasis in the country, it was difficult to give substance to these claims if the Springbok rugby team as such, consisting of white men only, looked suspiciously the same as before. Twenty years earlier some rugby administrators could happily proclaim that a black person would never don a Springbok jersey. In 1995, as a result of changed circumstances, there was an almost desperate search to find a black body who could on playing ability, be put into a Springbok jersey. Those who seek shall find. Forward stepped Chester Williams, a coloured winger from Western Province. Williams was certainly a good enough player to qualify on merit, but more important, on the public relations front, he was a priceless asset as the face that could launch the newly integrated South African rugby ship. Despite being a reserved person, Williams received a disproportionate amount of media attention as the only black player in the Springbok squad. Feted

---

366 Griffiths: *One Team*, p. 114; *The Star*, 20 June 1995.
367 For these developments see D. Booth: "Mandela and Amabokoboko: the Political and Linguistic Nationalisation of South Africa?", *Journal of Modern African Studies*, Sept. 1996, pp. 457–77.
368 For the "rainbow nation" notion see J.M. Coetzee: "The Rugby World Cup of Rugby", *Southern African Review of Books*, July 1995.

in the press and routinely referred to as the "black pearl", Williams rapidly became an icon for rugby in the "new" South Africa; he was the emblem of achievement, hope, reconciliation and recognition for the fledgling nation. That Williams played his earlier rugby under the auspices of the white dominated Rugby Board and not under the umbrella of the anti-apartheid activist unions – a fact which in the apartheid era would have made him a collaborator in many quarters – was conveniently forgotten. The only thing that counted was that Williams was black.[369]

But then disaster struck. Williams was injured and it seemed as if this would rule him out of the tournament; all too sudden the politically correct advertising campaign began to falter. It nevertheless started to build up steam again when Pieter Hendriks, Williams's replacement, was eliminated from the tournament as a result of dirty play. This opened up the way for Williams who in the meantime had recovered from injury to regain his place and to carry on where he had left off in the frontline of rugby's public relations campaign. It was strongly rumoured at the time, and also subsequently alleged by Luyt, that Griffiths had taken it on himself to offer Hendriks R15 000 not to appeal against the expulsion from the tournament as that could have jeopardised Williams's return.[370]

If Williams had to be kept in the centre of the frame, it is equally true that those with potential to sully the carefully constructed representation of rugby in post-apartheid South Africa, had to be kept outside. One such person was the Northern Transvaal forward, Henry Tromp, who had served a four-month jail sentence on a charge of manslaughter for his part in the death of a black youth who had been caught stealing from the Tromp family. Tromp was a strong candidate for inclusion in the Springbok World Cup squad. However, the opinion prevailed that it could do the public image of the Springboks infinite harm if a man with Tromp's past were to be part of the tournament.[371]

---

369 *Cape Argus*, 16 June 1995; *Rapport*, 23 July 1995; *Sowetan*, 15 June 1995; *Die Suid-Afrikaan*, May–June 1995; *Weekly Mail and Guardian*, 6–12 June 1997.
370 *Die Afrikaner*, 27 July–1 Aug. 1995; *SA Sports Illustrated*, 22 July 1996. Griffiths, *One Team*, pp. 81–82, does not address this allegation in his book.
371 On Tromp see *Beeld*, 10 April 1995; *Die Afrikaner*, 13–20 April 1995; *Rapport*, 16 April 1995; *Sunday Paper*, 17 August 1996; Griffiths: *One Team*, pp. 31, 203.

It was not only players like Tromp who were to be kept out of the public eye. In the "national interest", trade union and other disgruntled groups who threatened to disrupt the opening ceremony of the tournament at Newlands, Cape Town, were dissuaded from doing so; it would have been embarrassing for the new government if some of its own supporters were to be seen by the outside world as acting in a disruptive manner.[372] In trying to present a sanitised view of South Africa on the eve of the World Cup, the ANC government followed a pattern of well-established state behaviour in countries where international sporting events with a worldwide audience were to be staged. Similarly, pre-Olympian suppression of dissidents had occurred in Berlin in 1936, Mexico in 1968, Moscow in 1980 and Seoul in 1988.[373]

In events of this nature, the opening ceremony assumes a significance all of its own. Before the Olympics in Seoul the organising committee and international broadcasters had committed considerable resources to the planning and rehearsing of the opening ceremony. The reason for this, as the planners indicated, was that they had been well aware that the degree of favourable publicity for the country and the Games hinged in part on public reaction to the opening ceremony.[374]

For the Rugby World Cup organisers in South Africa, the opening ceremony of the tournament was even of greater importance as the principal vehicle for the self-representation of a newly born society. Given the country's deeply divided past, the whole ceremony had, as far as possible, to be drained from history. On a bright sunny day in Cape Town a colourful pageant unfolded as happy, smiling and dancing South African ethnic groups cavorted around the field, representing the "rainbow nation", while the official World Cup song "A world in union" was belted out. When President Nelson Mandela

---

[372] *Natal on Saturday*, 20 May 1995; *Die Burger*, 20 May 1995, *Citizen*, 21 April 1995.
[373] B. Houlihan: *Sport and International Politics*, (Prentice Hall, London, 1994), p. 13.
[374] J.F. Larson and H.-S. Park: *Global Television and the Politics of the Seoul Olympics* (James F. Larson, Boulder, 1993) 194–5. For a description of television coverage of the tournament see L. Strelitz and L. Steenveld: "Sport en Nasiebou in Suid Afrika: Die Betekenis van die 1995 Rugby Wêreldbeker", in *Ecqui Novi*, 17, 2 (1996), pp. 137–138.

appeared on the field to make a short speech he was warmly and enthusiastically welcomed with chants of "Nelson, Nelson".[375] The "rainbow nation" vehicle seemed to have clicked into gear.

Edward Griffiths described the ceremony in glowing terms as one of "outstanding quality, emotion and creativity", and as a most significant "expression of the new South Africa as a rainbow land at peace with its own diversity".[376] More soberly it can be seen as a well-choreographed public spectacle which gave the dark and dangerous South African past a wide berth, and as a result was able to create the illusion of a new country born and received without sin. Reflecting on the ceremony, the noted South African novelist and academic, J.M. Coetzee, pertinently observed that such a "de-historicised vision of Tourist South Africa" (consisting of "contented tribesfolk", "timeless Sotho in blankets", "timeless Zulu in ostrich feathers", "happy eighteenth century slaves and slave owners in kneebreeches" and "half-a-dozen lost looking lads in khaki shirts and shorts") should be viewed purely as the product of image makers and image managers intent on creating a consumable commodity for the World Cup tournament.[377] The public representation of South African society might have been a parody, but it was not a departure from the norm as far as such sporting occasions are concerned; the ceremony merely conformed to the way in which events of this nature are generally contextualised in the public domain. In the literature dealing with sport and identity it is described as "eternalisation", whereby "social-historical phenomena are deprived of their historical character by being portrayed as permanent, unchanging and ever-recurring..."[378] For example, in the opening ceremonies of the four Canadian Olympic and Commonwealth Games between 1976 and 1994, indigenous native cultures were also cast in a similar mould.[379]

However, the manufactured magic of unity created by the opening ceremony was shortly afterwards, in a rather unexpected way,

---

375 For example *Die Burger*, 26 May 1995; *Cape Times*, 26 May 1995.
376 Griffiths: *One Team*, pp. 62, 63.
377 *Southern African Review of Books*, July 1995. See also J. Maingard: "Imag(in)ing the South African Nation: Representations of Identity in the Rugby World Cup, 1995", *Theatre Journal*, 49, 1 (1997), pp. 15–28.
378 N. Blain, R. Boyle and H. O'Donnell: *Sport and National Identity in the European Media* (Leicester University Press, Leicester, 1993), p. 11.
379 Nauright: "Global Games", p. 1327.

exposed for what it really was – just a show. In the week after the ceremony, the "happy" representatives of the rainbow nation on the Saturday before, many of them black youngsters from Langa and Guguletu near Cape Town, complained bitterly that they were not compensated for their participation and threatened to disrupt further World Cup proceedings.[380] These threats did not materialise, but in a wider sense the unhappiness of the participants demonstrated the hollowness of the ceremony. The protests failed to attract much media attention, allowing the general public to continue basking in the afterglow of the ceremony sealed with a Springbok victory over the reigning Australian champions.

Purchasing the product

While it is important to identify those constitutive elements that at the time of the World Cup contributed to the remake of the South African rugby ethos, it cannot be regarded as a full explanation for the euphoria that swept South Africa and touched even those who earlier were either hostile to or apathetic about the game. In short, why did the South African public, white and black, endorse the refashioned product so enthusiastically? It does not follow that simply because image producers had carefully repackaged a product, it would necessarily have an impact on the cultural market place. A more searching explanation of the reasons why rugby appeared to transcend hitherto existing cultural boundaries is therefore required.

It would not be amiss, in this respect, to mention what actually happened on the rugby field itself. Often sports historians are so intent in exploring the wider dimensions of sport and society that the significance of the outcome of matches tends to go unnoticed. The fact that the Springboks won all their games leading up to the final ensured that the public interest was kept alive. To argue counterfactually, if the results were different there would not have been much cause for nationwide celebrations. What further added to the occasion was that the victory was achieved in South Africa's first participation in the World Cup tournament.[381] In assessing the on-field success of the team, the noted sports scientist, Tim Noakes, concluded

---

380 *Cape Argus*, 30 May 1995; *The Star*, 2 June 1995.
381 Griffiths: *One Team*, p. 114.

that the Springboks' 1995 triumph can be attributed to old-fashioned values of faith, discipline and teamwork, combined with supreme physical preparation and a clear understanding of the game plan, especially the defensive game plan. All these factors allowed the team to seize its moment of greatness and to add one of the greatest chapters to the legend of Springbok rugby.[382]

Casting a gaze away from the rugby stadium, one has to look at the prevailing public mood at the time of the tournament. The notion of public mood may perhaps be considered rather too nebulous for analytical purposes, yet it is a useful concept when understood as a category of social behaviour that "involves expectations about collective life or feelings of group efficacy".[383]

After years of apartheid and civil turmoil the country had in 1995 emerged from a tense period. The first democratic elections had taken place barely a year earlier and the fact that it was concluded without major upheavals was cause for considerable relief. The transition to democracy was widely hailed as a major achievement after all the earlier dire predictions of a bloodbath. The public mood was positive; for once it seemed as if South Africans of every hue had managed to succeed as a group. Accolades from the international community were all very novel. The satirist, Pieter-Dirk Uys commented gleefully:

> They no longer throw our Outspan oranges down London toilets, or our Granny Smith apples into the *grachts* of Amsterdam. They no longer secretly decant our KWV wine into Spanish plonk bottles or scream anti-South African slogans. In fact ... we are now the Good Guys ... We're the democratic, non-racial, non-sexist, non-sensical new South Africa. Hallelujah![384]

The World Cup tournament coincided with a ground swell of buoyant public opinion in 1995: "If ever a country was in need of a party, a good time ... it was South Africa."[385] It was indeed a rare historical moment. Public spaces for interaction at a different level than what

---

382 T. Noakes: *Challenging Beliefs: Memoirs of a Career* (Zebra Press, Cape Town, 2011), p. 157.
383 W.M. Rahn, B. Kroeger and C.M. Kite: "A Framework for the Study of Public Mood", *Political Psychology*, 17, 1 (1996), p. 49.
384 *Sunday Times Inside*, 22 October 1995.
385 Griffiths: *One Team*, p. 51.

was possible under apartheid had opened up; black and white could, in a relatively harmless way, express a common sentiment without either side sacrificing or risking too much.³⁸⁶

Most Afrikaners, excluding those on the right, adapted much quicker to the new dispensation than many observers had anticipated. In part this was because they still had representatives at the highest level in the Government of National Unity. They also believed, given the assurances of Vice-president F.W. de Klerk of weights and counterweights, that the transformation process was well under control. As such the new dispensation was not too threatening yet. On the contrary, as sociologist, Heribert Adam, explained at the time:

> By endorsing the ANC rule in a negotiated settlement, and in turn being praised for pragmatic foresight, Afrikaner nationalists wallow in a self-congratulatory mood of having achieved the ultimate triumph of survival as a recognised minority in a hostile environment. In their self-perception, Afrikaners have not handed over power, as it appears to the outside observer, but ... secured a much more stable and amiable environment for future greatness.³⁸⁷

The perception that political negotiations had worked to the benefit of Afrikaners, had its parallel in the connections between sport and society. There was more than an element of truth in the observation of one journalist that "Afrikaners had swapped apartheid for rugby, and there was every sign they thought it a fair deal".³⁸⁸

The ANC, in turn, had just moved into office and still had to demonstrate that they had effectively made the transition from a liberation movement to a responsible government committed to order and reconciliation. Furthermore, as far as economic and social policies were concerned, the ANC was put on "capitalist probation and subjected to unrelenting pressure to prove its reliability to business interests that will help shape its fate".³⁸⁹

At the time of the World Cup there was every reason for the ANC

---

386 Compare Griffiths: *One Team*, p. 113.
387 H. Adam: "Ethnic versus Civic Nationalism: South Africa's Non-Racialism in Comparative Perspective", *SA Sociological Review*, 7, 1 (1994), p. 26.
388 P. Waldmeir: *Anatomy of a Miracle: The End of Apartheid and the Birth of the New South Africa* (W.W. Norton and Company, Middlesex, 1997), p. 269.
389 M. Macdonald: "Power Politics in the New South Africa", in *Journal of Southern African Studies*, 22, 2 (June 1996), p. 227.

to conduct itself in an exemplary fashion. Steve Tshwete, the Minister for Sport and Recreation, was of the opinion that the "importance of the World Cup could not be overestimated". It offered "a wonderful opportunity and also sets a considerable test. If we pass this test, there could be important benefits for our country and people as a whole."[390] The ANC, like most other governments, clearly regarded sport as an essential element of foreign and domestic policy in as much as it could confer prestige and promote national unity.[391] All of this fed into the need for creating a favourable climate for international investments.[392] Through the publicity of the World Cup, the ANC could shore up its credibility "in a way that millions of advertisements worldwide would not have been able to buy".[393]

A central figure in the new government's blessing of the World Cup tournament was of course Nelson Mandela. It is common practice, as the American academic Allen Guttman has noted, for governments to "collect political prestige by staging extravagant sports spectacles and democratic leaders seldom miss an opportunity to throw out the first ball, to telephone congratulations to the winners, and generally to bask in the reflected glory of athletic achievement".[394] However, in the case of the South African rugby team, the Springboks probably stood more to gain by the association with Mandela than the other way around. Mandela already had a long established international reputation as an anti-apartheid icon, while the Springboks still had to prove their international credibility. Mandela's strategic appearances and his identification with the team helped elevate them, a virtually all-white team, to a symbol of nationhood.

It turned out to be a marketing masterstroke. One media specialist commented that Mandela – "he of the perpetual smile and the studied stoop of humility" – has "instilled and enthused the brand image of South Africa with his personality". What was particularly striking, was the break from the past. Gone was "the hateful image created

---

390 *Time*, 29 May 1995.
391 Compare D. Booth: "United Sport: An Alternative Hegemony in South Africa?", *International Journal of the History of Sport*, 12, 3 (Dec. 1995), p. 120.
392 *Economist*, 13 May 1995; *Productivity SA*, Mar.–Apr. 1995.
393 *Volksblad*, 27 June 1995. (Translation)
394 A. Guttmann: *Sports Spectators* (Colombia University Press, New York, 1986), p. 179.

over decades by the amorphous polymer of bald, grumpy old men pointing fingers and frowning under their black trilbies". Now a new perception was about to take root:

> Instead of that dull country with its dour leaders and bloody conflicts, the world sees Nelson Mandela adorned with the inevitable shirt from a selection – it becomes apparent – of infinite colour and variety, making a speech at the opening game of the Rugby World Cup. They hear the mostly white South African crowd ... chanting Nel-son, Nel-son, praising him in their own boorish rugby manner. Later infinitely compassionate and forgiving, he calls to wish the team luck – a subtle reminder of why they are playing in the tournament at all. The jibe missed, they are duly impressed and they win.[395]

Mandela's involvement with the team and the tournament generally, can also be seen as an excursion into the field of cultural politics. The closed cultural space occupied by rugby, hitherto a predominantly Afrikaner preserve, was sufficiently prised open to allow at

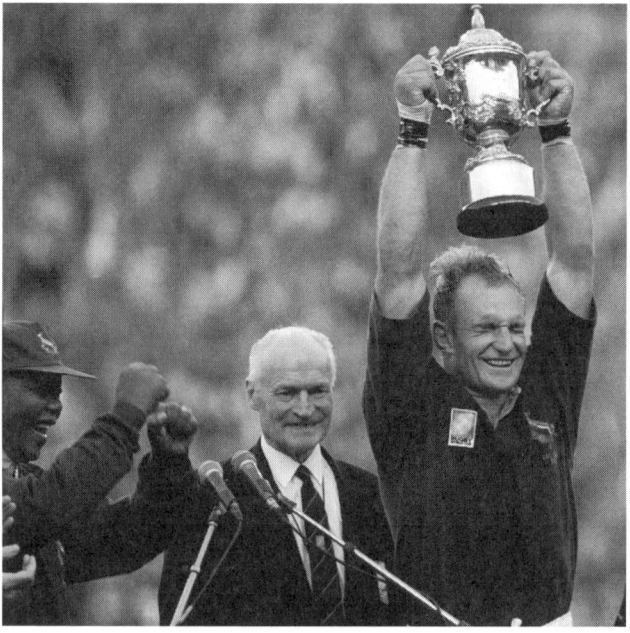

The magic moment: "We are all winners...?" *(Gallo images)*

---

395 *Living*, December 1995.

least a partial reinscription of the game's narrow cultural identity. In addition, the "public ownership" of rugby was symbolically democratised and extended. Afrikaner claims of possession were compromised with Mandela's anointment of the game; the metaphorical message was that the game belonged to the new South Africa and the old order had passed. Perhaps slightly exaggerated, a British journalist nevertheless made the point well:

> Mandela had ... pulled the political magician's trick of all times; to have allowed his rivals the most precious of prizes they could ever wish for and – swish – with one sweep of the cloak represented the prize unchanged, yet suddenly belonging to not the minority but the majority.[396]

Mandela's performance also drew calculated praise from Frederik van Zyl Slabbert:

> He [Mandela] was the master at exploiting the appropriate moment, making a conciliatory gesture, and persuading the international community that South Africa was 'on its way.'... Nobody must underestimate his performance at the Rugby World Cup final in 1995. I was there that day, and saw pot-bellied right-wing fanatics from the deep rural areas weeping when Mandela came up to present the victory cup at the end of the game. This was one of the final blows to exclusive right-wing Afrikaner nationalism. I saw and heard one of the pot-bellied brigade whispers through his tears: "That is my president."[397]

Ultimately the Springboks, their management and die-hard rugby devotees willingly played along, not fully realising that at a meta-level they were small players in a far greater bigger political drama than the World Cup. Wrapped up in their own limited sporting concerns, they were feted and momentarily ensnared by "Madiba magic".

During the tournament much was made of black support for the event, yet the dynamics of the support were seldom elucidated. There were those whites who believed that black enthusiasm was proof of rugby's, and by implication, white's proselytising power.[398] It was an oversimplistic view, conveniently ignoring shifts in power rela-

---

396 Quoted in *Cape Times*, 27 June 1996.
397 F. van Zyl Slabbert: *The Other Side of History: An Anecdotal Reflection on the Political Transition in South Africa* (Jonathan Ball, Johannesburg, 2006), p. 61.
398 For an example see *Cape Argus*, 23 June 1996.

tions. In fact, it was only because there was a black government in power that South Africa was able to host the tournament; the cultural trickle-down effect of this was that black South Africans could now afford to demonstrate greater largesse. The change was neatly explained by one commentator who pointed out that it was as if black people were in the position of "senior school kids, indulging the junior standards", and similarly with "benign generosity" black people "allowed white South Africa to have its fun while they applauded".[399]

The support that black people expressed for the Springboks was of a very specific nature. For historical reasons the majority of black people in the former Transvaal only had a superficial acquaintance with the culture of rugby; for many of them it was the spectacle of the occasion that mattered more than anything else. Aggrey Klaaste, well-known editor of *The Sowetan*, was surprised by the level of interest showed by his readers and he put it down to "the nature of the World Cup tournament. The people got swept along."[400] A poll conducted during one of the early matches of the Springboks showed that 44% of Soweto's inhabitants watched the game.[401] It was the first occasion of its kind in South Africa and even though it was a relatively unknown game to them, it did not mean they had to miss out on the extravaganza. The new South Africa had opened up a wider range of possible identifications than before. Under apartheid it was difficult to identify with a team associated with the oppressors, but with apartheid officially out of the way it was less problematic to support a team that claimed to represent the whole of South Africa. Black people could, some for the first time, revel in the novelty of the freedom of choice.

Culturally, black support for the Springboks generally found expression in uninhibited dancing and praise-singing of the Amabokoboko. However, the significance of such celebratory exuberance can be overestimated. One woman described her support for the Springbok team in a novel manner, delightfully capturing the strangeness

---

399 *Sunday Independent*, 25 June 1995. See also *The Star*, 25 May 1995.
400 D. Retief: *The Springboks and the Holy Grail: Behind the Scenes at the Rugby World Cup* (Zebra Press, Cape Town, 2011), p. 50.
401 S. Crawford: "Nelson Mandela, the Number 6 Jersey and the 1995 Rugby World Cup: Sport as a Transcendent Unifying Force, or a Transparent Illustration of Bicultural Opportunism" in R.R. Sands (ed.), *Anthropology, Sport and Culture*, (Bergin and Garvey, London, 1999), p. 129.

of the game for the uninitiated, but ultimately giving cause to reflect on the durability of support which is based only on a carnivalesque experience of the game:

> I have no idea of what they're doing or why, or which way they're supposed to be running. I can't see why they spend all that time on each other or making themselves into that tortoise thing. All I know is that I am glued to the screen and when I see the team in green hugging each other I get damp in my eyes; these are my boys, that's my team.[402]

Such sentiments constituted one of the elements of the social adhesive that bonded the nation during the World Cup tournament. But was the adhesive sufficiently strong to prevent the product, so carefully assembled by Griffiths and company, from disintegrating after the tournament?

From Boipatong to "Boer" – black bonhomie? *(From J. Carlin,* Playing the enemy, *London, 2008)*

Putting the product to test

The post-World Cup period did not start off very auspiciously. In his post-dinner speech Louis Luyt as the host suggested that had the Springboks participated in the two previous World Cup tournaments, they could have won those as well. Luyt later claimed that it was meant as a joke, but the All Blacks did not think so and some of them, taking umbrage at what they considered a gloating and arro-

---

402 *The Star*, 6 June 1995.

gant attitude, left the dining room.[403] The earlier well-oiled publicity machine of the World Cup tournament was beginning to splutter.

South Africa's rugby image was further tainted by a rather rough transition from semi-amateurism to full professionalism which involved drawn-out and often unsavoury wrangles over contracts and salaries. To the general public, not particularly concerned about the finer details, it seemed as if the players who had given life to the slogan "One Team: One Country" now had a far greater interest in money than in the team or the country.[404]

If the magical whitewash of the World Cup began to flake in the latter part of 1995, it was seen to be peeling off quite rapidly in 1996. During the 1996 All Black tour some rugby supporters in Bloemfontein dusted off their old South African flags, associated with the apartheid order, and merrily proceeded to wave these with gusto during the test match. It was in contrast to the World Cup tournament when very few old flags were seen and the new multicoloured South African flag attained almost cult status. It appeared as if there was still some symbolic life left in the old flag. Morné du Plessis as manager tried to undo some of the damage by claiming that the Springboks did not play for those who carried the old flag. This only served to create a furore in the Afrikaans press. Neither did the comments of Trevor Manuel, Minister of Finance, calm matters; he said that if certain rugby supporters behaved in the same way as they did during the apartheid days, he could not see his way clear to support the Springboks, but would as he had done under apartheid, shift his allegiance to those who opposed the Springboks. The incongruous situation of a Minister of State refusing to support his own country on the sporting field, and subsequent threats that the old flag may be banned, gave the impression that the harmonious image of a rainbow nation of barely a year before had been supplanted by a more discordant image of a nation rent asunder by thunder and lightning.[405]

---

403 For example *Sunday Times*, 2 July 1995.
404 *Business Day*, 5 July 1995; *Finansies en Tegniek*, 14 July 1995; *Weekly Mail and Guardian*, 21–27 July 1995; *Sunday Times*, 6 and 20 Aug. 1995; *Beeld*, 12 Aug. 1995; *Rapport*, 20 Aug. 1995; *Pretoria News*, 11 Sept. 1995; *SA Sports Illustrated*, 16 Sept. 1996.
405 *Volksblad*, 7 and 8 Aug. 1996; *Beeld*, 14 and 23 Aug. 1996; *Die Burger*, 15 Aug. 1996; *Citizen*, 22 and 31 Aug. 1996; *Die Afrikaner*, 16–22 Aug. 1996; *Sunday Times*, 18 Aug. 1996.

Not only was South Africa defeated by the All Blacks in the 1996 series, but key people of the 1995 triumph fell beside the wayside. Amidst fierce controversy the captain, Francois Pienaar, was dropped from the Springbok side, and so was Joel Stransky, the 1995 match winner. Moreover, the principal designers and purveyors of the refashioned rugby ideology during the World Cup tournament became casualties in 1996. Du Plessis more or less left out of his own accord, while Louis Luyt bluntly dismissed mastermind Edward Griffiths per fax as CEO.

Griffiths, as a skilled media person, was quick off the mark and made much of his dismissal in the press and elsewhere, projecting himself as the crusading saviour of South African rugby, fighting tirelessly against a reactionary establishment only to be stopped unceremoniously by that well-known and insensitive juggernaut, Louis Luyt. It subsequently became clear that Griffiths had oversimplified matters.

Although Luyt could undoubtedly have handled the situation with greater tact – an attribute that never seemed to come to him easily – the fact that he failed to do so did not necessarily mean that he was entirely in the wrong. Griffiths, fired up with missionary zeal after the World Cup, had apparently acted rather rashly on several occasions by making commitments to build stadiums in black areas for more than R14 million without ascertaining whether the funds were actually available for such projects. He also had altercations with Frikkie Erasmus, the attorney acting on behalf of Chester Williams, as to Williams's reluctance to sign a contract with the SARFU. Wiliams was in part Griffiths's own media creation, and the latter resented the fact that Williams had chosen to plan his financial future outside the structures of SARFU. Allegedly he then threatened to plant a story in the press that Williams was not prepared to assist rugby development in black areas. Besides these criticisms, Luyt also listed nineteen other reasons why Griffiths was dismissed.[406]

However, the niceties of the Griffiths case did nothing to dispel the growing impression that unity of spirit and purpose in South Afri-

---

406 *Sunday Independent*, 18 Feb. 1996; *Rapport*, 18 Feb. 1996; *Sunday Star*, 17 Feb. 1996; *Sunday Times*, 18 Feb 1996; *Cape Times*, 25 July 1996; *SA Sports Illustrated*, 22 July 1996; Griffiths: *One Team*, pp. 200–204, 212–213.

can rugby was merely a transient phenomenon. It was given further credence by ongoing accusations and counter-accusations over the pace and direction of rugby development. Some former activists who felt left out in the cold after the merger of the earlier 1990s, threatened to break away from SARFU, claiming that with the advent of full professionalism, even less than before was done for rugby development in disadvantaged rural areas.[407] If any additional evidence of disharmony was required, it was provided by the embarrassing resignation of Springbok coach, André Markgraaff. In an unguarded moment he was caught on tape railing against the "f*****g k*ff*rs" involved in the administration of sport.[408] Markgraaff's crude outburst was in sharp contrast to the silky smooth discourse which had emanated from the rugby management during the World Cup tournament.

To crown it all, by mid-1997 relations between sports administrators and the government had deteriorated to such an extent that the government was preparing a bill with a view to curbing the autonomy of sporting bodies and the almost unfettered power of people like Louis Luyt.[409] A legal fracas followed, even involving Mandela's appearance in court to defend his position pertaining to the inquiry into rugby affairs. Legally it might have been justifiable; politically it was a predictable public relations disaster to have the venerable Mandela appearing in the witness box. One commentator neatly summarised it as follows: "Challenging Mandela in court is like accusing Mother Teresa of child abuse."[410] Rugby in South Africa in 1997 was clearly not rugby in 1995. Perhaps the hubris of the victory of 1995 was just too much, engendering overconfidence in the rugby fraternity and allowing old traits to reappear with a vengeance.

But then, in a wider sense the South Africa of 1997 was not the South Africa of 1995. Black resentment has grown in reaction to what is considered an imperfect and inadequate process of societal transformation and little signs of greater overall economic equality. Afrikaners have become increasingly disenchanted with an ANC

---

407 *Weekly Mail and Guardian*, 7–13 Mar., 23–29 Aug. 1996; *The Star*, 22 Aug., 1996; *Sunday Independent*, 4 May 1997; SABC 3 programme, "Rugby Unity", 6 May 1997; *SA Sports Illustrated*, 14 Apr. 1997.
408 *Beeld*, 18 Feb. 1997.
409 *Sunday Times*, 8 June 1997.
410 Retief: *Holy Grail*, p. 98.

government. The National Party had left the Government of National Unity, and there was widespread concern about retrenchments in the civil service and semi-state organisations, affirmative action and the diminishing status of the Afrikaans language in public life. One Afrikaner who was involved in the flag controversy in Bloemfontein made a clear connection between political and social developments, and the resurgent support for the old flag when he stated that the "new South Africa has now become an embarrassment and a threat to us, so how can we identify with the new flag?"[411] Indeed, the public mood had changed. Consequently, Patti Waldmeir, an astute American journalist, felt compelled after a fairly optimistic and positive analysis of the South African transition, to add the following postscript to her book in 1997:

> South Africa's euphoria has faded leaving South Africans with a massive post-liberation hangover, and a painful case of depressed spirits. They have awakened to a world where Nelson Mandela has begun to lose his aura of sainthood: a world where corruption and incompetence have merged to taint the new administration; where fear of crime and violence is a constant companion; and where the arrogance of power has begun to claim its victims. (They even lost at rugby.)[412]

Given these shifts in the public mood, it was perhaps not at all surprising that rugby, already affected by internal divisions, found it difficult to maintain its position in the nation-building stakes. Ultimately, with the benefit of historical hindsight, the 1995 occasion has to be seen for what it was: "a transient moment of national euphoria gift-wrapped in rainbow nation romanticism".[413]

Conclusion

The fact that rugby's image had become tarnished after the World Cup cannot be considered an unusual occurrence in the world of sport and society. In the literature dealing with the social impact of sporting events, it is generally accepted that "while sport possesses

---

411 *Volksblad*, 22 Aug. 1996 (translation); See also *Rapport* 11 Aug. 1996; *Daily News*, 12 June 1995; *Sowetan*, 9 Aug. 1996.
412 Waldmeir: *Anatomy of a Miracle*, p. 287.
413 C. Merrett: "From Non-racial Sport to the FIFA World Cup: A Tale of Politics, Big Business and Hope Betrayed" in C. Thurman (ed.), *Sport versus Art: A South African Contest* (Wits University Press, Johannesburg, 2001), p. 74.

a powerful symbolism that can be exploited on occasion to great effect, the malleability of sports symbolism often undermines its capacity to exert a lasting effect on national identity".[414] However, what made the South African World Cup experience distinctive was that it had to deal with a deeply divisive past, and that it only had a narrow cultural resource base – in the public mind rugby before the tournament was mainly associated with Afrikaners and apartheid – to work from and to mould into a more encompassing whole upon which a degree of unity, however transient, could be constructed.

Writing on the dynamics of rugby and nation-building, the editor of the *Weekly Mail and Guardian* perceptively commented, albeit with a touch of chauvinism, on the state of play in 1996:

> When South Africa characterises itself as "one nation" it is less a statement of fact than the expression of an aspiration. Only a fool would imagine that ours is a united country. It was, in fact, the recognition of the fractured nature of our society – and the violently destructive consequences if we did nothing about it – that led us to the constitutional settlement. Inherent in that settlement was a vision of national unity fabricated in the hope that the wish would prove to be the father of a future reality – that if we repeated the mantra often enough on "one people, one nation" we would in time create the society that would allow the survival of our children. At this early stage in that exercise in nation-building it is easy to ridicule the pretension, to cry out like the little boy that "the emperor has no clothes on". Some foreign observers do so, priding themselves on their perspicacity in seeing through our delusions. They are also fools for failing to understand the desperate game we play.[415]

The way in which the Springbok victory embodied the often unexpressed aspirations of many South Africans and its implications adds a necessary cautionary note to any analysis simply wishing to dismiss the World Cup euphoria as a case of a gullible public being misled by a persuasive media. To be sure, as indicated, it was in many respects an orchestrated media affair, and there were also very specific reasons for the enthusiasm displayed by the public. But this should not be construed as reflecting negatively on the desire

---

414 For example B. Houlihan: "Sport National Identity and Public Policy" *Nations and Nationalism*, 3, 1 (1997), p. 113.
415 *Weekly Mail and Guardian*, 16–22 Aug. 1996.

of many South Africans to purchase a re-designed cultural product, with all its possible latent flaws, in the hope that it would serve the future better than the past. They could hardly be blamed for failing to read the small print that was to become operative as soon as the political and social context began to shift.

Furthermore, the setbacks subsequent to the World Cup tournament should not necessarily be seen as a complete reversal and a return to the earlier rigid positions. Joel Stransky, regarded by some journalists as a liberal, had a firm opinion on this: "We seemed to have turned the clock back 20 years. Guys who have done so much to improve the image at the World Cup were removed from office. It was as if you'd built up a million-dollar corporation and then just left it to go bust. It was a huge step backwards."[416] On face value Stransky's view was difficult to fault. But in making the exceptionalism of the World Cup tournament – a result of very special circumstances – the norm, all else is per definition bound to fail.

Although there were undoubtedly problems in building on the momentum of the World Cup, it does not necessarily follow that rugby returned to its former Afrikaner and apartheid enclave. A number of external forces ran counter to the possibility of such a development. Afrikaner culture has been so fragmented in the 1990s after its uncoupling from official political power that even if rugby wanted to return to the past, it would have been difficult to find a home at all.[417] Because of the world champion status of the Springboks and particularly because of the game's historical associations with the old order, it must also be borne in mind that rugby was more subjected to public trials of political correctness than some other sports. Rugby could not hide behind the perceived multiracial past of a game like soccer in South Africa or the liberal façade that cricket had erected so effectively.[418]

---

416 *Weekly Mail and Guardian*, 18–22 Aug. 1997.
417 On Afrikaner culture see W.A. Munro: "Revisiting Tradition, Reconstructing Identity: Afrikaner Nationalism and Political Transition in South Africa", in *Politikon*, 22, 2 (1995), 27; *Sunday Independent*, 6 Apr. 1997.
418 For a subtle and perceptive analysis of the underlying ideology informing cricket development see K. Johns: "A Second Innings for Cricket: The Political Economy, Nation-building and Cricket Development Programmes in South Africa" (Unpublished MA thesis, University of the Witwatersrand, 1995).

In addition, with the general globalisation of sport, rugby could no longer claim to be an exclusive Afrikaner project; ownership had now to a greater extent than before shifted to large television corporations and sponsors. "From Boere-glasnost came rugbystroika", one journalist commented, "the focus of rugby moved from the scrum to the criss-cross beauty of the fourth, fifth and sixth wave of rucking ... much more in tune with the cathode-ray world of computers and TV."[419] As it happened, in the post-World Cup years it was the professionalisation of the game that became a marked feature of the rugby landscape.

---

419 H. Pienaar: "The Boere and the Egg-Shaped Ball", *Sidelines*, (Sept. 1996), p. 17.

6
Rugby, rands and religion: Ramifications of the professionalisation of the game, 1995-2013

For rugby, both the external and internal environments changed dramatically after 1995. Externally, it had to adjust to a predominantly ANC government and as far as the internal dynamics were concerned, it was the dawn of a fully professional era.

This chapter explores the often unexamined linkages and at times often contradictory positions between two sets of evolving conditions as embodied on the one hand by the ANC government's insistence on greater black representations at the elite levels of the game and on the other hand the demands of professional sport. Furthermore, the impact of professionalisation is explored in terms of what the process meant for "ordinary" rugby clubs away from the revenue-generating urban centres as well as how "player culture" changed from the amateur era. In addition, the role of religion in professional rugby and its wider correlates in Afrikaner society is probed.

Advent of professionalism

Historically, rugby union in South Africa had an ambiguous relationship with money. While money fed the financial health of provinces and clubs, the most important commodity, the player, was left out of the equation. Danie Craven took a strong stand against players being paid to play the game. He regarded money as the "cancer that will kill rugby," arguing that the "old" values of loyalty and enjoyment of the game would fall along the wayside with the introduction of professionalism.[420] His views saw him embroiled in an intense battle during the late fifties and in the sixties to oppose the paid rugby league code of the game in South Africa.[421]

Yet, while Craven's opposition to rugby as a profession was steadfast, South Africa's sporting isolation during the eighties which led, as we have seen, to the so-called "rebel tour" by the New Zealand All Blacks under the name of the Cavaliers in 1986, forced the hand of rugby authorities to countenance the remuneration of players to a greater extent than they would have liked to admit at the time.[422] Described by some as an "expensively persuaded tour,"[423] this development was, perhaps unwittingly, a decisive step towards greater commercialisation of the game in South Africa. Sporting isolation also aided the process in other ways. In the general absence of international tours during this time, apart from the Cavaliers, the country lacked a national rugby identity and the game revolved around the provincial Currie Cup competition. Winning the Currie Cup became all-important as it represented the pinnacle of what could be achieved nationally. The result was that financial incentives were used to lure star players across provincial borders. The level of care and compensation that the South African players received surprised Rob Andrew, the English fly half who visited South Africa in the early nineties.[424] This did not necessarily include direct salary payments, but rather payment in the form of houses, cars, jobs and reimbursements. Besides this, players from South Africa and Australia regularly embarked on an off-season exodus to Italy and France, and it was not, as one official wryly noted, "because they liked pasta or the language".[425]

While a groundswell of local opinion already existed in South Africa that players should be properly and openly compensated for

---

420 Partridge: *A Life in Rugby*, p. 107.
421 H. Snyders: "Preventing Huddersfield: The Rise and Decline of Rugby League in South Africa, c. 1957–1965" in S. Cornelissen and A. Grundlingh (eds), *Sport Past and Present in South Africa: (Trans)forming the nation* (Routledge, London, 2012), p. 13.
422 Partridge, p. 114.
423 G. Teichmann and E. Griffiths: *For the Record: Gary Teichman* (Johannesburg, 2000), p. 76. See also chapter 4.
424 R Andrew: *A Game and a Half – An Autobiography* (Hodder and Stoughton, London, 1994), p. 154.
425 *Natal on Saturday*, 16 July 1994.

their labours on the field, the final push towards full professionalisation came from abroad. After putting formal apartheid irrevocably behind it, South Africa became more integrally part of wider globalisation trends, including immersion in global media processes with their penchant for centralising control. In 1995 South African rugby was one of the countries in the sights of the Rupert Murdoch News Corporation (NewsCorp), the fifth largest media corporation in the world at the time, which sought to acquire sole television rights for screening a new southern hemisphere competition between provincial franchises in South Africa, Australia and New Zealand as well as tests between these countries. Considerable rivalry with other corporations ensued before NewsCorp was able to clinch a deal worth US$555 million over ten years. In South Africa the deal was brokered in the face of other contenders and amidst much cloak-and-dagger activities which drove some administrators and players apart.[426]

The intensity of boardroom dramas was ample proof that the tide of the commercialisation of the sport could not be turned back. Rugby's insertion into the global sporting economy has been described as an "insidious link to consumer capitalism", but it is equally apparent that without it, the game in all likelihood would have stagnated as a "separate cultural island" in the international domain.[427]

Henceforth in a professional era greater pressure was to be exerted on administrators as well as players. Although players gradually had to perform to higher levels, it is misleading to claim that they now had to choose between a "love of the game or money". Joel Stransky claimed that the one does not necessarily rule the other out: "You play the game for the love it anyway, just as Tom Cruise goes out on stage or in a movie and acts because he loves doing that ... And I think that if you run out onto a field and put your body on the line week in and week out ... you deserve to be paid."[428]

---

426 For details see P. FitzSimons: *The Rugby War* (Harper Sports, Sydney, 1996), *passim*; L. Luyt: *Walking proud: The Louis Luyt Autobiography* (Don Nelson, Cape Town, 2003), pp. 266–279; T.J.L. Chandler and J. Nauright (eds): *Making the Rugby World: Race, Gender and Commerce* (Frank Cass, London, 1999), p. 156.
427 P. Horton: "Rugby Union Football in Australian Society: An Unintended Consequence of Intended Actions" in *Sport and Society*, 12,7 (2009), p. 173.
428 Interview with Joel Stransky by Alana Bolligelo, 11 April 2005. (Transcript in private collection)

The television rights for the new competitions were sold to pay-for-view channels which meant that viewership of the games constituted mainly the more affluent who could afford pay television while the mass market was excluded. In comparison to Australia and New Zealand, South Africa's Supersport channel made the biggest investment in purchasing the rights from NewsCorp. It has also been calculated that by 2004 more than 60% of the income of SA Rugby, the commercial arm of the South African Rugby Football Union, came from broadcasting.[429] Politicians dutifully, but to no avail, demurred about the exclusion of a large number of viewers. It was an early indication that in contrast to the pre-professional era where politicians could readily assert their authority, the advent of professionalism in 1995 meant that powerful competing stakeholders had appeared on the scene.

Professionalism and the politics of transformation

In other rugby-playing countries formal national politics may have impinged tangentially on the game, but in South Africa as a country constantly in the throes of transition, political pressures weighed far more heavily. It is therefore not possible to gauge the impact of professionalism without taking into account the vagaries of South African politics. The intention is not to provide a blow-by-blow account of rugby politics in the country, but rather to sketch the interplay between commercialism and the African National Congress government's drive to transform the racial composition of the teams and prevailing white culture of the game.

It is nevertheless a good starting point to emphasise that a hallmark of the politics of South African rugby is its often bewildering gyrations, its byzantine nature and perpetual boardroom machinations. Mark Keohane, a noted sportswriter and former communications officer for the Springbok team, has described the internecine clashes as "ugly" and all that is "consistent within the administration is the infighting, jockeying for positions and political agendas."[430] Given the country's history of race division, it is not surprising that

---

429 M. Keohane: *Springbok Rugby Uncovered: The Inside Story of South Africa's Rugby Controversies* (Zebra Press, Cape Town, 2004), p. 155.
430 Keohane, p. 236.

much of the politics is race based, but opportunistic office bearers have also switched allegiances under the sway of political expediency.

A salient matter that preoccupies rugby politicians and the press alike is the number of non-white players in the top teams. It would be misguided to see this in its entirety as an issue manufactured by the ANC; it is to a great extent a situation that they have inherited. As one journalist pointed out: "The notion that race might actually be a consideration in South African team selection is not a new one – it is as old as Springbok teams. Once upon a time, the quota was 100% white – never 100% of the best rugby players in the country."[431]

While this may be an accurate appraisal of the historical situation, it has to be borne in mind that the ANC's vision for sport also falls short of the ideal of the "best rugby players irrespective of race." In line with its general affirmative action policies, representative bodies should aim to reflect the demographics of the country. In theory, if not always in practice, this means that at least 80% of such bodies must consist of people of colour. This is an enduring problem for the government. The Minister of Sport in 2005, Makhenkesi Stofile, is even on record stating in parliament that the need to win should be made subordinate to the need to transform the racial composition of teams, because if a predominantly white sport team wins, South Africa still loses.[432]

It was unlikely that rugby would meet the preferred outcomes of affirmative action policies within any given time frame. Soccer has a much greater black following than rugby, and although the number of black (the term "black" used here includes coloured) rugby players constitutes a sizeable portion in relation to white players, black players are not yet in such numerical preponderance that they could be drafted to fill 80% of the positions in the top teams. In 2001, of the 694 registered professional rugby players in South Africa, 130 or 18,7% were black. In total there were 300 000 senior players in South Africa of whom 120 000 (40%) were black.[433] These figures

---

431 *Saturday Star*, 30 October 2004.
432 *House of Assembly Debates*, 16 February 2005.
433 A. Desai and Z. Nabbi: "'Truck and Trailer': Rugby and Transformation in South Africa" in S. Buhlungu, J. Daniel, R. Southall, and J. Lutchman (eds), *State of the Nation: South Africa 2007* (Human Sciences Research Council, Pretoria, 2007), p. 410.

indicate that there was not a big enough pool to satisfy transformation needs of 80%. It is furthermore instructive to note that from 1994 to 2005, in terms of overall Springbok test caps awarded, 149 went to black players and 747 to white players – in terms of percentages it meant that 16,6% were allocated to blacks.[434] This figure is very close to the 18,7% black professional rugby players in the country – an indication that in terms of what is available, there is a close alignment. The durability of black players at the top level is also a germane issue. The journalist Vuyisa Qunta has drawn attention to the "uncomfortable reality" that some of the black players who have reached the top faded away rapidly afterwards. The reasons for this he claims are "ill-discipline" in the form of "drunken and delinquent behaviour" and a "lack of basic fitness."[435] There may be deep-seated explanations for such behaviour and one can also assume that such a lack of performance was not restricted to black players only. However, the effect of this was that it further reduced the number of black players in the higher echelons.

Nevertheless, there is a perpetual insistence by the government for more blacks, particularly ethnic Africans, to be included in the top teams, especially the Springboks. While South Africa's 2007 Rugby World Cup victory was hailed by politicians of all stripes, there was also a thinly disguised admonishment that the racial composition of the team on the day which only included two coloured players, left much to be desired.[436] Wrapped up in this view is also a need to assert African self-esteem and self-worth, denied to many black people under apartheid. Stofile, for example, regards "sport as an instrument to free our people from the inferiority complex instilled by apartheid. It must also free white compatriots from a superiority complex or "baasskap" ("boss-ism").[437] In line with this, Stofile regards sport as essential to "kill the myth that ... black people cannot play certain sporting codes because they are black."[438] Such thinking has become entrenched in certain black circles and shows little sign of abating.[439]

---

434 Desai and Nabbi: "Truck and Trailer", p. 411.
435 *Business Day*, 16 November 2007.
436 *Cape Times*, 22 October 2007; *Rapport*, 28 October 2007.
437 M. Stofile: "Sport as a Human Right", in C. Thomas (ed.), *Sport and Liberation in South Africa*, p. 9.
438 *Cape Times*, 7 November 2007.
439 Compare *Mail and Guardian*, 16–23 March 2013.

Whether such assertions of presumed biological racism and superiority on the part of whites should be taken as a convincing argument as the real reason for the insistence of quotas is a moot point. Influential scholars on the history of sport in South Africa during the transition period are sceptical. Arguing from a non-racial perspective, they have suggested that quotas perpetuate racial thinking and are not about redress

> but rather about reinforcing the political dominance of a national government by a black elite. This has meant that nationalist politicians looking for a quick-fix glory on the international sports field are opportunistic ideologues: they want largely black teams to represent the country and win trophies that reflect the ascendancy of black athletes representing a new South Africa. Yet the whole notion of race is an ideologically powerful social construct previously employed for nefarious socio-political engineering that had a disastrous effect on the South African nation. Its use now is no more justified than it was in the apartheid era.[440]

The government, however, has cornered the ideological market on what transformation is supposed to mean. In 2007 they were well positioned to pressurise rugby to conform. Stofile's brother, Mike, was prominent in the South African rugby hierarchy as deputy president of the union, and in Butana Komphela, chairperson of the parliamentary committee on sport, they had an outspoken and combative advocate of transformation in rugby. In mid-2007, the union was threatened to render transformation charters for sport legally enforceable.[441]

However, the question is, given the government's overwhelming power, why it waited for such a considerable period after 1994 before considering the adoption of more stringent measures. Part of the answer may be that it regarded "friendly" persuasion as sufficient to have the desirable outcome, but given the fact that in the state bureaucracy and many other spheres of society, government had not hesitated to impose strict affirmative action codes, there may be some additional dynamics at work as far as rugby is concerned.

---

440 C. Merrett, C. Tatz and D. Adair: "History and its Racial Legacies: Quotas in South African Rugby and Cricket", *Sport and Society*, 14, 6 (2011), p. 768.
441 *SA Sports Illustrated*, July 2007, "Rugby Crisis".

Much of the discourse on rugby centres on arguments of race, demographics, power and the game as historically representative of a domineering Afrikaner presence under apartheid which in part is now seen to be carried over to the new dispensation. What is significantly absent is a fuller recognition of the impact of professionalism and its wider implications. Although provincial coaches may well be tardy, as is often claimed, to include promising black players as opposed to established white ones in their starting line-ups,[442] the pressing commercial environment in which they operate should also be taken into account. Writing on global sport sponsorship, T. Amis and T.B. Cornwell have made the pertinent point: "We must get beyond the conceptualisation of sponsorship as simply a neutral exchange process but instead more critically assess some of the broader outcomes that accompany such agreements."[443] In the South African context this implies that the debate about rugby ownership should be realigned to give greater precedence to financial imperatives.

Sponsors, though they might ostensibly endorse the government's vision, are more concerned about profits than in the number of black players in sporting teams. What concerns them primarily is the need to present rugby as a TV spectacle that would attract viewers, irrespective of the number of black players. This means that it is risky to experiment at the higher echelons of the game with players who for a variety of reasons did not have the necessary exposure at that level. One of the clauses of South Africa's agreement with NewsCorp stipulates that all the countries must field their best teams. This stems from the apprehension that a substandard team might have a negative effect on the entertainment value of TV broadcasts and on spectator attendance at matches.[444] A rigid insistence on a fast-track selection policy, it has been claimed, might also have a knock-on effect in spurring an exodus of quality white players to go and play abroad. If these players are not replaced by black players who are on par, it may result in a drop in standards of play and a drop in TV viewers and sponsorships.[445] This argument can perhaps be regarded

---

442 Desai and Nabbi: "Truck and Trailer", p. 410.
443 T. Amis and T.B. Cornwell (eds): *Global Sport Sponsorship* (Berg Publishers, Oxford, 2005), pp. 11–12.
444 J. Volschenk: *Struggle Rugby – A Sport in Crisis* (Solidarity, Johannesburg, 2002), p. 45.
445 *SA Rugby News*, March 2005, "Politics in Rugby Here to Stay."

as self-serving to protect white interests, but it is one which carries considerable weight with sponsors. In the world of sport sponsorship, objectives are clearly set out and finely calibrated.[446]

Furthermore, while government officials may insist that it is a "right" to play sport,[447] the professional era has complicated matters. It has been argued that the right to equal access to sport by all members of society can in general terms only apply to amateur sport. Professional sport, in contrast, is an industry, based on economic foundations and accordingly it has a different frame of reference pertaining to the access of sportspeople. Given the competitive nature of sport and the revenues collected by a winning team, it is not the kind of workplace environment where open access and long learning curves can be accommodated easily.[448]

It is clear that an inherent tension exists between the government's transformation drive and the financial dictates of the professional game. According to André Markgraaff, former Springbok coach and administrator, the government is "scared" of the sponsors who are not prepared to be hemmed in by government directives.[449] Markgraaff has stated his opinion boldly, but he is probably not too far off the mark. The government's own pronouncements reflect an admixture of circumspection and understanding, even bordering on deference towards sponsors. Addressing sport sponsors, Minister Stofile stated: "We know that your imperatives are about obtaining the maximum exposure for your products and the best return on investment for your marketing or advertising 'buck'." He then implored: "But please remember, these things are only possible if there is social cohesion and national pride in a country! Will you please help build those in South Africa?"[450] His predecessor, Ngconde Balfour, was less diplomatic and once in a state of exasperation threatened to reign in sponsors.[451] Significantly, it was an empty threat.

---

446 C.H. van Heerden and P.J. du Plessis: "The Objectives set by South African Sponsors for Sport" in *Equi Novi*, 24 (1), 2003, pp. 20–36.
447 *SA Rugby News*, March 2005, "Politics in Rugby Here to Stay".
448 A.M. Louw: "Sport Transformation in South Africa: A Critical Analysis of the Applications of Affirmative Action in Professional Sport" (Unpublished paper, International Association of Sport Law, XI, Annual Congress, Johannesburg, 2005), p. 25.
449 *Die Vrye Afrikaan*, 20 January 2006, "Wat is verkeerd met SA rugby?"
450 Opening address by Minister M.S. Stofile, Sandton Convention Centre, 7 June 2005, http://www.info.gov.za/speeches. (Accessed 7 November 2007)
451 Volschenk: *Struggle Rugby*, p. 25.

The role of powerful businessmen behind the scenes should not be underestimated. A journalist has recounted, albeit somewhat conspiratorially, on the tenor of a meeting between some officials of the rugby hierarchy and a few businessmen on a wine farm outside Stellenbosch in July 2004 to discuss the direction of rugby:

> All the big names in rugby were there ... and on the face of it the whole exercise seemed perfectly legitimate. What confused me was the presence of one individual, though...When I asked why he was present, I was told that he represented a powerful group of businessmen, who were all extremely wealthy and influential. "People with money like that," I was told, "hold the real power in South African rugby. They pull the strings." Needless to say, whatever the man asked for at the meeting, he got. All his suggestions were approved without question.[452]

The mysterious person in question was the Stellenbosch-based billionaire, Johann Rupert of Rupert International who has some business interest in the game.[453] Rupert, according to former Springbok coach Jake White, was also instrumental in arranging a meeting of the executives of sponsors such as Absa, Vodacom, Sasol, Ford, and Canterbury in 2006 at his farm to gain support for the beleaguered White who had several clashes with the rugby hierarchy.[454] White maintained his position and duly soldiered on to become a victorious Rugby World Cup coach in 2007. Despite the occasional murmurings from Absa in 2010 about the number of black players at the top level, there has not been a concentrated attempt on the part of big business to effect change.[455]

The age of professionalism meant the repackaging of old provincial loyalties in the form of new franchises with American-style brand names such as the Eagles, the Cheetahs and the Bulldogs. The rebranding of existing provinces also held other possibilities. By encouraging and endorsing the creation of a new team to play in the expanded Super 14 competition in 2006, the government saw in this a possible solution to its problem of too few black players in the ex-

---

452 *SA Sports Illustrated*, July 2007, "Crisis in Rugby".
453 For Rupert's interest see FitzSimons: pp. 206, 297; *Finansies en Tegniek*, 31 May 2002, "Steelkant agter die Ponde aan".
454 *Rapport*, 11 November 2007, "Jake White se Bom-boek"; C. Ray, *In Black and White: The Jake White Story* (Zebra Press, Johannesburg 2007), pp. 251–252.
455 On Absa see *Rapport*, 3 October 2010; *Rapport*, 14 August 2011.

isting higher echelons. This gave rise to a team with the name of the Southern Spears, to be based in Port Elizabeth, comprising players from the Southern and Eastern Cape where rugby had a long-standing tradition and where the most black rugby players are located. Butana Komphela was enchanted with the idea and stated: "No political argument could be made as to why the south-eastern Cape should not be awarded an opportunity to participate in the Super 14."[456] It was also strongly rumoured that the establishment of the Spears was a pre-condition for government's support for South Africa's bid (failed as it turned out) to host the 2011 World Cup.[457]

Plans for the Spears went ahead; players were contracted, jerseys and kit were designed and the concept was publicly launched in American razzamatazz fashion, replete with cheerleaders, called "Spearleaders". In 2006 the Chief Executive Officer, Tony McKeever, made much of what he dubbed "the rugby demographics" of the Spears. Compared to the Spears which could boast with 71% of its players as black, other Super 14 outfits in total only had 29%.[458] SA Rugby invested R4,6 million into the concept in the hope that sponsors would soon come on board. Reality turned out to be different. The team's performance in training matches buried any hope that it would be competitive in the Super 14 competition, and to top it all, charges of financial mismanagement surfaced.[459] A slightly cynical journalist remarked: "They were never the new South African rugby dream. They were simply a reminder of the nightmarish old South African rugby ways."[460]

Nevertheless, the idea of a top "people's" team from the heartland of black rugby players resurfaced in 2010, this time under the name of the Southern Kings. Boosted by the availability of a new stadium, a legacy of the 2010 Soccer World Cup, and what appeared as more competent leadership in the union, a fresh assault was launched. At the helm of this renewed attempt to gain admission to Super Rugby was Cheeky Watson, a well-known anti-apartheid sport activist during the 1980s and father of the controversial Luke Watson who was

---

456 *Mail and Guardian*, 31 March 2006.
457 *SA Rugby*, July 2006, "Eastern Extinction".
458 *Mail and Guardian*, 21 April 2006; *Die Burger*, 26 November 2005.
459 *Cape Argus*, 18 April 2006; *Die Burger*, 21 April 2006; *SA Rugby*, July 2006, "Eastern Extinction".
460 *SA Rugby*, July 2006, "Eastern Extinction".

reported to have voiced derogatory remarks about the symbolic value of the Springbok rugby jersey. A revamped squad managed to drag themselves up the ladder of the second tier (so-called first league) of the Currie Cup, but could not win the league. Its demographics also failed to mirror the aspirations of those who wished to see a predominantly black team. With only 11 out of a squad of 36 players (31%) being "non-white" – significantly less than in 2006 – the impression was created that instead of being the team that could present a more "acceptable face" to the world, it became a refuge of some white players (Luke Watson was also drafted) who otherwise might have struggled to obtain a Super Rugby contract. [461]

However, the Kings did improve in the 2012 season by marginally winning the second tier of the Currie Cup. Towards the end of 2012 SARU decided to allow the team to play in the 2013 Super Rugby league at the expense of the Gauteng Lions franchise which was at the bottom of the league table after the 2012 series. It meant that the Kings gained entrance to the league by skipping the Currie Cup Premier championship and other hoops normally associated with promotion. Not surprisingly, it was a controversial decision and taken under some duress. Cheeky Watson had no qualms about admitting that his political credentials and connections, rather than the Kings' rugby prowess on the field, played a significant part in the lead-up to the Kings attaining Super Rugby league status. "All this government intervention ensured that the region reached the goal of Super Rugby," he stated before a parliamentary committee on sport in February 2013.[462]

However, the Kings' participation in the Super Rugby league, so desperately canvassed by Cheeky Watson and his union, was a qualified concession provisionally granted for one year only and stood to be reviewed. Watson, perhaps not surprisingly so, harboured some suspicions that this arrangement meant that they were being set up to fail. The Kings were only able to attract limited local sponsorship when the season was already well under way and, moreover, despite

---

461 Statistics for the Kings have been obtained from E. Griebe, statistician of SA Rugby, on 16 February 2012. On the Kings see also *Die Burger*, 1 February, 2012; *Die Burger*, 16 February 2012; *Mail and Guardian*, 17 to 23 February 2012.
462 Parliamentary Monitoring Group, South African Rugby Union report on the Kings, 14 February 2013, http:/www.pmg.org.za.report. (Accessed, 28 February 2013)

the vociferous claims of being the "people's team from the Eastern Cape", only three black players appeared in the starting line-up for their first Super Rugby match. Watson confessed embarrassment, but blamed SARU for this state of affairs.[463]

The failed Spears experiment and the caution in allowing the Kings to participate in the Super Rugby league illustrated the dynamics of the professional era and the difficulties of overcoming sponsorship and performance hurdles. Big business interests, allied to major city provincial unions, regard the game as a merit-based enterprise which will only thrive as a commercial concern if the strongest teams are allowed to develop, regularly filling the stadiums and attracting the viewers. The Spears, weak on and off the field, lacked too many of the essential prerequisites for prospective sponsors to be interested.[464] The fortunes of its successor, the Kings, appear to be only marginally better. Their sponsorship is relatively limited and the team will have a daunting task to perform consistently well. Furthermore, bearing in mind the significant under-representation of black players in its first squad, the attempts to literally change the complexion of the game at the top level remains a chimera.

It has become a truism that for more black players to proceed to a higher level, more resources must be channelled to the development of the game. After the 1995 Rugby World Cup victory, much was made of the need to galvanise the development programme, but although the task was taken seriously enough, new obligations ushered in by the professional era militated against the best of intentions. Resources had to be diverted to facilitate and maintain a sharp competitive edge at international level and the structures of the game had to be overhauled to slot in with the new professionalism. In the process the promises that were made after the 1995 victory that 40% of the World Cup profits would be used to encourage mass participation in the sport faded away.[465] In the ensuing years, after professionalism was well established, the development programme regained focus, but its practical implications and results were less than anticipated.[466] Likewise, attempts by former black players from the pre-1994 anti-apartheid sporting bodies to promote rugby in black schools

---

463 *Die Burger*, 26 February 2013.
464 *Business Day*, 15 April 2006.
465 Desai and Nabbi: "Truck and Trailer", p. 407.
466 Keohane: *Springbok Rugby Uncovered*, p. 50.

were met with decided rebuffs from the teachers. Exclusively black schools have produced very few top players; they tend to come from traditional rugby-playing schools which are mainly upper class and predominantly white.[467]

In 2012 the South African Rugby Union reported to parliament that the majority of Springboks came from only 1,81% of the total number of schools in the country. Of the black Springboks two came from Rondebosch Boys High School, two from Peterhouse and individuals from Pretoria Boys High School, St Johns, Prince Edward, Queens College and Springs Technical High School.[468] While the potential rugby talent in ordinary schools in the Eastern Cape should not be doubted, the overall lack of facilities outside the charmed circle of elite schools, coupled with often insufficient nutrition for growing adolescents from poor homes, render the possibility of immediate and dramatic change remote.[469] The key to future change lies with schools that can produce healthy, muscular young rugby players. In February 2013, Jurie Roux, Chief Executive Officer of the union, made what may appear as a self-evident point – but one that is often lost in the swirl of politics – that a "Springbok team representative of the demographics of South Africa will only arrive when the demographics of rugby-playing schools reflect the national demographics".[470]

There is another important dimension that is often overlooked in analyses of the transformation of South African rugby. It can be argued that the government's vision for the game to encompass an increasing number of black players, especially in the higher echelons, is undermined structurally by the conditions generated by professionalism. If the amateur era had persisted after 1995, there might have been resistance against attempts to wrest ownership of the game away from a predominantly white Afrikaner establishment, but white opposition to such endeavours might have been based on cultural and historical reasons and to a lesser extent on financial considerations

---

467 *Business Day*, 16 November 2007.
468 Parliamentary Monitoring Group, South African Rugby Union Transformation Plan Progress Report, 23 May 2012, http://www.pmg.org.za.report. (Accessed 24 May 2012)
469 L. McGregor: *Touch, Pause Engage: Exploring the Heart of South African Rugby* (Jonathan Ball, Johannesburg, 2011), p. 81.
470 *Cape Times*, 20 February 2013.

as the latter would not have been that prominent. However, with the switch to professionalism, business imperatives injected a powerful new dynamic; it took the game to the global stage, but acted as an impediment to radical local change in the racial composition of the top teams.

Monied interests not only have an impact on the higher levels of the game, but in certain instances rugby has also become a commercial product at schoolboy level. This is particularly the case with the Easter weekend tournament of elite schools in Johannesburg. Large corporations, including banks, act as sponsors for the tournament and in the process turn the game into a commodity with a view on future dividends. The teacher in charge of rugby at one of these schools explained the arrangement: "It is all about business. The school's accounts are now held with the bank sponsoring them. For every million they spend on school rugby, they probably get back R13 million in business. The kids will most likely open accounts with that bank as well." [471]

As rugby has become a commodity, the way in which the product is presented to the public becomes equally important. This gave rise to strategic partnerships between SA Rugby as the professional arm of the South African Rugby Football Union and the television channel, Supersport, as well as the print media, under the somewhat misleading name of the Independent Group. Supersport, which owns the broadcasting rights of the Tri-nations, the Super 15, the Currie Cup and Vodacom competitions, also has an agreement pertaining to access to the Springbok team that only SA Rugby could provide. This had the effect of moderating criticism of the national team and rugby administration. Mark Keohane has clearly outlined the outcome of this agreement:

> Supersport, the dominant media force in South African rugby, wields the greatest influence on the average punter. Yet they are caught between two worlds: calling the game and selling the game. Their commercial motivation is to sell advertising and satellite decoders. They cannot tell the viewer too often that South African rugby is a circus, as it will have a direct effect on their own product. They have to lure the viewer to the game; rugby is their biggest investment.[472]

---

471 *Sunday Times*, 27 September 2006.
472 Keohane: *Springbok Rugby Uncovered*, p. 155.

Players who refused to be corralled by the twin forces of commercialism and SA Rugby, and who spoke out of turn were quickly brought to heel.[473]

Professionalism in South African rugby followed, as indicated, a particular trajectory which was to some extent divorced from the government's agenda for sport. In a sense though, it is ironic that professionalism can be viewed as retarding the process of societal transformation as envisaged by the ANC. If the seismographic political shifts of the early 1990s had not occurred and the ANC had not been elevated to a major political player, South Africa's sporting ban might well have continued and in the absence of credible international competition, the introduction of full and open professionalism in its current form in the country would have been difficult if not impossible to achieve. Yet the ANC, as one of the important protagonists in reversing the political order, has been unable to stamp its imprint on a game which is more likely to be swayed by financial considerations than political directives emanating from the government. The locus of control was increasingly slipping away from South Africa and the imperatives of global capitalism in the television age became correspondingly pressing. [474]

However, it would not be fitting for the government to cry foul as the ANC government's market-oriented economic policies structurally created the very conditions which allowed commercialisation of the game to flourish, from the top national team to certain sectors of school rugby as well as to the nature of media control over the game.[475] Overall it has been a heady mix as some scholars have pointedly observed:

> Healthy, participative recreation governed by fair rules and codes of morality has become a multimillion-rand enterprise run by ruthless businessmen, employing cynical players and watched by overwrought spectators. An unholy alliance of commercialism and nationalism, enhanced by a touch of circus, has provided politicians with plausible excuses to interfere.[476]

---

473 "Transformation in Rugby", April 2004. http://www.litnet.co.za/seminar/ollie.asp. (Accessed 1 September 2004)
474 Black and Nauright, *Rugby and the South African Nation*, p. 138.
475 For an analysis of ANC economic policy see for example R. Southall: "Black Empowerment and Present Limits to a more Democratic Capitalism in South Africa" in S. Buhlungu, J. Daniel, R. Southall and J. Lutchman (eds), pp. 175–201.
476 Merrett, Tatz and Adair: "History and its Racial Legacies", p. 769.

The outlook is unlikely to change. Ashwin Desai and Goolam Vahed's analysis of what happened in professional cricket in South Africa may just as well apply to rugby: "Commercial imperatives in the professional age, where television revenue is dependent on fielding successful teams, mean that despite the platitudes about transformation, the focus will remain on the elitist project of breeding champions."[477]

Clubs, players and professionalism

If commercialisation were to become the new cement that bonded the superstructure of the grand mansion of rugby, the question arises whether the supply of cement was sufficient to provide the outbuildings with at least one layer. In particular, this applies to rugby in the South African platteland. Under the amateur code and under the influence of the legendary Danie Craven, rugby on the platteland was nurtured as a possible breeding ground for future Springboks.[478] In the post-1995 dispensation, amateur rugby has remained fairly healthy in urban and semi-urban areas, but in more outlying areas the game has lost much of its former allure as a cohesive local force.

Amongst the white inhabitants of South Africa's remote *dorpe* (towns) rugby in the pre-professional era used to be one of the elements which added significantly to a sense of community: "The pride and joy of wearing the jersey and socks of the *dorp*'s rugby team, the selection squabbles, the dusty fields, the women on the committees, the transport arrangements and the struggle to find referees, were all part of a strong foundation..."[479] The game on the platteland had its own rituals and time-honoured peculiarities:

> ... the sound of aluminium studs on a cement floor, an eigthman with a sweatband, Olympic boots with ... points, the red cord of a referee's whistle, the smell of cinnamon sugar, a Ford 20 M on the touchline sounding its hooter, a knee guard that has sagged down to a calf, someone shouting from the pavilion: "Take his life, take his life!"[480]

---

477 A. Desai and G. Vahed: "Beyond the Nation? Colour and Class in South African Cricket" in A. Desai (ed.), *The Race to Transform: Sport in Post-Apartheid South Africa* (HSRC Press, Cape Town, 2010), p. 187.
478 Dobson: *Danie Craven*, p. 185.
479 G. Jooste: *Rugby Stories from the Platteland* (30 Degrees South, Johannesburg, 2005), p. 8.
480 D. Snyman: "Deep Heat Heroes and Forgotten Fields" (Unpublished manuscript, 2007), p. 9.

Many of the rugby strands that were woven into the fabric of small towns started to unravel rapidly with the advent of professionalism. Admittedly, other factors such as ongoing urbanisation also played their part, but the process was accelerated by professionalism. In some areas like the Northern Cape and the Karoo, provincial units were disbanded as being commercially unviable and this removed the incentive for club players to aspire to higher honours. In other areas, promising club players were lured by professional provincial teams and promising schoolboys were contracted before they even started playing club rugby. The stars and crowd-pullers in the local teams became fewer. Also, it became more difficult to find coaches and administrators who were prepared to become involved in the game without payment.[481] Finally, at times the local *dorp* team had to vie for attention on Saturdays with top level games broadcasted on television and it was only the most die-hard club supporter who was prepared to exchange the comfort of his or her TV lounge to venture out and watch a struggling team in wintry conditions. Admittedly, SARU has recently shown that it is well aware of the problem in the rural areas and the introduction of a club rugby championship is an attempt to stem at least part of the haemorrhaging.

The introduction of money into the game also had an impact on the relationship between players and spectators. Obviously, the larger unions attract the crowds and experience saturation TV coverage, but much of this depends on winning. Blind provincial loyalty, regardless of performance, cannot automatically be assumed. A big union on a losing streak is likely to see attendance figures falling. A corollary of this is the measure in which spectators identify with individuals in the team. In the amateur era players were associated with provincial unions for a longer period of time than in the professional dispensation where the transfers of players take place rapidly and routinely. The effect of this is noticeable in the growing absence of nicknames assigned to players. In the pre-professional period nicknames were a common practice as players stayed long enough in a province to endear them to the crowds and "earn" a nickname.[482]

---

481 *Rugby 15 International*, November 1995, "RIP: The Death of Rugby in the Country Districts"; *Vrye Afrikaan*, 20 January 2006, "Wat is verkeerd met SA rugby?"; *Die Burger*, 1 March 2004; *SA Rugby*, November 1995, "The Death of the Rugby Club".
482 For an analysis of nicknames see chapter 3.

In the professional era, with a few exceptions, players have become birds of a passage; in the first place they now belong to the union and only in a distant second place to the spectators.

The more clinical and carefully managed environment of the current professional era represents in the minds of some supporters a contrast to the amateur days where players, according to them, were rough-hewn characters who combined a working life and sport without being cosseted. It is claimed that the hard men of rugby did not necessarily spent hours in the gymnasium – they were naturals – and never complained about being tired and jaded like the "current bunch of pampered millionaire prima donnas".[483]

Underlying this thinking, one can argue, is the yearning for a simpler bygone era where one's heroes had a more conventional existence, apart from their rugby exploits not that far removed from the lives of ordinary mortals. During the amateur dispensation, spectators were also more of an integral part of the subculture of the game and often administrators and officials were drawn from their ranks or those of former players. Identity, loyalty and parochialism were key elements which cemented this culture and although these have not altogether disappeared, they have become eroded in the face of professionally run outfits, at least one step if not more removed from earlier informal managerial styles predicated upon a mutually understood sense of affiliation and obligation to a club or province.[484] "Rugby has lost its innocence," the journalist Dana Snyman observed recently. "It is now being run by chartered accountants, marketing people and sponsors." [485] His view was echoed by a newspaper headline: "Loyalty in rugby is dead; long live money."[486]

Intriguingly, this particular sense of loss was experienced across South Africa's racial lines. It was also the case in so-called coloured areas where rugby clubs under the banner of the anti-apartheid South African Council of Sport thrived before 1995. In the professional

---

483 *Saturday Star*, 19 September 2009. See also *Die Burger*, 15 March 2012; *Die Burger*, 24 February 2012. For a similar trend in New Zealand see G. Ryan: "The End of an Aura: All Black Rugby and Rural Nostalgia in the Professional Era" in G. Ryan (ed.), *Tackling Rugby Myths: Rugby and New Zealand Society, 1854–2004* (Otago University Press, Dunedin, 2005).
484 Compare Horton: "Unintended Consequences" p. 972.
485 *Die Burger*, 30 June 2012. (Translation)
486 *Rapport*, 28 April 2013. (Translation)

era, talented players were inclined to gravitate to clubs with more money and superior playing fields and better overall facilities.[487] Many clubs, it has been claimed, "with long and rich histories of social struggle were compelled to collapse or combined to form hybrid mergers to ensure survival. This contributed to the devaluation, and sometimes demise of the history, ethos, traditions and contributions they had made to the fight for emancipation."[488] This development gave rise to nostalgic recollections of a vanished rugby culture and a hankering for a lost sense of community.[489]

Overall the impact of professionalism on provincial unions had favoured those in the bigger cities: Western Province in Cape Town, the Sharks in Durban, the Lions in Johannesburg, the Blue Bulls in Pretoria. These franchises had turnovers of more than R100 million per year in 2004, in comparison to the smaller unions like the Border Bulldogs in East London with R11,3 million and the Boland Cavaliers with R6,7 million per year.[490] In the absence of a player-capping mechanism, limiting the number of players a province may contract, richer provinces tend to monopolise the available players and in addition siphon off players, particularly promising black ones from smaller unions to fulfil their quota requirements.[491] The result is that the less well-endowed unions are continuously at a disadvantage. Players' salaries vary considerably: in 2007 the top 1% of provincial players (excluding Springbok income) earned R83 300 per month and those at the lower end of the scale a minimum salary of R5000 per month for the smaller unions and R8000 per month for the wealthier unions.[492]

Professionalisation of the game has not only brought an inter-

---

487 Y. Ebrahim: "Comments on the Future of South African Sport", in Thomas (ed.), p. 174.
488 F. van der Horst: "The South African Council on Sport: the Sports Wing of the Liberation Movement" (Unpublished paper, Sport and Liberation Conference, Universtiy of Fort Hare, East London, 15 October 2005), p. 15.
489 J. Nauright: "Rugby, Carnival, Masculinity and Identities in 'Coloured' Cape Town" in T.J.L. Chandler and J. Nauright (eds), *Making the Rugby World: Race, Gender and Commerce* (Frank Cass, London, 1999), p. 40.
490 *Saturday Star*, 21 February 2004.
491 *Cape Argus*, 19 September 2006; *Vrye Afrikaan*, 20 January 2006, "Wat is verkeerd met SA rugby?"
492 C. Schoeman: *Player Power: A History of the South African Rugby Players Association* (Sarpa, Rondebosch, 2009), pp. 97, 107.

nal transfer market, but South African players also plied their trade abroad in increasing numbers. In 2006 there were 300 South Africans in different leagues around the world in comparison with almost 700 in the country itself. Reasonable calibre provincial players were snapped up by overseas clubs for R1,1 million and good players for up to R1,53 million. The best Super Rugby league player only stood to earn a little over half of that in South Africa.[493] The favourable overseas exchange rate to the Rand made rugby abroad an attractive proposition. However, it has been argued that the South African race-quota system also forced white South African players to investigate possibilities elsewhere.[494] While this may perhaps have been the case in some instances, it is unlikely to be the norm given the fact that there are relatively few black players in the top teams.

Apart from the migration of players, the game itself had to adapt to professionalism. Partly as a result of rule changes, stoppage time

"A new ball game? Chasing pounds on the blind side".
(Finansies en Tegniek, *31 May 2002*)

---

493 *Sunday Times*, 2 April 2006; *Rapport*, 22 July 2007.
494 "Montpelliers swoops on 'quota' victim", http://www.planet-rugby.com. (Accessed 24 October 2007); see also *Finansies en Tegniek*, 31 May 2002, "Steelkant agter die Ponde aan".

in comparison with the amateur era has been significantly reduced, but as players became fitter, heavier, quicker and more muscular, defensive patterns – some borrowed from rugby league – became tighter, and as fewer line breaks occurred, the game ran the risk of becoming less spectacular. To satisfy supporters and the all important financial interests, the question of how to alter the game in order to provide sufficient entertainment value is one that continues to occupy the thinking of top administrators.[495]

In comparison to the amateur era, the interactions between rugby players have become qualitatively different. Professional players are more circumspect about socialising than was the case with players in the amateur era. In the pre-1995 dispensation, rugby incorporated a greater deal of male bonhomie: beers, *braais*, and late nights were not unusual. Under professionalism and the added commercial interest and public exposure, the focus has shifted to regeneration, rehydration, ice baths and massages.[496] Players hardly get to know their opponents off the field. "These days," a provincial player lamented, "the visiting teams just get into their buses and speed off into the night."[497] Keith Andrews, a former Springbok front rower who had experienced both eras elaborated on the way the social side of rugby has changed: "Ja, I reckon a problem these days is that the guys are not mates ... I'd play and enjoy a few good drinks afterwards; it was part of playing rugby ... But the youngsters now have all bought nice houses and have to pay the bonds. They must play to get the bucks. They don't go out for a few drinks and build some spirit – they go home and sleep."[498] At the top level, it has been remarked, professional rugby has become a most exacting occupation with its own set of demands:

> The intensity of the physical, psychological, temporal and travel demands and the single-mindedness required of playing a game as a job, as opposed to engaging in it, albeit obsessively, as a pastime, has thrust the modern elite players very clearly into the world of economic rationalism, accountancy and marketing.[499]

---

495 *Die Burger*, 7 April 2012. See also *Beeld*, 24 July 2009, *Die Burger*, 30 June 2012.
496 *Daily News*, 22 July 2002.
497 *Rugby World South Africa*, April 2006, "Werner Lessing: Leopard".
498 *SA Rugby*, April 1996, "Six Beers with Keith".
499 Horton: "Unintended Consequences", p. 973.

The texture and experience of international tours have changed likewise. Tours in the professional era are about achievement to the exclusion of much else, including imbibing the local culture. Week in and week out a "monstrous must-win clash" awaits the professional player, a brief period of rest and then a repeat and often improved performance is expected. This is in contradistinction to a somewhat more relaxed attitude during international tours in the amateur era where greater space existed for interaction with the local population, a fuller sense of camaraderie developed and more occasions arose for merrymaking and participation in what has been described as "pure unadulterated fun".[500]

In the first years of professionalism, some players in the lower ranks combined an occupation with playing professional rugby.[501] As the demands of the game intensified, it was no longer a feasible proposition. In order to play competitive rugby, one had to regard it as full-time occupation. Because of the structure of South African rugby with 14 provincial unions and various cup games, the country has a relatively high number of professional players. For many of these players it is an insecure, high-risk working environment. Apart from the ever-present threat of injuries which may damage or end a career, the demands of the game are such that the development of life and occupational skills, besides playing rugby, are at times underdeveloped. It has been noted that too many "schoolboys see rugby as a 'quick financial fix'" and that there are too many "punch-drunk journeymen seeking out sponsorship and endorsement under the guise of professional rugby. Our workforce does not need any more failed rugby players turned fax-machine salesmen at the age of thirty."[502]

For some players who have come to the end of their careers the thought of life without rugby can be a daunting one. One player who has played provincial rugby for a less glamorous province for 12 years and made 161 appearances, admitted to a journalist that "he knows that he'll have to find a job but he's not sure what," and that "at night he lies awake, wondering what will happen to him once it's

---

500 *SA Rugby*, April 1996, "Editorial".
501 *SA Rugby*, October 1997, "Rugby Men at Work".
502 http://www.keo.co.za/2006/02/15-sas-professionalism-promotes-mediocrity.html. (Accessed 21 July 2006)

all over."⁵⁰³ Closely aligned to this is the need to adjust socially in a world removed from the excitement of rugby. As a retired player explained: "For ten years you train twice a day and suddenly it is all gone." Others find it "difficult to sit at home suddenly without the 'rush' of rugby".⁵⁰⁴

The demands of the transition from the sealed-off and rarefied world of top professional rugby to an ordinary much more humdrum life took their toll on some. Joost van der Westhuizen, the noted Springbok scrumhalf who had a long career from 1992 to 2003 is a case in point. Professionalism substantially altered his fortunes in life. From living in a modest Pretoria flat and working part-time as a security guard he moved to a luxury mansion, and from driving a *bakkie* he upgraded to several fast cars.⁵⁰⁵ But as he later reflected, his perceptions of reality became skewed during this period as everything was catered for and he lost track of everyday mundane matters such as the cost of bread or a litre of milk. During his playing days he thought:

> … being a successful sportsman was all there was: everybody wanted your autograph, your picture, your attention. It was all about you. Even when I was playing, even when I got married, all I knew was how to get away with it. I stuffed up, and when I think back, I wish other players could learn from my mistakes. Because I fell on my ass. Hard.⁵⁰⁶

Van der Westhuizen's personal life spiralled out of control after rugby and he was the subject of intense media coverage, which still continues today after he was diagnosed with a life-threatening motor neuron disease in 2011.

Another case of post-rugby maladjustment was that of Japie Mulder, team mate of Van der Westhuizen in the victorious 1995 Rugby World Cup team. In December 2007 Mulder was found guilty in a court of law for statutory rape of his friend's 14-year-old daughter. He was fined R120 000 or three years' imprisonment. Mulder paid the fine with a smile, left the court room with a swagger and

---

503 *Rugby World South Africa*, April 2006, "Werner Lessing – Leopard".
504 *Rapport*, 13 November 2005. (Translation)
505 Griffiths: *Captains*, pp. 507–508.
506 J. van der Westhuizen: "In Retrospect" in A. Powers (ed.), *Rugby in Our Blood* (Tafelberg, Cape Town, 2011), p. 121. See also p. 123.

rode off in a luxury vehicle. Whilst the reasons for his appalling conduct may be psychologically deep-seated, his behaviour left the impression that as a former rugby hero he was untouchable. The father of the daughter commented: "He has an enormous ego. And this is the problem with all these so-called celebrities… They think they can get away with everything." [507]

Of course it can be argued that many did adapt sensibly to life away from the cauldron of professional rugby, but the contrast with amateur days remains stark. In 2006 Mark Irwin, the New Zealand prop forward of 1956, encapsulated the difference in terms which may equally well apply to South Africa:

> Today it is rugby 24/7 and I would not have liked that. There is no opportunity to play a summer sport… Worse than that, there is no opportunity to get out into the world and prepare one for the future. I couldn't have trained to be a doctor, as I did then, in today's rugby world. So there were much wider horizons in our day, you could live life not just play rugby.[508]

There is some concern in administrative circles in South Africa about rugby players being contracted at a very young age and then not being developed properly, nor acquiring any other skills. It is claimed that they may train a bit, but never appear in games and then just drink and while away their time in front of the television.[509] In 2007 statistics revealed that 78,18% of all professional rugby players in South Africa were totally dependent on rugby for their income and had no alternative financial sources and 57,75% had not at all considered what the future beyond rugby may hold for them.[510]

To be sure though, for some players exposure on the rugby field may open up networks and opportunities in the wider world[511]. However, it is not a given outcome for the great bulk of players. The fairly recent introduction of rugby academies by certain unions with the intention of not only shaping potentially top players, but also to add

---

507 *Rapport*, 2 December 2007. (Translation)
508 *The Sunday Independent*, 30 July 2006.
509 *Die Burger*, 9 December 2006.
510 C. Schoeman: *Player power*, p. 99, 107.
511 For testimonies of players who have successfully made the transition to the world of work, see R. van Reenen: *From Locker Room to Boardroom: Converting Rugby Talent into Business Success* (Zebra Press, Cape Town, 2012).

life skills and provide educational qualifications is an attempt to address the issue of life after rugby.[512]

Furthermore, some of the concerns and interests of the players were taken into consideration with the establishment of the South African Rugby Players' Association. Standard contracts were negotiated and every player had access to full medical cover and was able to contribute to a pension fund.[513] Given the increased physical demands of the game and the risks involved, a players' association was a necessary outcome of professionalisation and presented another departure from the amateur era where players had no official representation. The association is of course not a perfect safety net in the volatile sporting environment, nor is "player power" as yet sufficiently developed to move beyond threats of strikes to large-scale strikes.[514] To be sure, in 2010 the South Western Districts Eagles refused to play in a Vodacom match because of financial irregularities in the union, but this was a one-off affair and rapidly contained. In a way serious strike action would be the logical result of full professionalism and should this occur one of the last vestiges of the amateur ethos of loyalty to the game would be finally buried. But important as material welfare may be, the professional era also seemed to have engendered specific religious correlates.

On a wing and a prayer? Exploring the interface between professional rugby and religion in Afrikaner society

Although deemed dissimilar in terms of spheres of influence and appeal, tacit understandings in the public mind of the connections between rugby and religion are not uncommon and have a long history in South Africa. Going down the years one can point to a 1999 Rugby World Cup game when the flyhalf, Jannie de Beer, succeeded with a remarkable five drop goals in a match against England. Understandably, the media made much of this, including an insinuation

---

512 For example SWD rugby academy.co.za, http://www.news/saru. (Accessed on 18 February 2013)
513 Teichmann and Griffiths: *For the Record*, p. 53.
514 For an account of a threatened strike in the Springbok camp see R. van der Valk and A. Colquhoun: *Nick and I: An Adventure in Rugby* (Don Nelson, Cape Town, 2003), pp. 100–104.

that De Beer had said that God was on the side of the Springboks. It transpired though that his comment after the match was far less contentious and much more laconic: "God gave me the talent, and the forwards the ball."[515] Earlier in 1978 a perturbed Christian from Bloemfontein voiced his displeasure that the "game has become a God, worshipped by players and spectators alike".[516] Such concerns were perhaps not quite unwarranted as is evident from the curious comment in 1970 of Gert Yssel, a teacher and lay preacher in the former Western Transvaal. He displayed a baffling notion of logical cause and effect when he attributed a Springbok defeat in a test match to God's wrath at Afrikaner women wearing what Yssel considered indecent miniskirts.[517]

Less bizarre and cast in a more thoughtful anthropological mode is the observation in 2007 by Johann Symington, director of communications in the Dutch Reformed Church, that outwardly rugby may resemble religion in that it has

> ... its own pantheon of gods and sacred traditions. It is true that players do not kneel or pray in the passageways of the stadia, but the absolute dedication of the supporters to the game and the team, the symbolic changing of clothing and the faces painted to look like totem figures reveal something of the immanent religious status of the sport.[518]

Such analogies are not unique to South Africa and academic observers in America have in much the same vein likened sport stadia to "cathedrals where followers gather to worship their heroes and pray for their success".[519] From a Marxian perspective, the well-known adage of "religion as the opium of the people" has been adapted to ask: "Do massified sports displace religions as mythic forms, as the model of morality, as the answer to the fundamental human questions of value and purpose?"[520]

---

515 *Beeld*, 27 October 1999. (Translation)
516 *The Friend*, 17 June 1978.
517 *Sunday Times*, 14 June 1970.
518 *Die Burger*, 23 May 2007 (Translation). See also *Rapport*, 26 August 2012.
519 D. Wamm, L. Melznick, M.J. Russell, G.W. & D.G. Pease: *Sport Fans: The Psychology and Social Impact of Spectators* (Routledge, New York, 2001), p. 198.
520 T. Young: "The Sociology of Sport: Structural Marxist and Cultural Marxist approaches", *Sociological Perspectives*, 29, 1 (January 1986), p. 26.

While comparisons of this nature may alert us to certain similarities, they can just as easily be misleading. Historians Tara Magdalinski and Timothy Chandler have sounded a cautionary word, pointing out that the supposed affinity between sport and religion cannot be insinuated "simply because the ritualistic character of one resembles that of the other". They make the salutary point that ultimately "athletes are not gods, regardless of media treatment, and sport stadia for the most part are not places of worship".[521] Even if sporting heroes are elevated to a higher plane, Johann Symington has warned, they are best viewed as "gods of inconsequence". [522] Beyond the immediacy of their fame they have no enduring influence, nor, of course, does the discourse of sport even begin to ask questions of profound existential significance. Sport has no exegetic qualities and in itself cannot pretend to provide a representation of the world or attempt to provide salvation. If the liminal area of sport and religion is to be explored, the challenge is to take the argument further than superficial comparisons and to shift the focus to the embedded social logic which allows for changing forms of engagements and specific process-driven dimensions of interaction.

Before professional rugby, the religious affiliations of players were mainly a private matter. Although many belonged to the Dutch Reformed Church – the mainline Afrikaner *volkskerk* – it was not a matter to be highlighted in the media. (This was the case despite the fact that a number of Afrikaner clergy helped to spread the gospel of rugby in the first half of the twentieth century in the countryside and that nine minsters of religion played for South Africa.[523]) Springbok rugby players might have prayed before a match, but it all happened discreetly and whatever religious fervour there might have been was not meant for public consumption.[524] The first major sign that religious performativity was no longer restricted to the cloakroom but could assume a public face happened during the 1995 Rugby World Cup victory when the Springbok team huddled on the field for a

---

521 T. Magdalinski and T. Chandler (eds): *With God on Their Side: Sport in the Service of Religion* (Routledge, London, 2002), pp. 1–2, 197–198.
522 *Die Burger*, 23 May 2007.
523 See chapter 3: E. Grieb and S. Farmer: *The Springbok Handbook* (Jonathan Ball, Cape Town, 2011), p. 115.
524 Anon: *Agter die Doellyn*, (CUM Publications, Vereeniging, 2011), p. 35.

"Getting it off his chest." Jaco van der Westhuizen makes his belief clear. *(From Anon,* Agter die Doellyn, *Vereeniging, 2011.)*

thanksgiving prayer after their narrow win.[525] "We had won and, in a surge of emotion, I sunk to my knees," Francois Pienaar recalled. "The players gathered in a tight circle and, with bedlam breaking out around the stadium and around the country, we quietly gave thanks to God for our victory."[526] On the eve of the professional era, apart from the players' obvious gratitude in winning the game it in retrospect signalled that a new space has opened up for players to publicly embrace religion if they chose to do so.

With the advent of professionalism and its saturation of media and television coverage, some players gradually became more forthright in public testimonies of their faith. The actions of Jaco van der Westhuizen, a former Springbok and utility back for the Bulls, provided the most visible demonstration of this when he stripped off his rugby jersey after the Bulls victory in the 2007 Super Final and clambered up the rugby posts to proudly display a T-shirt with the words: "Jesus is still King!" He later explained: "I was obedient. It was something the Lord wanted for that day. The morning before the game, I felt how He told me that today is the day you are going to do

---

525 *Die Kerkbode*, 30 June 1995, "Springbok-oorwinning".
526 F. Pienaar (with E. Griffiths): *Rainbow Warrior* (Collins Willow, London, 1999), p. 182.

something for me." Van der Westhuizen also later expressed belief in a charismatic faith healer in Nigeria.[527]

Van der Westhuizen's brazen individual demonstration on the field might have been a one-off event, but it can nevertheless point towards a more widely held belief system amongst other players. Several Springboks with a penchant for charismatic movements attended evangelical campaigns such as the Mighty Men movement initiated by the farmer-turned-lay preacher, Angus Buchan.[528] Significantly, some of these rallies took place at rugby stadia such as Ellispark in Johannesburg and Loftus Versfeld in Pretoria, respectively the homes of the Lions and the Bulls rugby team. At Loftus Versfeld more than 70 000 enthusiasts filled the stadia, many of them rugby supporters who lined the stands in replica rugby jerseys. When Buchan's fiery sermon reached a crescendo, big men in their rugby outfits were seen to sob.[529]

While Buchan professed the need for a return to family values, his preachings were heavily laden with conservative patriarchal notions and the need for men to reassert themselves in the household and broader society.[530] Peter de Villiers, the Springbok rugby coach till the end of 2011, has claimed that he had regular contact with Buchan and openly aligned himself with Buchan's ideas. "When you [a man] enter the front door," he said, "you are the head. She [the wife] has to listen to you."[531]

The Mighty Men movement showed remarkable similarities to that of Promise Keepers in America in the early 1990s. The latter sought to "develop Christian men" and aimed at offering a sacralised version of "Iron John" culture. As was the case with Mighty Men, it attracted men in their thousands to rallies being held in sport stadia. Here it has been argued they could "affirm their phallic, warrior and fathering instincts" and create a new reverence for the "tribal man", infused by a "patriarchal religious identity that is further empow-

---

527 *Agter die Doellyn*, p. 143.
528 *Rapport*, 26 April 2009.
529 http://www.iol.co.za/news/south-africa/more-than-70 000-gather-at-Loftus-for-Jesus. (Accessed 7 February 2012)
530 S. Nadar: "Palatable Patriarchy and Violence Against Women in South Africa – Angus Buchan's Mighty Men's Conference as a Case Study of Masculinism", *Scriptura*, 102 (2009), pp. 551–661.
531 *Rapport*, 19 February 2012 (Translation). See also *Rapport*, 26 April 2009.

ered by notions of spiritual fulfilment."[532] Although it is not possible to prove direct contact between Buchan and the Promise Keepers movement, in a world of instant communication, charismatic ideas are known for their rapid dissemination.[533] Moreover, the parallel manifestations in terms of discourse and subliminal dynamics that illustrate the linkages between sport, religion and masculinity are revealing. Rugby players who attended the Mighty Men mass rallies did not make any announcements nor can it be claimed that they subscribed to all the tenets of the movement, but their mere presence did speak at least of general support for the revivalism preached by Buchan.

Several rugby luminaries were more forthright in testifying in print. A book with their testimonies was an instant success for a Christian publishing house and sold more than 20 000 copies in four months, a firm indication of the profitable blend of rugby and religion.[534] From the book it is clear that a spiritual system of belief helps to provide sustenance to some of those who are expected to perform at the highest level physically and mentally. The need to be "reborn" is evident in several of these public declarations, particularly in that of Pierre Spies, a strapping Springbok loose forward.[535] Gio Aplon, an elusive fullback and wing who is of smaller size than most other professional rugby players is another case in point. He moved from the mainline Anglican Church to His People, a charismatic congregation. In joining this church he claimed he was spiritually born again and he believed it boosted his confidence. Commenting on his position as a Springbok he explained: "Every day I realise how privileged I am to be here." Every day I wake up thinking of the blessing the Lord gave me. It takes hard work and discipline, but the main factor for me is God."[536] According to Peter de Villiers the Springboks also held regular Bible study groups on the Friday before test games and 17 out of the 22 players participated.[537]

---

[532] M. Taylor and R. Taylor: "Something for the Weekend, Sir? Leisure, Ecstacy and Identity in Football and Contemporary Religion", *Leisure Studies*, 16, 1 (1997), p. 41.
[533] S. Coleman: *The Globalisation of Charismatic Christianity: Spreading the Gospel of Prosperity* (Cambridge University Press, Cambridge, 2000), p. 55.
[534] *Beeld*, 17 November 2011. The book is *Agter die Doellyn*.
[535] *Agter die Doellyn*, p. 57.
[536] Quoted in Macgregor, p. 229
[537] *Die Kerkbode*, 22 January 2010, "In God se hande".

In the Bulls camp the question of religion is discussed guardedly. The franchise regards itself foremost as a professional sporting organisation and not as an Afrikaner Christian organisation, the Chief Executive Officer Barend van Graan was at pains to explain.[538] Heyneke Meyer, a former successful Bulls coach and appointed Springbok coach in 2012, regards it as a "sensitive" subject. "We are Christian-driven but there is no pressure to conform," he said about the atmosphere at the Bulls. "Before games, we pray, we pray that we play very well and to our full talents and let the Lord shine… If they [the players] pray, they go onto the field feeling good and feeling that they are protected."[539] Frans Ludeke, Meyer's successor expands on this by claiming that religion can help one to be a "better person" and that better people "make better Bulls". It entailed more than just doing the "church thing on Sunday" but rather gave them the opportunity to "let our lives speak".[540] In his autobiography Victor Matfield, the Bulls and Springbok icon, had fewer qualms than others and stated frankly: "Religion plays an important part in many of the Bok and Bulls players' lives. We always try to set a good example and live according to the right principles."[541] The Bulls also emphasise Bible study in their junior academy, albeit almost in a kind of formulaic fashion according to one observer.[542]

What emerges from this, despite all the qualifications about the role and extent of religion, is that a Christian belief system features in professional rugby and that it fulfils a certain purpose. It also carries a perceptible tinge of the charismatic which distinguishes it from the amateur era where it was unheard of for rugby players to publicly proclaim their affiliation. With professionalism in rugby, sports have become entertainment businesses and many of the elite performers have evolved into celebrities where the boundaries between private and public life have become extremely porous.[543] Therefore, it is not surprising that players themselves are more forthcoming in profess-

---

538 Macgregor, p. 175.
539 Quoted in Macgregor, p. 152.
540 Quoted in Macgregor, p. 145.
541 V. Matfield: *Victor: My Journey* (Zebra Press, Cape Town, 2011), p. 222.
542 Macgregor, p. 100.
543 P. Kelly and C. Hickey: "Player Welfare and Privacy in the Sports Entertainment Industry", *International Review for the Sociology of Sport*, 43, 4 (2008), p. 384.

ing their faith. At the same time such testimonies have dovetailed with the performativity found in charismatic churches.

These developments have not happened in a vacuum and can be aligned with shifts in church affiliations in Afrikaner ranks. In the post-apartheid era the Dutch Reformed Church experienced considerable haemorrhaging as its pre-eminent status as a *volkskerk* was being called into question along with the fragmentation of ethnic Afrikanerdom. Under National Party rule there was a close relationship between church, party and state and one which many ministers of religion sought to uphold. Although some sermons during this period do reflect attempts to move away from rigid apartheid, by and large the ministers were also implicated in the system to make a significant difference. One theologian has explained that preachers fell prey to a kind of national theodicy which rendered their attempts impotent. They "wanted to unlock the Gospel for the situation; instead the Gospel was locked up in the situation".[544] Having to face a markedly different situation in the new South Africa and one for which the church had not adequately prepared its congregations, this state of affairs brought about a stark disillusionment and along with growing secularisation it contributed to a discernible decline in numbers.[545]

Yet some of those who deserted the Dutch Reformed Church did not abandon religion per se but turned towards less dogmatic and more charismatic churches for spiritual guidance.[546] These churches are perceived to be more in touch with the needs of disenchanted people. They tap into modern media technology, and liturgical practices are cast in spectacular theatrical formats while theological messages emphasise emotionality, immediacy and the embodiment of the spirit as opposed to cerebral rationality, delayed gratification and salvation.[547] Another key component is the weight being given to

---

544 J. Cilliers: *God for Us: An Analysis and Assessment of Dutch Reformed Preaching During Apartheid* (Sunmedia, Stellenbosch, 2006), pp. 77–78.
545 J. Cilliers: "Preaching Between Assimilation and Separation: Perspectives on Church and State in South African Society". Unpublished paper, Homiletics Seminar for Danish pastors, Copenhagen, June 2008, 10; C. Lombaard: "Die Charismatiserende Afrikaanse Kerke – Enkele Gedagtes", 1 January 2005; http://www.teo.co.za. (Accessed 4 February 2012); *Beeld*, 18 November 2010; *Rapport*, 19 February 2012.
546 I. Nell and J. Cilliers: "Within the Enclave: Profiling South African Social and Religious Developments" (Unpublished paper, Stellenbosch University, 2011), *passim*. See also *Insig*, December 2003, p. 46, "'n Nuwe Lewe in 'n ou Kerk".
547 Cilliers: "Preaching Between Assimilation and Separation", p. 10.

prosperity – God wants you to be wealthy and even if you are battling financially, allowing God to enter into your life will make a difference. Material wellbeing bestowed on one by God is an important marker of one's earthly and spiritual success.[548] These interpretations have their roots in American Pentecostal movements centering on the Bible book 3 John: 2 with its message that "thou mayest prosper and be in health, even as thy soul prospereth".[549]

This trend is pronounced though not restricted to urban areas such as the western edges of Johannesburg where numerous young and relative wealthy Afrikaners have settled in modern Tuscan-style townhouses on Roodepoort Ridge, leaving behind the "old-fashioned" suburbs of Krugersdorp, Westonaria and Randfontein which their parents used to inhabit. A more functional style of living brought with it not only a migration to a different physical space, but the new lifestyle also contributed to the search for an appropriate spiritual home commensurate with the demands of contemporary urban existence. In the marketplace of denominations, the Dutch Reformed Church appeared decidedly dated and the Pentecostal churches with their flashy technological flair, lively music and emphasis on prosperity much more appealing.[550]

In Pretoria, however, in the generally well-to-do eastern suburbs innovative Dutch Reformed Church leadership realised that the challenges presented by the slick spectacles of the charismatic denominations can be warded off by incorporating similar elements into their services. This has contributed to the Moreletapark congregation becoming a megachurch complex serving 15 000 members and with 8000 members attending three different services on Sunday.[551] On the internet it is billed as "a real local business".[552] Coincidentally

---

548 Lombaard: "Charismatiserende Afrikaanse kerke", *passim*. See also J. Theron: "Money Matters in Pentecostal Circles", *Studia Historiae Ecclesiasticae*, 37 (2), September 2011, pp. 153–171.
549 S. Coleman: *The Globalisation of Charismatic Christianity: Spreading the Gospel of Prosperity*, 41.
550 I. Chipkin and A. Leatt: "Religion and Revival in Post-Apartheid South Africa", *Focus*, 62 (August 2011), p. 45.
551 *Rapport*, 5 February 2012. For a general discussion of the challenge posed for the Dutch Reformed Church see N. van Staden: "Gereformeerd en Charismaties? 'n Liturgiese Ondersoek na Kontemporêre Tendense in die Nederduits Gereformeerde Kerk, (M.Div thesis, Stellenbosch University, 2007), pp. 1–38.
552 www.http://za.wowcity.com/centurion/locbus2/2608424657405141430/n-g-kerk-moreleta-park. (Accessed 8 February 2012)

(or not) in its gigantism and flamboyance it merges with the rest of the urban landscape as it is located in close proximity to one of the biggest shopping malls in South Africa, namely Menlyn Park which prides itself on shoppertainment.[553] The religious yearning, "nearer my God to thee", and the consumerist adage, "nearer my mall to thee", almost seemed to have acquired a seamless quality.

In one of its marketing ploys of biblical literature, Moreletapark church uses the famous Victor Matfield, who on cue in an interview is seen enthusiastically to endorse a book on faith in action.[554] While we cannot read too much in this kind of association – there is nothing peculiar about rugby players having church affiliations – it does form a contrast with the pre-1994 era where profile-raising linkages between sport and an Afrikaner church with charismatic tendencies would have been beyond the pale. Equally so, it would have been unthinkable for a minister of religion, as has happened in Pretoria in 2008, to substitute his formal frock for a replica rugby jersey and appear on the pulpit.[555] In a wider understanding, the confluence of sport, religion and urban living is not unique to the South African situation. It has been a marked feature of changing trends in America where during periods of social flux in the twentieth century "evangelical forms combined with other strategies of creating urban lifestyles that were adapted to urbanism, in the process incorporating sport both as a morally positive activity and an edifying spectacle".[556]

In terms of the relationship between rugby and religion it seems that the emergence of a particular kind of religious expression in professional rugby has been facilitated and mirrored by parallel trends in Afrikaner religious life. The convergence relates not to outwardly superficial similarities between sport and religious practice but to a deeper and more profound social understandings of function and form which have permeated both sport and religion as indicators of broader change. To some degree rugby, though still supported by

---

553 J. van Eeden: "'All the Mall's a Stage': The Shopping Mall as Visual Culture" in J. van Eeden and A. du Preez (eds), *South African Visual Culture*, (Van Schaik Publishers, Pretoria, 2008), p. 46.
554 www.http://moreleta.org.video/video/search?q=Matfield
555 This incident is mentioned in J. Jansen, *Knowledge in the Blood*, p. 74.
556 S. Coleman: "Of Metaphors and Muscles: Protestant 'Play' in the Disciplining of the Self" in S. Coleman and T. Kohn (eds), *The Discipline of Leisure: Embodying Cultures of 'Recreation'* (Berghahn Books, New York, 2007), p. 42.

many Afrikaners, is no longer the sole preserve of Afrikanerdom the way it was before 1994, as the professional era saw a shift in ownership to financiers and sponsors with modified objectives in which the profit motive has become an important consideration. At the same time the Dutch Reformed Church as the once powerful Afrikaner theological colossus had to contend with charismatic challenges promoting a new spiritual way of living in a world where achievement and affluence are foregrounded. Despite their political distaste for the African National Congress, in terms of financial wellbeing, it has been suggested that entrepreneurial Afrikaners have benefited considerably from the opening up of the economy after 1994.[557] The journalist Chris Louw has made the astute observation that this contributed to a situation where "wealthier Afrikaners increasingly seek solace in materialism. Without idealism that is all that remains. Money, swanky houses and fancy cars have become surrogate replacements for everything else."[558] He could also have added that that this was bound to have an influence on religious outlook.

Beliefs and aspirations which were formerly confined to a circumscribed Afrikaner domain and infused with a particular set of related values have now acquired a more public, materialistic and consumerist dimension. Religious adherence has become more charismatic with its emphasis on performativity, success and prosperity; professional rugby has become inscribed as a form of commodified mass entertainment with a relentless emphasis on victory and substantial financial rewards for the players and various unions. Perhaps then, given the overlapping and underlying bases of both practices, it is not surprising that to some extent a process of cross pollination in respect of expression and social logic can be perceived. It might well be a non-linear connection and uneven in its manifestation. Nevertheless, whatever its exact shape, it was spawned by the erosion of the struts in post-apartheid Afrikaner society to allow for the emergence of new templates of understanding involving the reworking or displacement of earlier beliefs which were once predicated upon a watertight and discrete ordering of all segments of society.

---

557 S. Terreblanche: "Mag en Onverdiende Rykdom in SA", www.http://vrye-afrikaan.co.za/leesphp?id=815. (Accessed 20 February 2012)
558 Quoted in H. Giliomee: *Die Afrikaners van 1910–2010: Die Opkoms van 'n Moderne Gemeenskap*, (Die Erfenistigting, Pretoria, 2011), p. 31. (Translation)

Conclusion

It has been shown that the advent of professional rugby had an impact on several levels: the politics of transformation, the business management of the game, the game itself, player-spectator relations, and the players themselves of course – while it has also been argued that the role of religion assumed a new dimension. Yet it is necessary to enter a caveat here; in an overall assessment it cannot be claimed that professionalisation brought about a complete rupture. As a game, despite all the changes, it is not indistinguishable from what went on before and although it has broadened its support base, its long-standing and intimate relationship with Afrikaners is still clearly discernible. At its most visible is the crowd at Loftus Versfeld stadium in Pretoria which has been described as the supreme liminal space for Afrikaner expression.[559]

Equally telling is the fact that almost 63% of the 2011 World Cup squad could be considered Afrikaners or came from a white Afrikaans background – a significant figure if it is considered that Afrikaners comprise only about 6% of the total South African population. To be sure, it can be taken as an indication of the lack of transformation or it can bear testimony to a very durable relationship between a particular game and a relatively small community. The roots of this relationship, even though they were historically well watered and planted in the best soil, did weather some serious storms in a new sporting climate to keep on flowering in a most conspicuous way in the garden of international rugby.

---

559 *Beeld*, 5 April 2012. See also J. Jansen: *Knowledge in the Blood*, pp. 8, 74.

7
Diffusion and depiction: How Afrikaners came to play cricket in twentieth-century South Africa

A cursory survey pertaining to the literature on cricket in South Africa will reveal that for very good reasons, given the country's volatile history, much has been made of the impact of segregation and apartheid on the game.[560] While perfectly understandable, this perhaps had the effect of preventing a more even spread of attention covering other dimensions. A surprising omission in this respect, when one takes into account the crucial role of Afrikanerdom in shaping the contours of twentieth-century South African history, is that the changing Afrikaner interest in the game has not been subjected to a sustained analysis.[561]

This chapter attempts to address this shortcoming by focusing on the trajectory of Afrikaner involvement in cricket, trying to account for the initial reticence to embrace the game as enthusiastically as they did with rugby. Afrikaner interest though, grew apace during the 1960s and the conditions which facilitated such a turnabout are explored. Equally, the intricacies of the way in which prominent cricketers from an Afrikaans background have been portrayed and represented in terms of identity politics are outlined.

---

560 For a bibliographical overview see South African Sports Documentation and Information Centre, *South African Cricket, 1889–1989* (Human Sciences Research Council, 1989).
561 However, for a brief but suggestive account see A. Odendaal: "Turning History on its Head: Some Perspectives on Afrikaners and the Game of Cricket", in C. Day (ed.), *Cricket – Developing Winners* (United Cricket Board, Illovo, 2001), pp. 29–34.

Ambivalence

Cricket has long been regarded as the quintessential English game, synonymous with the British upper classes and dispersed throughout the British Empire as part of the cultural glue that helped to bond the "mother" country with the colonies, and wherever the game was played it was to be closely associated with the imperial heritage and ethos. For all the physical skills and mental challenges the game demanded, it also carried with it the overtones of ritualised behaviour, at times an exaggerated sense of what was considered gentlemanly conduct and was often thinly disguised elitist snobbery.[562] As cricket could be time-consuming, its upper-class status was at least in part linked to the availability of free time, a commodity in plentiful supply to those who were not compelled to work long hours. This, as well as the leisurely pace of the game, caused one sceptic to dub it as a form of "organised loafing".[563]

In the South African context, cricket was imported in the nineteenth century by British soldiers, imperial administrative functionaries, missionaries and immigrants who were all in their own way part of the imperial project and instrumental in the diffusion of the game.[564] The animosities and associations spawned by South Africa's turbulent past meant that the very disseminators of the game were also often deemed to be adversaries of or at least at loggerheads with the local Afrikaner population which had developed divergent political and cultural orientations. Throughout the nineteenth and well into the twentieth century, Afrikaner attitudes towards British cultural forms and their carriers were carefully weighted, ambiguous and at times openly dismissive. Cricket was bound to suffer the same fate.

---

562 The literature on symbolism of the game is extensive. See for example, R. Holt: *Sport and the British: A Modern History* (Clarendon Press, Oxford, 1990), pp. 204–209, and B. Stoddart and K.A.P. Sandiford (eds): *The Imperial Game: Cricket, Culture and Society* (Manchester University Press, Manchester, 1998), pp. 58–59 and *passim*, J. Mangan (ed.), *The Cultural Bond: Sport, Empire, Society* (Frank Cass, London, 1992), pp. 1–10.

563 J. Simons: "The 'Englishness' of English cricket", *Journal of Popular Culture* 29, 4 (Spring 1996), p. 45.

564 J. Nauright and C. Merrett: "South Africa" in Stoddart and Sandiford, *Imperial Game*, p. 55.

English speakers for their part did not view Afrikaners as natural recruits to the game. Writing shortly after the devastating Anglo-Boer War of 1899–1902, John Buchan forcefully vented such views. "It is worth considering the Boer at sport," he wrote, "for there he is at his worst. Without a tradition of a fair play, soured and harassed by want and disaster, his sport became a matter of commerce (shooting game for profit)." Afrikaners to him "were simply not a sporting race".[565] Such essentialist views are of course more revealing of the imperial mindset than Afrikaner prowess at sport.

Cricket had some appeal among Afrikaners in the nineteenth-century Cape Colony, but while the game penetrated the interior, especially in the wake of the discovery of diamonds and gold, it held no real attraction to the Boers of the republics. Those Afrikaners who played the game in the republics, such as Pieter de Villiers and G.P. Kotzé, were mainly migrants from the Cape. The game nevertheless featured in the politics of the day in what must count as one of the first attempts in South African history to use sport as a so-called nation-building tool. Cricketing officials planning a tour of a South African team to England in 1894 argued that besides English speakers, cricketers of "Dutch descent" should also be included in the team in order to ensure that it was a team representative of the country, albeit whites only. Furthermore, during the volatile politics in the Transvaal preceding the Anglo-Boer War with *Uitlanders* agitating for full citizenship and racking up the tension with the Boer government of President Paul Kruger, it was emphasised in the local English press that the tour should "assume its true importance as a national affair" and they called upon Kruger to contribute towards the funding of the tour. Such a gesture, it was claimed, "would show the *Uitlanders* that he sympathises with their old national game … a game which will do more to merge Boer and *Uitlander* into good Transvalers than any elaborate measure that can be devised by the Volksraad. Boers and *Uitlanders* must not only work together but play together…"[566] There is no evidence that Kruger responded to this.

---

565 Quoted in Holt: *Sport and the British*, p. 227.
566 J. Winch: *Sir William Milton: A Leading Figure in Public School Games, Colonial Politics and Imperial Expansion, 1877–1914* (Unpublished D.Phil thesis, Stellenbosch University, 2012), pp. 122–123.

During the Anglo-Boer War, the British employed their prisoner-of-war and concentration camps to transmit British culture to the Boers, and in Ceylon in 1901 a celebrated game between the Boer POWs and a Colombo Colts XI, the Ceylonese champions, was staged.[567] This event has bulked large in the writing of the history of South African cricket, mainly because it was regarded as unique to find such an event taking place during wartime, but especially because of its white-brown dimension. While intriguing, it certainly was not evidence of a widespread Boer fondness of cricket. Overall, the bitter animosities generated by the Anglo-Boer War fuelled general Afrikaner resentment and antipathy towards British cultural practices and leisure pursuits.

This differed somewhat from the situation before the war in the Cape Colony where to some extent British influences had over a considerable period seeped into the cultural outlook of Cape Afrikaners. At Stellenbosch there was a fairly strong cricket team and N.J.H. Theunissen, an Afrikaner theology student from Stellenbosch University represented South Africa as a fast bowler in the second test in Cape Town against the English during the first international series in South Africa in 1889. Although chosen for the first test in Port Elizabeth, his university professor showed complete disdain for such secular frivolities as cricket and refused to give him time off to play.[568] A few others followed Theunissen, most prominently J.J. Kotzé, nicknamed "Boerjong", a farmer from the Western Province who was described as a "Boer who preferred cricket to war".[569] As a fast bowler he "hated being punished by the batsman" but was considered a poor batsman and a clumsy fielder.[570] He played in England

---

567 H. Schulze: "Boer Prisoners of War in Ceylon" in B. Murray and G. Vahed (eds), *Empire and Cricket: The South African Experience, 1884–1914* (Unisa Press, Pretoria, 2009), pp. 179–196; and D. Allen, "Bats and Bayonets": Cricket and the Anglo-Boer War, 1899–1902", *Sport in History*, 25,1 (April 2005), pp. 34–35.
568 G.B. Stander: "Die Geskiedenis van Matie-Krieket" (Unpublished MA thesis, Stellenbosch University, 2000), p. 108.
569 Merret and Nauright: "South Africa" in Stoddart and Sandiford (eds), *Imperial Game*, p. 58. See also W.G. Schulze: "The Boer Prisoners of War in Ceylon and the 'Great and Grand Old Manly Game of Cricket'" in B. Murray and G. Vahed (eds), *Empire and Cricket: the South African Experience, 1884–1914* (Unisa Press, Pretoria, 2009), p. 185.
570 C. Martin-Jenkins: *The Complete Who's Who of Test Cricketers* (Orbis Publishing, London, 1980), p. 263.

while the war was still in progress and visited England again for the test series of 1907. During this tour, sections of the British press invoked the stereotypical imagery of rural village cricket where the farmer, blacksmith and squire all harmoniously indulged themselves in a game during a long summer day. Kotzé was seen to fit this scenario perfectly; given his rural background he was described as taking life "calmly and deliberately", despite his fearsome qualities as a bowler. Kotzé also became a symbol of wider import: his presence in the team was taken as evidence that Afrikaners had taken to the British cultural ways and was a tribute to successful anglicisation.[571] Sporting identity could clearly be manipulated to serve the discourse of the day.

Rugby, equally, though with a different slant, served a similar purpose. The first and highly successful Springbok rugby tour of the United Kingdom in 1906, under the captaincy of Paul Roos, was acclaimed as a major venture in nation-building, with Afrikaners being accepted on par with their British counterparts. Initially, cricket was assigned a noticeably modified role by the game's leaders, who represented this particular sport as "the Empire's game", played primarily by those of British stock on their own terms where someone like Boerjong Kotze could only appear in the guise of a successfully assimilated Englishman. The primary symbolic political object of tours between South Africa and England was to help integrate post-war South Africa into the British Empire, and to reassure the "mother country" that South Africa was now safely British. In 1909, on South African initiative, the Imperial Cricket Conference was founded, which firmly and officially tied the game even closer to the imperial project. "Subsequently," it has been argued, "the Boers did not feel either welcome or inclined to participate in the game, which remained very much an expression of Anglo-Saxon separateness and superiority in the eyes of Afrikaner farming people."[572]

For the greater part of the first half of the twentieth-century, cricket amongst Afrikaners remained in the doldrums.[573] For those who bought into cricket's symbolism it was a deplorable situation,

---

571 G. Levett: "Constructing Imperial Identity: The 1907 South African Cricket Tour of England" in Murray and Vahed (eds), *South African Experience*, p. 248.
572 Holt, *Sport and the British*, p. 227.
573 Nauright and Merrett: "South Africa" in Stoddart and Sandiford (eds), *Imperial game*, p. 59.

as a potential opportunity of establishing closer bonds between the two white groups through sport was being wasted. It occupied the mind of at least one dignitary, J.H. Hofmeyr, Administrator of the Transvaal who in the late twenties, besides being a protégé of Premier Jan Smuts, was also a cricket fanatic. Cricket appealed to Hofmeyr's higher sensibilities: "It satisfied his moral sense, for here was a human activity, governed by the rule of law, competitive in nature, yet devoid of rapacity or fear or cruelty, and pleasurable to enjoy." Infused with such enthusiasm, he was convinced of the power of cricket to draw men together. Accordingly, he was instrumental in arranging school cricketing tours which had one of its aims to promote the game at certain Afrikaans schools.[574] However, greater white unity and a common interest in cricket were a distant chimera only destined to manifest themselves as reality several decades later. As late as 1951 there was among certain members of the Afrikaner elite an almost complete ignorance of the game. Therefore, the first post-1948 Afrikaner National Party premier, D.F. Malan, a rotund, bespectacled, former minister of religion to whom sport was decidedly otherworldly, told Dudley Nourse, the astonished captain of the South African cricket team which consisted of English speakers only, on the eve of their departure on a tour to England in 1951 that he hoped they had enjoyed their stay in South Africa.[575]

While the anti-cricket ideology of many Afrikaners can be understood at one level, it does, however, raise the question of why cricket was rejected but at the same time Afrikaners readily took to rugby which was also a British upper-class import. This apparent paradox calls for some elucidation. While avoiding the trap of arguing that certain ethnic groups are genetically programmed for specific sports, it can be pointed out that rough-and-tumble contact sport like wrestling has since the days of the Boer republics been a popular pastime for young Afrikaners which could have acted as a bridging platform for making the transition to a physical game like rugby.[576] The nature of cricket can also have a bearing on the matter.

---

574 A. Paton: *Hofmeyr* (Oxford University Press, Oxford, 1964), pp. 140–141.
575 D. Woods: "African Sunrise" in *Wisden* (Wisden and Co., London, 1993). See also E. Robins: *This Man Malan* (SA Scientific Publishing, Cape Town, 1953), p. 56.
576 D. Allen: "Beating Them at their Own Game: Rugby, the Anglo-Boer War and Afrikaner Nationalism, 1899–1948" in *International Journal of the History of Sport*, 20, 3 (September 2003), p. 50.

Writing on immigrant sporting acculturation in Australia, academic authors have pointed out that "undoubtedly it is more difficult for immigrants to acquire complex cricket skills than it is to learn simpler football skills, especially if one is not brought up on the intricacies of cricket".[577] Similar comments have been made by another observer pertaining to Afrikaners: "Cricket is a game that takes a long time to learn, it is not like rugby or soccer which you can learn quite quickly ... You have to start playing very young. Afrikaner schools did not promote it..."[578] These arguments may have their own validity, but cannot claim to provide a comprehensive explanation.

Cricket must also be positioned in the wider socio-economic context. The first few decades of the twentieth century were difficult ones for some Afrikaners as successive droughts and increasing commercialised farming forced many off the land and into the cities.[579] It was a debilitating trek for many and the luxury of playing a relatively expensive game like cricket and belonging to an English club where most of the cricket was being played was not a realistic proposition for Afrikaners who had more pressing financial needs and less leisure time. Likewise, in the countryside the lack of facilities and competitive structures inhibited the spread of the game. In comparative perspective it was a situation which closely and illuminatingly resembled similar circumstances in New Zealand where the Maori section of the population experienced the same kind of barriers which prevented a large-scale entry into the game and which made it easier for them to turn to rugby as a sport of choice.[580]

In addition, one should consider the symbolic dynamics of a game like rugby. As we have seen earlier, it can be argued that the combative nature of the game appealed to the evolving self-image of nationalist Afrikaners during a period of accelerated growth of nationalism in the 1930s and 1940s. Having said that, the situation was not static. Although rugby's position as the premier Afrikaner sporting code was not to be seriously challenged, in the ensuing decades

---

577 P.A. Mosely, R. Cashman, J. O'Hara, H. Weatherburn (eds): *Sporting Immigrants: Sport and Ethnicity in Australia* (Walla Walla Press, Sydney, 1997), p. 182.
578 R. Archer and A. Bouillon: *The South African Game* (Zed Press, London, 1982), p. 87.
579 H. Giliomee: *The Afrikaners: Biography of a People*, pp. 315–354.
580 Compare G. Ryan: "Few and Far Between: Maori and Pacific Contributions to New Zealand Cricket", *Sport and History*, 10, 1 (January 2007), p. 88.

as the political and economic landscape changed, Afrikaner interest in sport was set to broaden.

Embracing the game

Concomitant with the historic National Party victory of 1948 was an incremental Afrikaner rapprochement with British cultural manifestations. While Afrikaner cultural interests still occupied pride of place, the acquisition of power meant that sufficient confidence prevailed for the opening up of spaces to explore areas of leisure pursuit which up till then had at best only elicited lukewarm responses. Furthermore, power also meant the assertion of Afrikanerhood in areas where it was previously absent.

Hence, in language reminiscent of current black demands that sporting teams should reflect the composition of the "nation", it was argued in 1956 in Afrikaner circles that "until the Afrikaner takes his place on our cricket fields, no Springbok team can be said to be truly representative of our country's cricketing ability". Yet this quest was not formulated in terms of present-day transformational charters, but a different route was suggested. Emerging Afrikaner interest had to be channelled into the "establishment of Afrikaans clubs, or rather clubs where the atmosphere is Afrikaans so that the newcomer will readily feel at home and will be able to concentrate all his endeavours on the mastery of the game itself".[581] The need for such an Afrikaans cricketing environment stemmed from antipathy towards what was regarded as snobbish English-speaking clubs where Afrikaners were often deemed to be marginalised.[582] What was ideally required, was an opportunity for "Piet van der Merwe and Jan Burger to learn the game" in an enabling context.[583] Given such stepping stones, the assumption was that eventually Afrikaner cricketers would be able to hold their own at national level.

Although some predominantly Afrikaner clubs were formed, in a broader context Afrikaner interest in the game benefited from socio-

---

581 *South African Cricket Review*, December 1956, "Need for Afrikaans Cricket Clubs".
582 Archer and Bouillon: *The South African Game*, p. 87.
583 *South African Cricket Review*, December 1956, "Need for Afrikaans Cricket Clubs".

economic and attendant cultural changes which permeated white society during the 1960s. With an average growth rate of 6% during most of the decade, South Africa experienced a period of unprecedented prosperity. In tandem with this there was a trend among Afrikaners to move away from unskilled or semi-skilled relatively poorly paid labour to skilled and better remunerated positions with stable career prospects in the burgeoning nationalist bureaucracy and other associated enterprises. In addition, the business world saw greater collaboration between English companies and rapidly emerging Afrikaner concerns along with a general realignment of the ownership of the urban economy. While Afrikaners still lagged behind English speakers in terms of total income (45% against 55%), overall they made significant strides in the 1960s. These developments brought in its trail a set of gradually unfolding cultural correlates, reflected for example in the greater acquisition of material goods such as expensive cars, architecturally designed houses and also as a new marker of status, overseas tours.[584]

Along with lifestyle changes facilitated by increased wealth, recreational patterns showed greater differentiation and there was a deliberate attempt to master new kinds of sport. Golf was one sporting code which increasingly attracted Afrikaner players and at the same time Afrikaner interest in cricket showed a steady upward curve. Between 1955 and 1970 the number of white cricketers, many of them from Afrikaans homes, more than doubled.[585] This was underpinned by the emergence of a slowly convergent and more homogenous Afrikaans- and English-speaking youth culture. "White children increasingly began to share the same middle-class interests," it has been observed, "pop music, shopping mall fashions and games, including cricket".[586] What is more, there was a significant growth in the number of educational institutions during this period. The number of white school teachers, many of them Afrikaners, grew by 34,6% between 1960 and 1972.[587] Such an expansion of the educa-

---

[584] A. Grundlingh: "'Are we Afrikaners Becoming too Rich'? Cornucopia and Change in Afrikanerdom in the 1960s", *Journal of Historical Sociology*, 21, 2/3 (June–September, 2008), pp. 144, 148–151.
[585] Archer and Bouillon: *The South African Game*, p. 87.
[586] Odendaal: "Turning History on its Head", p. 30.
[587] Grundlingh: "Cornucopia and Change", p. 145.

tional field held in turn the potential for exploring variegated ways of self-expression by overseeing the introduction of new sporting codes at school level.

In 1975 it was possible to report that during "the last ten years the Afrikaner's involvement in the game has increased rapidly. Afrikaans schools where the word cricket has sometimes hardly been heard started organising and playing the game."[588] Greater financial resources available to schools in the wake of the 1960s also aided the process as more schools were able to afford expensive equipment and the upkeep of the grounds.[589]

While the game in general gained more popular appeal, it was left mainly to more established and elitist schools with a traditionally strong sporting ethos to come into their own and catapult a number of Afrikaans players onto the provincial and national scene. The name of Grey College in Bloemfontein stands out in this regard. Grey, a leading school in the Free State, was established in 1855 and attracted the sons of elite Afrikaners in the province. It was a bilingual school with a fair amount of cross-cultural fertilisation between English and Afrikaans speakers.[590] For Afrikaners with a talent for ball games it was an ideal environment to be exposed to sports other than rugby and with dedicated teachers who in the 1960s had a particular interest in cricket, and somewhat later the introduction of professional coaches, the foundation was laid for the emergence of new talent. Corrie van Zyl, a national player explained the connection bluntly: "I started playing cricket because of Grey."[591]

Others elevated the connection to an even higher level. Two gifted Afrikaans players, Kepler Wessels and Hansie Cronjé, both destined to become South African captains, were illustrious sons of Grey College who bestowed on the school a special aura in the South African cricketing world and helped to foster a closer identification of Afrikaners with the game.[592] Almost equally so, Allan

---

588 *South African Cricketer* (February 1975), "Krieket, Lekker Krieket".
589 *The Independent*, 11 December 1993.
590 *Grey College Centenary Publication* (Juta, Cape Town, 1955), *passim*.
591 G. King: *The Hansie Cronjé Story: An Authorised Biography* (Global Creative, Cape Town, 2005), p. 56.
592 Interview with Ewie Cronjé, Bloemfontein, 5 September 2008. See also D. Gouws: *... and Nothing but the Truth?* (Zebra Press, Cape Town, 2000), pp. 65–75.

Donald, though not from Grey College, was despite his surname an Afrikaans speaker from lower middle-class Bloemfontein whose exploits as a lightning-fast bowler in the 1990s bequeathed him legendary status.[593] In the decades from the 1970s onwards, Afrikaans speakers started to be chosen more frequently for the provincial Free State Nuffield team, the tournament which showcased South African schoolboy cricket. Besides, some Grey College cricketers not only performed well during the tournament but also impressed with their leadership skills, so that increasingly they were appointed as captains of the South African Schools Nuffield team.[594] Grey's success spilled over into senior cricket and in 1995 the entire Free State senior provincial team was Afrikaans speaking.[595] The province also became a force to be reckoned with. In the late 1980s a previously lacklustre Free State team was transformed by an increasing number of Afrikaans-speaking Old Greys. "The fresh young men, brains washed clean, bodies hardened in the Grey ethos, started to turn Free State around," it was claimed.[596]

Grey College might have nurtured a special relationship between Afrikaners and cricket, but there were similar, if less concerted, developments in other places. Gradually players from several Afrikaans schools elsewhere in the country started making an impact in senior cricket; for example, Nantie Hayward from Eastern Province, Albie Morkel and André Nel from the East Rand, Francois Herbst from Gauteng, Arno Jacobs from North West Province, Tertius Bosch and Fanie de Villiers from Pretoria all came into prominence from the 1990s onwards.[597]

Indicators of an increased Afrikaner presence and skill in the higher echelons of the game had already become evident in the early 1970s as the social yeast of the 1960s started to foment in the form of a new generation of Afrikaners. In the Nuffield tournament of 1972, Afrikaans speakers constituted about 20% of the total number of players – a marked increase from earlier tournaments where the

---

593 A. Donald: *Allan Donald: The Biography: White Lightning* (Collins Willow, London, 2000), pp. 6–9.
594 *Millennium Magazine*, (April 1996), p. 95, "A Whole New Ball Game".
595 Interview with Ewie Cronjé, Bloemfontein, (5 September 2008).
596 King: *Cronjé*, p. 60.
597 Odendaal: "Turning History on its Head", p. 32.

percentage of Afrikaans speakers was negligible. "Afrikaner boys," it was reported at the time, "are currently busy making a name for themselves... The teams of Griquas and Northern Transvaal are now being captained by Afrikaners while the strength of a few other teams is in their Afrikaans players." [598] Afrikaners also started to make their presence felt in other areas of the game. In the early 1980s Willie Basson of the then Northern Transvaal was the first Afrikaans speaker to be named administrator of the year for his role in making the province – described as the "ugly stepchild of the Currie Cup scene: the unwanted Cinderella" – a more competitive force.[599]

In assessing the reasons for the growth of cricket among Afrikaners, it is useful to factor in that besides the socio-economic and cultural developments of the 1960s, political developments were propitious for greater integration of Afrikaans and white English speakers. South Africa's departure from the Commonwealth in 1961 and the establishment of a republic, although initially rued, had over time the effect of forging closer identification with Afrikaners as English speakers gradually came to terms with the irretrievable loss of former imperial ties. Coupled with this realisation and also fearful of the winds of change which had started to blow in Africa, English speakers started to shift their allegiance away from the struggling United Party towards the National Party.[600] Afrikaners for their part welcomed the move as it signalled newfound parity between the two groups and opened the possibility for greater white cohesion. With these developments, playing a British game no longer had the same kind of perceived negative association it might have had earlier. In 1970 a sport analyst was able to write: "The game is no longer an English game and therefore an alien institution: it is a South African game and now that the political connection with England has been severed, the Afrikaner can play cricket with a quiet conscience."[601]

What happened on the field was also of considerable importance. In 1966/67 South Africa won an epic series against Australia which sparked a general sense of sport euphoria and triumphalism. It was a

---

598 *Transvaler*, 5 January 1972. (Translated)
599 *SA Protea Cricket Annual*, 1984, p. 37.
600 Giliomee: *Afrikaners*, p. 542.
601 R. Bowen: *Cricket: A History of its Growth and Development throughout the World* (Eyre and Spottiswoode, London, 1970), p. 216.

most ebullient team, brimful with confidence and talent and singularly expressive in its cricketing ways.[602] Its prowess captured the imagination and its enthusiastic pursuit of victory was contagious. That's why an Afrikaner reporter reflected in 1975: "Like everybody else, we like winning. We are proud of the successes of our national teams. So when the Springboks emerged as a world power in cricket in the early years of the previous decade, the Afrikaners were very much behind them. That was where support of the game really started."[603] Cricket books were published in Afrikaans and in one such book, Peter van der Merwe, an Anglo-Afrikaner and the victorious captain against the Australians, prefaced the book by saying that "there has never before been such an interest in cricket among Afrikaans speakers as is the case currently. As a player it has been clear to me from the numerous telegrams I have received from [Afrikaans] enthusiasts over the whole of the country."[604] Other players concurred. Ali Bacher, Springbok captain in 1970 and destined to become a prominent cricket administrator recalled: "What was very significant to me was that, for the first time, thousands of Afrikaners came to watch cricket and show their support. This continued throughout the test series when Afrikaans folk became very committed cricket fans. I believe they were attracted by our success."[605] In a similar vein Peter Pollock, a fast-bowler and one of the heroes of the 1960s predicted that the Afrikaner's enthusiasm for cricket would come into good stead in the future, explaining that "such is his temperament and personality that in years to come he will become an even more faithful patron than his less volatile English counterpart".[606]

The Afrikaans press reported widely on the cricketing feats of the national team. At a symbolic level it appeared that Afrikaans speakers had laid equal claim to these victories as part of the achievements of a new white republican nation. Along with economic prosperity, political dominance and the initial illusion that apartheid provided the answer to South Africa's racial issues, Afrikaners now had the

---

602 *Millennium Magazine* (April 1996), "A Whole New Ball Game", p. 94.
603 *South African Cricketer* (February 1975), "Krieket, Lekker Krieket".
604 N. Steyn: *Sesse tot Oorwinning: Suid-Afrika se Krieketsege, 1966–1967* (Voortrekkerpers, Johannesburg, 1967), p. 9. (Translation)
605 R. Hartman: *Ali: The Life of Ali Bacher* (Viking, Cape Town, 2004), p. 91.
606 P. Pollock and G. Pollock: *Bouncers and Boundaries* (Sportman Enterprises, Johannesburg, 1968), p. 154.

confidence to regard themselves on par with English speakers and this realisation extended to the cricket field where successes in the sporting arena ensured wider traction, providing the opportunity of showcasing and appropriating sporting talents to demonstrate the fruits of National Party rule. In addition, with the looming prospect of international isolation as anti-apartheid forces gathered strength abroad, sporting prowess was a way to keep South Africa prominently before the eyes of those who might be considered potential allies.[607]

Looking at the diffusion and non-diffusion of cricket in a global context, American sociologists, Jason Kaufman and Orlando Patterson, have isolated a number of factors which under certain conditions can facilitate or retard the adoption of the game where there was a significant British presence. Probably because of a lack of detailed research on southern Africa, the area is dismissed in a rather cursory fashion. Nevertheless, they came to the conclusion that of the multiple factors that can play a role, "it is social stratification that lies most fundamentally at the heart of the matter. The extent to which an elite cultural practice like cricket was shared with or shielded from the general population was a direct result of the elites' own sense of their place atop the social hierarchy."[608] Equally pertinent here is the finding of Boria Majumdar and Sean Brown that cricket in twentieth-century India became part of the nationalist project and accomplishment in the game was a cultural response to outdo the British elite, while the absence of cricket in America can be ascribed to the fact that the USA has achieved independence a century and a half earlier than India, which meant that the need to use a specific sport as a cultural form of self-assertion did not arise.[609]

These observations can be tweaked as far as South Africa is concerned. Cricket was not really part of the Afrikaner nationalist armoury and Afrikaners generally only showed an interest in the game once the movement had peaked in the 1960s. Its earlier ab-

---

607 Bowen: *Cricket*, p. 216; and Archer and Bouillon: *The South African Game*, p. 88.
608 J. Kaufman and O. Patterson: "The Cross-National Cultural Diffusion: The Global Spread of Cricket", *American Sociological Review*, 70 (February 2005), p. 105.
609 B. Majumdar and S. Brown: "Why Baseball, Why Cricket? Differing Nationalisms, Differing Challenges", *The International Journal of Sport History*, 24, 2 (February 2007), pp. 139–156.

sence was at least in part a result of antagonism between English speakers and Afrikaners and also because, as we have seen, rugby has already been harnessed to serve nationalistic causes. However, as English-speaking businessmen started to mix with their newly arrived Afrikaner counterparts and politically English speakers edged closer to the Afrikaner government, tensions between whites in general gradually began to dissipate. These societal shifts contributed to a cultural space potentially opening up for cricket to broaden its base. Such a structural approach to the issue had the salutary effect that essentialisms about the acquisition of a sporting culture could at least be moderated if not totally discarded. The sport historian André Odendaal has argued the trajectory of an Afrikaner entry into the game succinctly: "Afrikaners did not get their place in the sun in cricket because they practised hard for fifty years and eventually acquired a cricket 'culture'. It was political power, increasing wealth and greater social opportunities and confidence that broadened the base and paved the way..."[610]

While Afrikaners started to assert themselves more forcefully in several spheres of society, it did not imply that all underlying English/Afrikaner animosities evaporated overnight or that Afrikaners rapidly started playing at the top level. In the 1960s Afrikaners were still invisible in the national team. It was the "Englishness" of the game that caused Prime Minster B.J. Vorster to quip when told what the English batting score between England and South Africa was: "Their English or our English?"[611] On the field Afrikaners were at times riled by ethnic jibes from English speakers; some might have been good-natured, others not. Albert Morkel who played in the Transvaal Premier League during the 1970s recounts how he was treated by some fellow team members: "I used to play for Old Johannians [the club associated with the elite South African private school St Johns College] with players like Don Mackay-Coghill. He always used to joke that I wasn't part of the team. They only brought me along so that I could make the *braai* after the game. We were called everything during those days, rock-spiders, hairy-backs, you name

---
610 Odendaal: "Turning History on its Head", p. 31.
611 B. Murray and C. Merrett: *Caught Behind: Race and Politics in Springbok Cricket* (Wits University Press and University of KwaZulu-Natal Press, Johannesburg and Durban, 2004), p. 79.

it."[612] Kepler Wessels, known for his intensity, was outspoken on the kind of treatment he received during his first few years of provincial cricket. He recalled that many players "thought I was a stupid Dutchman from the Free State. They can say what they like now but that's how it was. There is no doubt that Afrikaans-speaking guys were not regarded that highly."[613] These were not isolated incidents and several such observations found their way into the press.[614] In time though, as players mingled to a greater extent and along with broader shifts in South African society as the country lurched towards full democracy, petty white ethnic rivalries receded in the face of larger issues. Afrikaner representation at the highest level grew steadily and it was calculated that out of the 86 white players to represent South Africa between 1991 and 2012, a total of 30 (35%) were from an Afrikaans background.[615] However, before this point could be reached, a number of other developments occurred.

Emerging on the international scene: Kepler Wessels, Hansie Cronjé and the question of representational Afrikaner identity

One of the issues which emerged in the early 1970s was the international sporting boycott of South African cricket teams which was destined to span just over two decades. South African cricketers were for all intents and purposes stranded as far as official international cricket was concerned.[616] It has been argued, admittedly conjecturally, that one of the effects of this was that a fair number of promising Afrikaans cricketers were deprived of the opportunity to represent their country.[617]

---

612 L. Alfred: *Lifting the Covers: The Inside Story of South African Cricket* (Spearhead, Cape Town, 2001), p. 143.
613 E. Griffiths: *Kepler: The Biography* (Pelham Books, London, 1994), p. 30.
614 Several such stories are recounted in *Volksblad*, 1 November 2000.
615 *Die Burger*, 18 January 2012.
616 A great deal has been written on the sporting boycott. For an example of an evaluative account see D. Booth: "Hitting Apartheid for a Six? The Politics of the South African Sports Boycott", *Journal of Contemporary History*, 38, 3 (July, 2003), pp. 477–493.
617 Schulze: "Boer Prisoner of War in Ceylon" in Murray and Vahed, *South African Experience*, pp. 104, 303.

It was not a prospect which appealed to Kepler Wessels. As an Afrikaans-speaking youngster from Bloemfontein he had from an early age become used to extending himself in a game which Afrikaners had only recently taken an interest in and which had been dominated by English customs and traditions for a considerable period. He was intent on furthering his quest and that meant that he had to play international cricket in order to compete against the best. After a spell of playing county cricket in England, he moved to Australia, obtained citizenship and was chosen to represent his adopted country in 1982, scoring 162 runs on debut and carried on to represent Australia for 24 official tests and 59 one-day internationals. Later in the 1980s he also played in the rebel Australian tour to South Africa, designed to circumvent the boycott. In 1986 he returned to the country. To crown his extraordinary career, once the epochal political changes of the early 1990s allowed South Africa's readmission to the international fold, he was captain of the national team at the World Cup of 1992.[618]

Wessels was a driven professional and determined to rise above what he considered the politics that impacted on his game of choice. To some extent he was an early example of the trend in commercial cricket of players plying their trade irrespective of the ties to countries in which they were born. Hilary Beckles, the West Indian scholar, commented on this in 2004:

> Today's cricket hero ... now wishes to be identified as a professional craftsman with only a secondary responsibility to the wider socio-political agenda carried out by his predecessors ... He sees himself as an apolitical, transnational, global professional aiming to maximise financial earnings within an attractive market, and is principally motivated and guided by these considerations ...[619]

Yet for all of this Wessels was unable to escape being ethnically tagged in his career. Despite the fact that he played for Australia, he was originally from Afrikaner stock, and also the first Afrikaner to reach such exalted heights as to represent a country other than his own on the cricket field. The interconnectedness between sport, society and politics meant that his feats on the cricket field could not be separated from the wider politics that swirled around him.

---

618 For material on Wessels see Griffiths: *Kepler* and K. Wessels: *Cricket Madness*, (Aandblom Publishers, 1987).
619 Quoted in S. Scalmer: "Cricket, Imperialism and Class Domination", *Working USA: The Journal of Labour and Society*, 10 (December 2007), p. 440.

His biographer, Edward Griffiths wrote in glowing terms about his achievement to be selected for Australia, not refraining from injecting an ethnic element:

> Of all the South African cricketers who had been led into isolation by the politics of their government, only one man had shown the will and strength to get up and do something about it, emigrate to a country where he had no ties, wait through the period of qualification and earn a place in the Test team. They had said he was mad, but now he had done it. The loneliness, the sadness of leaving his home: it had all paid off. He had won. Just as he had been taught as a young Afrikaner in the Free State, he had not shrunk from the massive task, and he had seen it through.[620]

"From Bloemfontein to Brisbane": Kepler Wessels received his certificate of Australian citizenship in October 1980. *(K. Wessels,* Cricket Madness, *Port Elizabeth, 1987.*

---

620 Griffiths: *Kepler*, p. 72.

Not everybody was that impressed. Malcolm Fraser, the Australian prime minister who was all in favour of the boycott of South African sport, deliberately snubbed him at a ceremony in honour of new Australian team members.[621] Sections of the press also homed in on his background. He was regarded as "an implausible Australian" and moreover: "He is an Afrikaner, and a remote and sullen seeming one."[622] While he was fully accepted by his team members in his career of eight years in Australia, at times some cricket supporters sorely tested his patience. Despite the fact that he usually excelled on the field, he was called a "weak South African bastard" who should "bugger off" to where he came from.[623] Besides some friction which developed between him and the Australian Cricket Board on issues of payment, his return to South Africa was also prompted by what he considered insulting spectator behaviour. He claimed in 1986: "Whenever I went out to bat or play at any ground, I always got some abuse referring to my country of birth. I have been playing in Australia, doing my best and I don't think I should have to put up with that."[624] Once in South Africa and after the country's readmission to international cricket, Wessels's selection as captain of the World Cup squad of 1992 sparked its own round of ethnic comments. The wheel, so it seems, had come full circle as it was reported: "For much of his career as an Afrikaner in an Englishman's game, as a South African in an Australian dressing room – he has had to stand alone. Now, at the end of a long and difficult road, he will have the support of a nation."[625]

What is of interest here, is the variety of ways and the durability of the notion of "Afrikaner" as it unfolded in the context of the evolving Wessels saga. Despite the many twists and turns of Wessels's career, his exploits in the international cricketing arena and the fact that he understandably preferred to keep a low political profile, the notion of him as an Afrikaner remained constant. Although the reasons for and the intentions of the usage might have differed, it was the case as much in Australia as it was in South Africa. In his

---

[621] Griffiths: *Kepler*, pp. 77–78; R. Marsh: *The Inside Edge* (Landsdowne, Sydney, 1983), p. 127.
[622] Wessels: *Cricket Madness*, p.72.
[623] Wessels: *Cricket Madness*, p. 62.
[624] *The Star*, 8 August 1986.
[625] *Leadership SA* (March 1992), "Kepler".

home country it was considered "sad to see an Afrikaans-speaking guy 'forsaking' the land of his birth when so few Afrikaners had made it to the top in cricket".[626] In the volatile and politically charged atmosphere of South Africa in the 1980s the term of "Afrikaner" could not be uncoupled from wider politics. In this swirl of politics Wessels was destined to remain a branded individual. Referring to controversies surrounding Wessels, it was reported in the Afrikaans press that though one could change one's nationality, one could not alter one's identity.[627] While the Afrikaans reportage on Wessels was sympathetic, academic analysts, even though making the same point, adopted a more critical stance. Wessels's subversion of the sporting boycott was questioned and it was concluded that his "brief stint as an 'Australian' represented only a hiatus enforced by the international ban on competition with the apartheid state; Wessels's true national status was as valid in an apartheid South Africa as it was in a post-apartheid society".[628]

In what seems like a strange irony, Wessels's successor as South African captain was fellow Grey College old boy, Hansie Cronjé. His career was even more controversial, albeit for a different set of reasons. In a changed context, the notion of "Afrikaner" nevertheless once again emerged to serve a variety of discursive and explanatory functions.

When Cronjé was chosen to lead South Africa in 1994, he was the second youngest captain in the country's cricketing history to do so. He was destined to embark on an outstanding career with 68 tests and 188 one-day internationals, and was described as "one of the most astute captains in the game, and South Africa's most successful".[629] Cronjé was deemed a charismatic figure that captured the public's imagination. He held out the hopes of a sporting nation which had just recently emerged from the woes of apartheid and isolation to become a symbol of what South Africa was capable of in a new era. Reflecting on the immediate post-apartheid period, a sport journalist commented on the dynamics at work:

---

626 Wessels: *Cricket Madness*, p. 58.
627 *Beeld*, 4 November 1987.
628 G. Farred: "The Nation in White: Cricket in Post-Apartheid South Africa", *Social Text*, 50 (Spring 1997), p. 21.
629 R. Hartman: *Hansie and the Boys* (Zebra Press, Cape Town, 1996), p. 303.

This positive investment in the future by all of cricket's many constituencies, found a natural emotional locus in Cronjé and his successful test and one-day side. There might have been an element of fantasy and willed delusion in South African's adoration of their national captain ... but the national side remained a team worth following, a team which contained a part of us – however small.[630]

All of this was to be overshadowed though in the year 2000 with startling revelations that Cronjé was implicated in and had benefited financially from shady bookmaking deals relating to match-fixing. Subsequent to a commission of inquiry, the disgraced captain was banished from the cricketing world. Not long afterwards, in a pilot error of judgement, Cronjé met his ultimate and tragic fate when he died in 2002 in a plane crash close to George in the Southern Cape.

In the projection of the Cronjé saga and the discourse which enveloped Cronjé, his ethnic background became a significant strand. At one level, before his fall, he was seen as the embodiment of white nationhood, fully merging different sections in what used to be a game dominated by white South African Anglo-Saxons. Reflecting on what Cronjé had represented before his fall from grace, a journalist commented in April 2000: "Cronjé – unusual for a test cricketer, let alone a captain – is an Afrikaner. In his unflinching ... person, he thus symbolised the coming together of Afrikaans- and English-speaking whites after a century of conflict." His cricketing exploits had a wider reach and represented what was considered the best of two worlds: "a flinty Afrikaner who behaved like an honourable Englishman".[631]

Special pride of place though was reserved for Cronjé in Afrikaner ranks. He came into prominence precisely at a point when Afrikaners had all but ceded complete political power to the African National Congress; in the absence of political heroes the world of sport had opened up for a new set of icons to fill the void. "Nowadays," it was said in 2000, "South Africa only has sporting heroes as the ANC erased the rest of the *volk* through all kinds of chicanery. Therefore, it is a double blow for those who had regarded Hansie Cronjé as a hero – they now have no other heroic figures!"[632]

---

630 Alfred: *Lifting the Covers*, p. 159.
631 *New Statesman*, 17 April 2000.
632 *Die Afrikaner*, 20 April 2000. (Translation)

Cronjé's cricketing feats seemed to fit the bill perfectly for a re-fashioned Afrikaner symbol of derring-do in the brave new and increasingly globalised post-apartheid world. Coming from the heartland of the Free State, which was often viewed as somewhat of a backwater, he could do his people proud by adding new international dimensions to their world views. He was "Afrikanerdom's golden boy".[633] The qualities ascribed to him and his emblematic significance assumed larger-than-life proportions. He was

> a man of his times, a cosmopolitan, dashing figure, whose toughness was respected by men and whose appearance was admired by women... He was rich, sexy, uncompromising and successful... He reassured a tribe that the world had not come to an end. He expressed the yearning of his folk... Till his story was contaminated, Cronjé seemed like a colossus amidst a compromised people. He was a hero in uncertain times. A religion had abandoned its most basic tenets, a strong nation has been forced from its enclave, the pillars upon which life had rested for generations had been shattered. And there, upon the field, was a remote and unyielding figure, a conquering son reminding all and sundry that the possibilities of life endured. And then came the fall. And a terrible fall it was. Afrikaners, especially, were stunned.[634]

The tidings of Cronjé's wrongdoings were initially met with disbelief; the shock, one journalist claimed, was on par with the dismayed responses 34 years ago when it was solemnly announced that Dr Hendrik Verwoerd, for many whites the powerful and revered prime minister of the Afrikaner National Party government, had been murdered in parliament in 1966.[635]

Besides the way in which Cronje's demise was constructed in Afrikaner consciousness, his background from an Afrikaner home in the Free State also provided food for speculation as to his commitment to what was perceived as the ethos of the game. In English-speaking journalistic circles it was a topic of discussion whether Cronjé as an Afrikaner had fully imbibed what they regarded as cricket's sporting traditions. Accordingly it was a matter of conjecture that

> the further cricket had been disseminated from its English roots, the further certain aspects of the game had been devalued. The spiritual

---

633 Max du Preez quoted in Gouws: "... *and Nothing but the Truth?*", pp. 76–77.
634 *The Hindu*, 7 July 2004.
635 Max du Preez in Gouws: *Truth*, p. 76.

and ethical dimension of the game, the paraphernalia of "it's just not cricket" didn't seem to be that important in Afrikaans cricket-playing circles ... and young Afrikaans cricketers seem to treat it more or less mechanically, as a sport which had a host of techniques that need to be mastered in order to attain competence and progress through the ranks.[636]

While such speculation can be understood in a country where cultural differences between Afrikaners and English speakers have had a long history, it runs the risk of veering towards essentialist ethnic thinking. The way in which "Afrikanerness" was invoked is nevertheless revealing. Cronjé, like Wessels before him, could not be judged as a cricketer *per se*, but his ethnic origins had to be foregrounded. On an even grander scale, an academic linked Cronjé's transgressions to a version of Afrikaner history assumed to be dominated by persistent political deception and moral turpitude, implying that Cronjé's conduct was a corollary of that perceived history.[637] Cronjé's errant behaviour, so it seems, had to be yoked to the fact that he was considered to be an Afrikaner and that this provided an explanatory key.

In a slight variation of this theme, Cronjé's upbringing in the Free State was also brought to bear on another dimension of the saga. At issue here was his extensive dealings with Indian bookmakers and his condescending attitude towards the young Indian female investigator, Shamila Batoyi, who interrogated him during the commission of inquiry. Under apartheid the Free State had long prohibited Indians from settling in the province. Growing up in such an environment, it was argued that he had no previous experience of Indians and was therefore out of his depth and unsure how to deal with them.[638] This kind of discourse also acquired another layer. Some sections of the press homed in on perceived Indian characteristics and pitted the stereotype of the God-fearing Afrikaner against the devious Orientals.[639] The reflexive response as an academic author has explained, was that

---

636 As reported in Alfred: *Lifting the Covers*, p. 143.
637 J. Wardrop: "Fixing a Match or Two: Cricket, Public Confession and Moral Regeneration" in *The Australian Journal of Anthropology*, 13, 3, 2002, pp. 337–348.
638 Alfred: *Lifting the Covers*, p. 157.
639 For an analysis of this perception see J. Nauright: "White Man's Burden Revisited: Race, Sport and Reporting the Hansie Cronjé Cricket Crisis in South Africa and Beyond" in *Sport History Review*, 36 (2005), pp. 61–75.

the heroic, patriotic, Christian athletes like Cronjé could never be guilty of such chicanery and Indian investigators were incompetent and malicious. When it became impossible to evade the fact that Cronjé was in fact guilty, blame was subtly shifted away from the Indian investigators and athletes towards what might be described as the Indian milieu. "We all know that these things happen on the subcontinent" became a common refrain, implying that it was the innate immorality of the subcontinent that had ensnared, seduced, and corrupted an erstwhile icon of white moral purity.[640]

Such typecasting on both sides did not facilitate a deeper understanding of the reasons behind Cronjé's avarice and the general phenomenon of match-fixing, but it did show how easily recourse was taken to presumed ethnic qualities.

The discourses spawned by Cronjé's inglorious departure from cricket and their focus on the ethnic dimension as embodied by the portrayal of Cronjé as an exceptional Afrikaner, compel further attention. It is helpful to view this as a case of exaggerated identification. The mantle of overrepresentation was draped around Cronjé in the sense that he had become the heroic cricketer who in unsettled times symbolically shouldered the burden and aspirations of the whole of the Afrikaner community in search of someone like him.[641] This had the effect of obscuring more than it revealed. The Cronjé that was constructed by his community did not necessarily bear a close resemblance to the actual man and cricketer Cronjé. The man in question, though he did not turn his back on his home language, had largely refrained from casting himself as an Afrikaner and did not self-consciously generate the qualities attributed to him. In this respect, as one observer soberly noted, he carried "no discernible baggage".[642]

He was a professional cricketer who sought the highest financial returns, legitimate or otherwise, for his skills, sporting insight and knowledge. The adulation from the community that appropriated him and the fact that Afrikaners had established a profile in a

---

640 S. Sen: "Enduring Colonialism in Cricket: From Ranjitsinhji to the Cronjé Affair", *Contemporary South Asia*, 10, 2 (2001), pp. 238–239.
641 For the use of the term "overrepresentation" in sporting analyses see Ferred: "Nation in White", p. 21.
642 Hartman: *Ali: The life of Ali Bacher*, p. 317.

game in which they were largely absent earlier on was accepted as a lower-order given; he craved much more than gratifying ethnic ties and affirmation. His brother Frans, interviewed ten years after Cronje's death, added a further dimension emphasising the hidden reality of an international cricketer's almost hermetically sealed-off world: "He [Hansie] always had an adventurous part of him that was inquisitive. Playing cricket year in and year out, living in hotels and airports I think becomes a bit tedious and boring after a while. Maybe a bit of boredom set in and maybe this [transgression] was something a bit interesting."[643] It is an explanation that may perhaps be prosaic, but one that is more plausible than making Cronjé the victim of a particular version of Afrikaner history. It is also an explanation that dovetails neatly with the analysis of a sport psychologist, Greg Wilmot, who argued that Cronjé's statement at his hearing, namely "that the devil made me do it" is less of a religious confession and more of an indication of daring behaviour and the risks that some elite sportsmen are prepared to take. Cronjé has achieved much on the cricket field and out of boredom was looking for a new challenge, a new "high" or sporting thrill through a different kind of manipulation of the game.[644]

"A last lusty swing": Hansie Cronjé's final game at Newlands, Cape Town before the betting issue became public. *(From D. Gouws, ... and Nothing but the Truth? Cape Town, 2000)*

643 *The Independent*, 12 June 2012.
644 *Daily Maverick*, 16 May 2013.

International sporting stars often cannot control the attributes ascribed to them. Hence they can be placed in positions where their sporting stature assumes wider political and cultural dimensions. It has been said that Sachin Tendulkar, the prolific Indian batsman, is to Indian cricket what Gandhi was to the history of the Indian freedom struggle and that his image and influence have been used to promote Hindu religious identity and the exclusionary politics of Hindutva. The celebrity status of sport stars "allows individuals to transcend their occupational locales, conferring upon them an ongoing popularity which often manifests itself within a range of alternative social settings".[645] In this respect prelapsarian Cronjé, like Tendulkar, were cast in comparable roles, albeit with different emphases in divergent contexts. The similarities, however, disappeared with Cronjé's fall.

Conclusion

The trajectory of diffusion of cricket among Afrikaners correlated closely with their ascendancy to power in 1948 and subsequent economic advancement especially during the 1960s. Although these considerations were of paramount underlying importance, other considerations such as the success of the national team in the mid-1960s also contributed to greater press coverage and wider interest. However, this did not imply that Afrikaners made cricket their own in the same visceral way in which they embraced rugby. Cricket though enthusiastically supported, lacked the feverish intensity of the appeal of rugby. The general imagery of the Afrikaner's relationship with cricket is more disjointed; an overall pattern of involvement can be readily discerned, but the levels of symbolic symbiosis and emblematic investment of meaning are more muted.

As discussed, two outstanding cricketers to emerge from an Afrikaans background were Kepler Wessels and Hansie Cronjé. For different reasons their controversial careers gave rise to a set of discourses in which ethnic affiliation loomed large and in which identities were assigned which did not necessarily accord with their aspirations as professional cricketers. The historian Bill Nasson has

---

[645] A. Nalapat and A. Parker: "Sport, Celebrity and Popular Culture: Sachin Tendulkar, Cricket and Indian Nationalisms" in *International Review for the Sociology of Sport*, 40 (2005), pp. 440, 442.

recently encouraged members of the guild to "consider sport's historical meaning through a wider range of registers, taking the measure of its eternal virtues of triumph, honour and heroism as well as its ignominy and disgrace. And which also gets to grips with what it is to be a big hit, not merely on the field, but off it, too".[646] One way of doing this will be to take note of the way in which sporting identities, as alluded to in this chapter, have been refracted and constructed through particular discourses.

---

646 B. Nasson: "'Not Quite Fair Play, Old Chap': The Complexion of Cricket and Sport in South Africa," *Kronos*, 35 (2009), p. 256.

Afterword

This book had as its main *leitmotif* the interconnections between sport and leisure on the one hand and Afrikaner political and cultural projects on the other. There were different ways in which these linkages manifested themselves over time and the processes also had divergent outcomes.

During the 1930s the aim was to rescue the Afrikaner poor from the "evils" of dog racing. The agitation against dog racing had a clear middle-class character and was driven by *dominees* of the Dutch Reformed Church in particular. Those on whose behalf the battle was fought were indifferent at best if not antagonistic towards these efforts of upliftment. On an overarching meta-level one can discern a connection between attempts to terminate dog racing and the establishment of Hartenbos. Although at the time not necessarily planned that way, it can in retrospect be seen as a case of cultural displacement: the reprehensible indulgence in dog racing in the foul city of Johannesburg was to be substituted by the wholesome sea breezes of Hartenbos, supplemented by a range of activities designed to promote nationalistic constructions of Afrikaner popular culture. Hartenbos turned out to be a successful long-term enterprise and although the Afrikaner ambiance of the town in recent years might have been less conspicuous, its Afrikaner roots are not far below the surface.

While the Afrikaner middle class had overseen the demise of dog racing and the establishment of Hartenbos, rugby as a middle- and upper-class English game was deemed more compatible with Afrikaner aspirations than dog racing which carried an underclass stigma. But although the game had a sufficient class pedigree, its cultural ethos had to be refurbished and re-invested with presumed Afrikaner values prevalent from the 1930s onwards. The University of Stellenbosch was the ideal environment and launching pad for such a project.

Cricket took longer than rugby and had to wait for a particularly propitious set of conducive socio-economic and political conditions in the 1960s before Afrikaners could assert themselves in the most quintessential of English games. However, the notion of Afrikaner in this respect should not be viewed as a timeless construct, or else it can have a distorting effect of trying to refract the sporting lives of cricketers such as Kepler Wessels and Hansie Cronjé through the prism of Afrikanerhood, excluding other possible explanatory devices.

Returning to rugby, from the 1990s onwards – after the corrosive effects of the international sporting boycott of apartheid in South Africa – seismographic political changes in the country as well as the professionalisation of rugby helped to shape the dynamics of the game to a considerable degree. It was not, however, a completely new ball game. As real as these changes were, their impact should not be exaggerated. Afrikaner interest in the game turned out to be more than durable and given the kind of media attention continuously bestowed on rugby, often disproportionate to other more pressing political and social matters, one can be forgiven for thinking that some Afrikaners tried to make good the loss of power with an all-consuming enthusiasm in the game as a symbolic surrogate of significance. In this respect the euphoria of the 1995 Rugby World Cup victory can be seen as an embryonic indicator of the game's enduring emblematic cultural and political potency. Despite various pressures, rugby's sustainability and the continued discernible Afrikaner presence on and off the field bears testimony to a cultural manifestation which had not only succeeded in assuming an important place in Afrikaner popular culture, but has also become a major force on the stage of world rugby.

Underlying the connections between sport and leisure as explicated here are three fundamentals: ethnicity and its different inflections (including a specific sense of masculinity) at different historical junctures, the imperatives of material conditions, and middle-class aspirational initiatives. These can be inferred from the cultural politics of dog racing, the dominant concerns apparent in the development of Hartenbos, the diffusion of rugby and cricket and ultimately in the professionalisation of rugby. In refracting these through the paradigm of social history, it is clear that at different stages, depending on the overall configuration of interests, these factors asserted their influence in varying degrees, be it sometimes in unison or otherwise operating relatively independent. Al in all, they contributed substantially to shaping the Afrikaner world of sport and leisure.

Acknowledgements

I have been fortunate to live in a world where I could relatively successfully cloak my interest in sporting and leisure matters as actual work. My family (Annamari, Mauritz, Marizanne and Mia) knows me well enough to allow me the illusion that I have fooled them all these years.

My colleagues at the History Department at Stellenbosch University and elsewhere may have had their reservations, but were either too polite (a form of intellectual gamesmanship perhaps?) or too wrapped up in their own esoteric concerns to challenge me outright. I nevertheless benefitted considerably from the collegiality and interest of my immediate colleagues and acquaintances beyond: Anton Ehlers, Hermann Giliomee, André Odendaal, Christopher Merrett, Bruce Murray, Bill Nasson, Hendrik Snyders, Sandra Swart, Charles van Onselen, Vivian Bickford-Smith and Wessel Visser. Leschelle Morkel and Wouter Hanekom good-naturedly tried to shore up my status as a technocratic peasant. Danél Hanekom was an efficient and supportive editor.

I am also institutionally indebted to Stellenbosch University who has provided me with the academic space to follow my own bent. The National Research Foundation has generously funded my project and allowed me for once in my academic life not to live off the smell of an oil rag whilst doing research.

Some of the material in this book has been reincarnated from seeing the first light of day in article form in journals such as the *South African Historical Journal*, the *International Journal of Sport History* and *Sporting Traditions*, and chapters in books which have appeared in obscure places or which are long out of print. For this publication the material has been updated and substantially reworked – in certain respects they differ unrecognisably from the original versions – and then there is also work that now appears in print for the first time.

Albert Grundlingh
Stellenbosch
July 2013

Glossary
Abbreviations of rugby bodies mentioned in this study

SARFB – South African Rugby Football Board (1889–1978)
SARB – South African Rugby Board (1978–1991)
SACFB – South African Coloured Rugby Football Board (1897–1966)
SABRFB – South African Bantu Rugby Football Board (1935–1959)
SAARFB – South African African Rugby Football Board (1959–1978)
SARA – South African Rugby Association (1978–1991)
SARU – South African Rugby Union (1966–1991)
SARFF – South African Rugby Football Federation (1959–1991)
SACOSRU – SA Council on Sport Rugby Union (1992–1994)
SARFU – South African Rugby Football Union (1992–2004)
SA RUGBY (Pty) Ltd – South African Rugby Proprietary Limited (2002–2010)
SARU – South African Rugby Union (2004–present)

Sources

Books

Adam, H. and Giliomee, H.: *The Rise and Crisis of Afrikaner Power* (D. Philip, Cape Town, 1979).

Albertyn, J.R., Du Toit, P., and Theron, H.S.: *Kerk en Stad* (Pro Ecclesia, Stellenboch, 1948).

Alfred, L.: *Lifting the Covers: The Inside Story of South African Cricket* (Spearhead, Cape Town, 2001).

Amis, T. and Cornwell, T.B. (eds): *Global Sport Sponsorship* (Berg Publishers, Oxford, 2005).

Anderson, B.: "Imagined Communities" in J. Hutchinson and A.D. Smith (eds), *Nationalism* (Oxford University Press, Oxford, 1995).

Anderson, B.: *Imagined Communities: Reflections on the Origins and Spread of Nationalism* (Verso, London, 1983).

Anderson, S: "Introduction: Pleasures of Taking the Waters" in S. Anderson and B.H. Tabb (eds), *Water, Leisure and Culture: European Historical Perspectives* (Berg, Oxford, 2003).

Andrew, R.: *A Game and a Half – An Autobiography* (Hodder and Stoughton, London, 1994).

Andrewes, F.: "'Demonstrable Virility': Images of Masculinity in the 1956 Springbok Rugby Tour of New Zealand", in G. Ryan (ed.), *Tackling Rugby Myths: Rugby and New Zealand Society* (University of Otago Press, Dunedin, 2005).

Anon: *Race Relations Survey*, 1991/92 (South African Institute of Race Relations, Johannesburg, 1992).

Anon: *Who's Who in the Sporting World: Witwatersrand and Victoria: Rugby* (Johannesburg, 1933).

Anon: *Sport in the RSA* (Human Sciences Research Council, Pretoria, 1982).

Anon: South African Sports Documentation and Information Centre, *South African Cricket, 1889–1989* (Human Sciences Research Council, Pretoria, 1989).

Anon: *Agter die Doellyn* (CUM Publications, Vereeniging, 2011).

Archer, R. and Bouillon, A.: *The South African Game: Sport and Racism* (Zed Press, London, 1982).

Baker, A.: Greyhound Racing with "the Lid Off" (Routledge, London, 1953).

Barnard, L. and Stemmet, J-A.: *'n Lewe van sy Eie: Die Biografie van Volksblad* (Tafelberg, Cape Town, 2004).

Barnard, R.: "Contesting Beauty" in S. Nuttal and C.A. Michael (eds), *Senses of Culture: South African Cultural Studies* (University of Cape Town Press, Cape Town, 2000).

Beinart, W.: *South Africa in the 20th Century* (Oxford University Press, Oxford, 1994).

Black, D.R. and Nauright, J: *Rugby and the South African Nation: Sport Cultures, Politics and Power in the Old and New South Africas* (Manchester University Press, Manchester, 1998).

Blain, N., Boyle, R. and O'Donnell, H.: *Sport and National Identity in the European Media* (Leicester University Press, Leicester, 1993).
Booth, D.: *The Race Game: Politics and Sport in South Africa* (Frank Cass, London, 1998).
Booth, D.: "Theory" in S.W. Pope and J. Nauright (eds) *Routledge Companion to Sports History* (Routledge, London, 2010).
Booyens, B.: "Studentelewe – die Jongste Tydperk", H.B. Thom (ed.), *Stellenbosch, 1866–1966: Honderd Jaar Hoër Onderwys* (Stellenbosch, 1966).
Bowen, R.: *Cricket: A History of its Growth and Development throughout the World* (Eyre and Spottiswoode, London, 1970).
Brickhill, J.: *Race against Race: South Africa's "Multi-National" Sports Fraud* (International Defence and Aid Fund, London, 1976).
Brink, E.: "'Maar 'n Klomp Factory Meide': Afrikaner Family and Community on the Witwatersrand during the 1920s" in Bozzoli, B. (ed.) *Class, Community and Conflict: South African Perspectives* (Ravan Press, Johannesburg, 1987).
Brink, E.: "Man-made Women: Gender, Class and Ideology of the Volksmoeder", in C. Walker (ed.) *Woman and Gender in Southern Africa to 1945* (David Philip Publishers, Cape Town, 1990).
Callinicos, L.: *A Place in the City* (Ravan Press Johannesburg, 1993).
Cashman, R.: "Cricket and Colonialism: Colonial Hegemony and Indigenous Subversion?" in J.A. Mangan, *Pleasure, Profit, Proselytism: British Culture and Sport at Home and Abroad*, 1700–1914 (Frank Cass, London, 1988).
Chandler, T.J.L. and Nauright, J. (eds): *Making the Rugby World: Race Gender and Commerce* (Frank Cass, London, 1999).
Cilliers, J.: *God for Us: An Analysis and Assessment of Dutch Reformed Preaching During Apartheid* (Sunmedia, Stellenbosch, 2006).
Claassen, W.: *Kaalvoetklong tot Rugbytoks* (Lapa Publishers, Pretoria, 2011).
Claassen, W.: *More Than Just Rugby* (H. Strydom, Johannesburg, 1985).
Clapton, M.: *A Bit of a Flutter: Popular Gambling and English Society, c 1823–1961* (Routledge, London, 1998).
Clarke, F.C.: *Greyhounds and Greyhound Racing: A Comprehensive and Popular Survey of Britain's Latest Sport* (Routledge, London, 1934).
Coleman, S.: "Of Metaphors and Muscles: Protestant 'Play' in the Disciplining of the Self" in S. Coleman and T. Kohn (eds), *The Discipline of Leisure: Embodying Cultures of Recreation* (Berghahn Books, New York, 2007).
Coleman, S.: *The Globalisation of Charismatic Christianity: Spreading the Gospel of Prosperity* (Cambridge University Press, Cambridge, 2000).
Collins, T.: *A Social History of English Rugby Union* (Routledge, London, 2009).
Couzens, T.: "An Introduction to the History of Football in South Africa" in B. Bozzoli (ed.), *Town and Countryside in the Transvaal: Capitalist Penetration and Popular Response* (Ravan Press, Johannesburg, 1983).
Craven, D.: "'n Eeu van Sport", H.B. Thom (ed.), *Stellenbosch, 1866–1966: Honderd Jaar Hoër Onderwys* (Stellenbosch, 1966).
Craven, D.: *Die Leeus Keil Ons Op* (Johannesburg, 1956).
Craven, D.H.: *Oubaas Mark* (Afrikaanse Pers-Boekhandel, Cape Town, 1959).
Crawford, S.: "Nelson Mandela, the Number 6 Jersey and the 1995 Rugby World

Cup: Sport as a Transcendent Unifying Force, or a Transparent Illustration of Bicultural Opportunism" in R.R. Sands (ed.), *Anthropology, Sport and Culture* (Bergin and Garvey, London, 1999).

Davies, R.H.: *Capital State and White Labour in South Africa, 1900−1960: An Historical Materialist of Class Formation and Class Relations* (Harvester Press, Sussex, 1979).

Day, G. and Thompson, A.: *Theorizing Nationalism* (Palgrave, London, 2005).

Desai, A. and Nabbi, Z.: "'Truck and Trailer': Rugby and Transformation in South Africa" in S. Buhlungu, J. Daniel, R. Southall, and J. Lutchman (eds), *State of the Nation: South Africa 2007* (Human Sciences Research Council, Pretoria, 2007).

Desai, A. and Vahed, G.: "Beyond the Nation? Colour and Class in South African Cricket" in A. Desai (ed.), *The Race to Transform: Sport in Post-Apartheid South Africa* (HSRC Press, Cape Town, 2010).

Dobson, P.: *Rugby in South Africa* (South African Rugby Board, 1989).

Dobson, P.: *Rugby in South Africa: A History, 1861−1988* (South African Rugby Board, Cape Town, 1989).

Dobson, P.: *The Life of Danie Craven* (Human & Rousseau, Cape Town, 1994).

Donald, A.: *Allan Donald: The Biography: White Lightning* (Collins Willow, London, 2000).

Dreyer, N.: *Voorbladnooi: Van Pleinstraat tot Parys* (Protea Boekhuis, Pretoria, 2011).

Dunning, E.: "The Development of Modern Football" in E. Dunning (ed.), *The Sociology of Sport: A Selection of Readings* (Frank Cass, London, 1971).

Ebrahim, Y.: "Comments on the Future of South African Sport", in C. Thomas (ed.), *Sport and Liberation in South Africa* (University of Fort Hare, East London, 2006).

FitzSimons, P.: *The Rugby War* (Harper Sports, Sydney, 1996).

Fourie, J.J.: *Afrikaners in die Goudstad, 1886−1924* (Johannesburg, 1979).

Gaitskell, D., Kimble, J. and Unterhalter, E.: "Historiography in the 1970s: A Feminist Perspective", *Southern African Studies: Retrospect and Prospect* (Centre of African Studies, University of Edinburgh, 1983).

Gerber, G.: *Dok Craven: Agter die Kap van die Byl* (US Press, Stellenbosch, 2000).

Gerber, H.: *Craven* (Tafelberg, Cape Town, 1982).

Giliomee, H.: "Die Soeke na 'n Sinvolle Afrikaanse Verlede" in J. Tempelhoff (ed.), *Historical Consciousness and the Future of the Past* (Kleio Publishers, Vanderbijlpark, 2003).

Giliomee, H.: *Die Afrikaners van 1910−2010: Die Opkoms van 'n Moderne Gemeenskap*, (Die Erfenistigting, Pretoria, 2011).

Giliomee, H.: *The Afrikaners: Biography of a People* (University of Virginia Press, Virginia, 2003).

Gouws, D.: *... and Nothing but the Truth?* (Zebra Press, Cape Town, 2000).

Grey College Centenary Publication (Juta, Cape Town, 1955).

Grieb, E. and Farmer, S.: *The Springbok Handbook* (Jonathan Ball, Cape Town, 2011).

Griffiths, E.: *Kepler: The Biography* (Pelham Books, London, 1994).
Griffiths, E.: *Kitch: Truimph of a Decent Man* (CAB publishers, Johannesburg, 1997).
Griffiths, E.: *One Team, One Country: The Greatest Year of Springbok Rugby* (Viking, Johannesburg, 1996).
Griffiths, E.: *The Captains* (Jonathan Ball, Johannesburg, 2001).
Grobbelaar, P.W. (ed.): *Die Afrikaner en sy Kultuur: Ons Volksfeeste* (Cape Town, 1977).
Grundlingh, A., Odendaal, A. and Spies, B.: *Beyond the Tryline: Rugby and the South African Society* (Ravan Press, Johannesburg, 1995)
Guelke, A.: "Sport and the End of Apartheid" in L. Allison (ed.), *The Changing Politics of Sport* (Manchester University Press, Manchester, 1993).
Guttmann, A.: *Sports Spectators* (Colombia University Press, New York, 1986).
Hain, P.: *Outside In* (Biteback Publishing, London, 2012).
Hartman, R.: *Hansie and the Boys* (Zebra Press, Cape Town, 1996).
Heydenrych, D.H.: *Tukkie-Rugby 75* (Pretoria, 1983).
Hobsbawm, E.J.: *Nations and Nationalism since 1780: Programme, Myth and Reality* (Cambridge University Press, Cambridge, 1990).
Hofmeyr, I.: "Building a Nation from Words: Afrikaans Language, Literature and Ethnic Identity, 1902–1924" in S. Marks and S. Trapido (eds), *The Politics of Race, Class and Nationalism* (Longman Ltd, London, 1987).
Holt, R.: *Sport and the British: A Modern History* (Oxford University Press, Oxford, 1990).
Houlihan, B.: *Sport and International Politics* (Prentice Hall, London, 1994).
Hutchinson, J.: "Cultural Nationalism and Moral Regeneration" in J. Hutchinson and A.B. Smith (eds), *Nationalism* (Oxford University Press, Oxford, 1995).
Jansen, J: *Knowledge in the Blood: Confronting Race and the Apartheid Past* (UCT Press, Cape Town, 2009)
Johnstone, R. and Neville, C.: *Rugby in South Africa* (Cape Town, 1964).
Jooste, G.: *Rugby Stories from the Platteland* (30 Degrees South, Johannesburg, 2005).
Kaljee, R.: *Hartenbos Bakens* (Privately published, Hartenbos, 1993).
Kellas, J.G.: *The Politics of Nationalism and Ethnicity* (Palgrave Macmillan, London, 1991).
Keohane, M.: *Springbok Rugby Uncovered: The Inside Story of South Africa's Rugby Controversies* (Zebra Press, Cape Town, 2004).
King, K.: *The Hansie Cronjé Story: An Authorised Biography* (Global Creative, Cape Town, 2005).
Kombuis, K.: *Afrikaans my Darling* (Human and Rousseau, Cape Town, 2003).
Kotze, D. (ed.): *Professor H.B. Thom* (Universiteitsuitgewers, Stellenbosch, 1969).
Kotze, G.: *Sport en Politiek* (Perskor, Pretoria, 1978).
Laidlaw, C.: *Mud in your Eye: A Worm's Eye View of the Changing World of Rugby* (Timmins, Cape Town, 1974).
Larson, J.F. and Park, H-S.: *Global Television and the Politics of the Seoul Olympics* (James F. Larson, Boulder, 1993).

Le Roux, H.: *Sportpourri: Ervarings van 'n Joernalis* (Van Schaik, Pretoria, 1998).
Levett, G.: "Constructing Imperial Identity: The 1907 South African Cricket Tour of England" in B. Murray and G. Vahed (eds), *Empire and Cricket: The South African Experience, 1884–1914* (Unisa Press, Pretoria, 2009).
Lodge, T.: "The African National Congress in the 1990s" in G. Moss and I. Obery (eds), *South African Review 6: From "Red" Friday to Codesa* (Ravan, Johannesburg, 1992).
Louw, R.: *For the Love of Rugby* (Johannesburg, 1987).
Luyt, L.: *Walking Proud: The Louis Luyt Autobiography* (Don Nelson, Cape Town, 2003).
MacClancy, J.: "Sport, Identity and Ethnicity" in J. MacClancy (ed.), *Sport, Identity and Ethnicity* (Berg, Oxford, 1996).
Magdalinski, T. and Chandler, T. (eds): *With God on Their Side: Sport in the Service of Religion* (Routledge, London, 2002).
Mangan, J. (ed.): *The Cultural Bond: Sport, Empire, Society* (Frank Cass, London, 1992).
Marsh, R.: *The Inside Edge* (Landsdowne, Sydney, 1983).
Martin-Jenkins, C.: *The Complete Who's Who of Test Cricketers* (Orbis Publishing, London, 1980).
Matfield, V.: *Victor: My Journey* (Zebra Press, Cape Town, 2011).
McGregor, L.: *Touch, Pause, Engage: Exploring the Heart of South African Rugby* (Jonathan Ball, Johannesburg, 2011).
Merrett, C.: "From Non-racial Sport to the FIFA World Cup: A Tale of Politics, Big Business and Hope Betrayed" in C. Thurman (ed.), *Sport versus Art: A South African Contest* (Wits University Press, Johannesburg, 2001).
Moodie, D.: *The Rise of Afrikanerdom: Power, Apartheid and the Afrikaner Civil Religion* (University of California Press, Berkeley, 1975).
Morrell, R.: "Forging a Changing Race: Rugby and White Masculinity in Colonial Natal, c 1870–1910" in J. Nauright and T.J.L. Chandler (eds), *Making Men: Rugby and Masculine Identity* (Frank Cass, London, 1996).
Morrell, R.: "The Times of Change: Men and Masculinity in South Africa" in R. Morrell (ed.), *Changing Men in Southern Africa* (Natal University Press, Durban 2001).
Morris, M. and Hindson, D.: "The Disintegration of Apartheid: From Violence to Reconstruction" in Moss and Obery (eds), *South African Review 6: From "Red" Friday to Codesa* (Ravan, Johannesburg, 1992).
Mosely, P.A., Cashman, O'Hara, R.J., and Weatherburn, H. (eds): *Sporting Immigrants: Sport and Ethnicity in Australia* (Walla Walla Press, Sydney, 1997).
Mostert, D. (ed.): *Gedenkboek van die Ossewaens op Pad van Suid-Afrika* (Nasionale Pers, Cape Town, 1940).
Murray, B. and Merrett, C.: *Caught Behind: Race and Politics in Springbok Cricket* (Wits University Press and University of KwaZulu-Natal Press, Johannesburg and Durban, 2004).
Nauright, J. and Black, D.: "'Hitting Them Where it Hurts': Springbok – All Black Rugby, Masculine National Identity and Counter-Hegemonic Struggle,

1959−1992" in J. Nauright and T. Chandler (eds), *Making Men: Rugby and Masculine Identity* (Frank Cass, London, 1996).

Nauright, J. and Merrett, C.: "South Africa" in Stoddart, B and Sandiford, K.A.P. (eds): *The Imperial Game: Cricket, Culture and Society* (Manchester University Press, Manchester, 1998).

Nauright, J.: "Rugby, Carnival, Masculinity and Identities in 'Coloured' Cape Town" in T.J.L. Chandler and J. Nauright (eds), *Making the Rugby World: Race, Gender and Commerce* (Frank Cass, London, 1999).

Noakes, T.: *Challenging Beliefs: Memoirs of a Career* (Zebra Press, Cape Town, 2011).

Nothling, F.J.: "The Pioneering Years" in M.C. van Zyl (ed.), *Northern Transvaal Rugby 50* (Pretoria, 1988).

O'Meara, D.: *Volkskapitalisme: Class, Capital and Ideology in the Development of Afrikaner Nationalism, 1934−1948* (Cambridge University Press, Cambridge, 1983).

Odendaal, A.: "Turning History on its Head: Some Perspectives on Afrikaners and the Game of Cricket", in C. Day (ed.), *Cricket ... Developing Winners* (United Cricket Board, Illovo, 2001).

Odendaal, A.: "Sport and Liberation: The Unfinished Business of the Past" in C. Thomas (ed.), *Sport and Liberation in South Africa: Reflections and Suggestions* (University of Fort Hare, Department of Sport and Recreation, Pretoria, 2006).

Odendaal, A.: "The Thing that is Not Round: The Untold Story of Black Rugby in South Africa" in A. Grundlingh, A. Odendaal and B. Spies: *Beyond the Tryline: Rugby and South African Society* (Ravan Press, Johannesburg, 1995).

Özkirimli, U: *Theories of Nationalism: a Critical Introduction* (Palgrave, Hampshire, 2000).

Parker, A.C.: *Giants of South African Rugby* (Cape Town, 1956).

Paton, A.: *Hofmeyr* (Oxford University Press, Oxford, 1964).

Partridge, T.: *A Life in Rugby* (Southern Book Publishers, Johannesburg, 1991).

Pearson, M.N.: "Heads in the Sand: The 1956 Springbok Tour to New Zealand in Perspective" in R. Cashman and M. McKernan (eds), *Sport in History: The Making of Modern Sporting History* (University of Queensland, Sydney, 1979).

Pienaar, F. (with E. Griffiths): *Rainbow Warrior* (Collins Willow, London, 1999).

Phillips, Murray G. (ed.), *Deconstructing Sport History: A Postmodern Analysis* (State University of New York Press, Albany, 2006).

Pirie, G.: "White Railway Labour in South Africa, 1873−1924" in R. Morrell (ed.), *White but Poor: Essays on the History of Poor Whites in Southern Africa, 1880−1940* (Unisa Press, Pretoria, 1993).

Pollock, P. and Pollock, G.: *Bouncers and Boundaries* (Sportman Enterprises, Johannesburg, 1968).

Ramphal, S. (ed.), *Misson to South Africa: The Commonwealth Report* (Penguin, London, 1986).

Ray, C.: *In Black and White: The Jake White Story* (Zebra Press, Johannesburg, 2007).

Retief, D.: *The Springboks and the Holy Grail: Behind the Scenes at the Rugby World Cup* (Zebra Press, Cape Town, 2011).
Robins, E.: *This Man Malan* (SA Scientific Publishing, Cape Town, 1953).
Roger, W.: *Old Heroes: The 1956 Springbok Tour and the Lives Beyond* (Hodder and Stoughton, London, 1991).
Ryan, G.: "The End of an Aura: All Black Rugby and Rural Nostalgia in the Professional Era" in G. Rynam (ed.), *Tackling Rugby Myths: Rugby and New Zealand Society, 1854–2004* (Otago University Press, Dunedin, 2005).
Sampson, L.: "Yesterday's Heroes", in Anon, *Laughing Through the Turmoil* (Johannesburg, 1990).
Schoeman, C.: *Player Power: A History of the South African Rugby Players Association* (Sarpa, Rondebosch, 2009).
Schulze, W.G.: "Boer Prisoners of War in Ceylon and the 'Great and Grand Old Manly Game of Cricket'" in B. Murray and G. Vahed (eds), *Empire and Cricket: The South African Experience, 1884–1914* (Unisa Press, Pretoria, 2009).
Scholtz, G.D.: *Hendrik Verwoerd* (Perskor, Johannesburg, 1974).
Sewell, E.H.D.: *Rugger – The Man's Game* (Hollis & Carter, London, 1950).
Snyders, H.: "Preventing Huddersfield: The Rise and Decline of Rugby League in South Africa, c. 1957–1965" in S. Cornelissen and A. Grundlingh (eds), *Sport Past and Present in South Africa: (Trans)forming the nation* (Routledge, London, 2012).
Southall, R.: "Black Empowerment and Present Limits to a more Democratic Capitalism in South Africa" in S. Buhlungu, J. Daniel, R. Southall, and J. Lutchman (eds), *State of the Nation: South Africa 2007* (Human Sciences Research Council, Pretoria, 2007).
Stals, E.L.P.: *Afrikaners in die Goudstad, 1924–1961* (HAUM, Johannesburg, 1986).
Steyn, N.: *Sesse tot Oorwinning: Suid-Afrika se Krieketsege, 1966–1967* (Voortrekkerpers, Johannesburg, 1967).
Stoddart, B. and Sandiford, K.A.P. (eds): *The Imperial Game: Cricket, Culture and Society* (Manchester University Press, Manchester, 1998).
Stofile, M.: "Sport as a Human Right", in C. Thomas (ed.) *Sport and Liberation in South Africa* (University of Fort Hare, East London, 2006).
Struna, N.: "Social History and Sport" in J. Coakley and E. Dunning (eds), *Handbook of Sport Studies* (Sage publications, 2000). (Electronic version, Accessed 13 September 2011)
Teichmann, G. and Grifiths, E.: *For the Record: Gary Teichman* (Johannesburg, 2000).
Theron, E.: *Sonder Hoed of Handskoen* (Tafelberg Uitgewers, Kaapstad, 1983).
Thompson, R.: *Retreat from Apartheid: New Zealand's Sporting Contacts with South Africa* (Oxford University Press, Wellington, 1975).
Van der Valk, R. and Colquhoun, A.: *Nick and I: An Adventure in Rugby* (Don Nelson, Cape Town, 2003).
Van der Westhuizen, J.: "In Retrospect" in A. Powers (ed.), *Rugby in Our Blood* (Tafelberg, Cape Town, 2011).

Van Eeden, J.: "All the Mall's a Stage": The Shopping Mall as Visual Culture in J. van Eeden and A. du Preez (eds), *South African Visual Culture* (Van Schaik Publishers, Pretoria, 2008).
Van Jaarsveld, C.: *Spoorwegkinders en die Depressie* (Fishwicks, George, 2010).
Van Reenen, R.: *From Locker Room to Boardroom: Converting Rugby Talent into Business Success* (Zebra Press, Cape Town, 2012).
Van Rooyen, Q.: *Springbok-triomf* (Tafelberg, Cape Town, 1972).
Van Waart, S.: *Mosselbaai: Seepoort van die Tuinroete* (Lapa, Pretoria, 2003).
Van Zyl Slabbert, F.: *The Last White Parliament* (Sidgwick & Jackson, Johannesburg, 1985).
Van Wyk, J.: *So Was Dit: Stories van Gister en Vandag* (Tafelberg, Cape Town, 2013).
Van Zyl Slabbert, F.: *The Other Side of History: An Anecdotal Reflection on the Political Transition in South Africa* (Jonathan Ball, Johannesburg, 2006).
Viviers, G.: *Rugby Agter Doringdraad* (HAUM, Pretoria, 1970).
Volschenk, J.: *Struggle Rugby – A Sport in Crisis* (Solidarity, Johannesburg, 2002).
Waldmeir, P.: *Anatomy of a Miracle*: *The End of Apartheid and the Birth of the New South Africa* (W.W. Norton and Company, Middlesex, 1997).
Walton, J.K.: *The English Seaside Resort: A Social History, 1750–1914* (Longman, London, 1983).
Wamm, D., Melznick, L., Russell, M.J. and Pease, G.W. & D.G.: *Sport Fans: The Psychology and Social Impact of Spectators* (Routledge, New York, 2001).
Wessels, K.: *Cricket Madness* (Aandblom Publishers, 1987).
Wilkins, I. and Strydom, H.: *The Super-Afrikaners* (Jonathan Ball, Johannesburg, 1978).
Woods, D.: "African Sunrise" in *Wisden* (Wisden and Co., London, 1993).

Academic journals

Adam, H.: "Ethnic versus Civic Nationalism: South Africa's Non-Racialism in Comparative Perspective", *SA Sociological Review*, 7, 1 (1994).
Allen, D.: "'Bats and Bayonets': Cricket and the Anglo-Boer War, 1899–1902", *Sport in History*, 25,1 (April 2005), 17–40.
Allen, D.: "'Beating Them at their Own Game': Rugby, the Anglo-Boer War and Afrikaner Nationalism, 1899–1948" in *International Journal of the History of Sport*, 20, 3 (September 2003), 37–57.
Anderson, E. and McGuire, R.: "Inclusive Masculinity Theory and the Gendered Politics of Men's Rugby," *Journal of Gender Studies*, 19, 3 (2010), 249–261.
Booth, D.: "Mandela and Amabokoboko: The Political and Linguistic Nationalisation of South Africa?", *Journal of Modern African Studies* (September 1996), 459–478.
Booth, D.: "Escaping the Past? The Cultural Turn and Language in Sport History" in *Rethinking History: The Journal of Theory and Practice*, 8, 1 (2004), 103–125.

Booth, D.: "Hitting Apartheid for a Six? The Politics of the South African Sports Boycott", *Journal of Contemporary History*, 38, 3 (July, 2003), 477–493.

Booth, D.: "United Sport: An Alternative Hegemony in South Africa?", *International Journal of the History of Sport*, 12, 3 (December 1995), 105–124.

Booth, D: "Beyond History: Racial Emancipation and Ethics in Apartheid sport", *Rethinking History: The Journal of Theory and Practice*, 14, 4, (2010), 461–481.

Botma, G.J.: Lightning Strikes Twice: The 2007 Rugby World Cup and Memories of a South African Rainbow Nation, *Communicatio: South African Journal of Communication Theory and Research*, 36, 1 (2010), 1–19.

Chipkin, I. and Leatt, A.: "Religion and Revival in Post-Apartheid South Africa", *Focus*, 62 (August 2011), 45–48.

Coetzee, J.M.: "The Rugby World Cup of Rugby", *Southern African Review of Books*, 38 (July 1995).

Collins, T.: "Work, Rest and Play: Recent Trends in the History of Sport and Leisure" in *Journal of Contemporary History*, 42, 397 (2007), 397–410.

Cordery, S.: "Mutualism, Friendly Societies and the Genesis of Railway Trade Unions", *Labour History Review*, 67, 3 (December 2002), 273–281.

Farred, G.: "The Nation in White: Cricket in Post-Apartheid South Africa", *Social Text*, 50 (Spring 1997), 9–32.

Du Preez, D.: "Die Calvinistiese Beskouing van Arbeid," *Koers*, 14, 2 (October 1946).

Farquharson, K. and Majoribanks, T.: "Transforming the Springboks: Re-imagining the South African Nation through Sport", Social Dynamics, 29, 1 (2003), 27–48.

Forster, J.: "'Land of Contrasts' or 'Home We Have Always Known'? the SAR&H and the Imaginary Geography of White South African Nationhood, 1910–1930", *Journal of Southern African Studies*, 29, 3 (September 2003), 657–680.

Grundlingh, A. and Sapire, H.: "From Feverish Festival to Repetitive Ritual? The Changing Fortunes of Great Trek Mythology in an Industrialising South Africa, 1938–1989", *South African Historical Journal*, 21 (1989), 19–38.

Grundlingh, A.: "'Are we Afrikaners Becoming too Rich'? Cornucopia and Change in Afrikanerdom in the 1960s", *Journal of Historical Sociology*, 21, 2/3 (June–September, 2008), 143–165.

Gupta, A.: "The Globalization of Cricket: The Rise of the Non-West", *International Journal of the History of Sport*, 21, 2 (March 2004), 257–276.

Horton, P.: "Rugby Union Football in Australian Society: An Unintended Consequence of ntended Actions" in *Sport and Society*, 12, 7 (2009), 169–184.

Houlihan, B.: "Sport National Identity and Public Policy", *Nations and Nationalism*, 3, 1 (1997), 113–137.

Jeffrey, I.: "Street Rivalry and Patron-Managers: Football in Sharpeville, 1943–1985", *African Studies*, 15, 1 (1992), 68–94.

Kaufman, J. and Patterson, O.: "The Cross-National Cultural Diffusion: The Global Spread of Cricket", *American Sociological Review*, 70 (February 2005), 92–110.

Kelly, P. and Hickey, C.: "Player Welfare and Privacy in the Sports Entertainment Industry", *International Review for the Sociology of Sport*, 43, 4 (2008), 383–398.

Kutcher, L.: "The American Sport Event as Carnival: An Emergent Norm Approach to Crowd Behavior" in *Journal of Popular Culture*, 16 (1982), 34–41.

Macdonald, M.: "Power Politics in the New South Africa", *Journal of Southern African Studies*, 22, 2 (June 1996), 221–233.

Maguire, J.A.: "Studying Sport through the Lens of Historical Sociology and/or Sociological History" in *Sport and Society*, 14, 7–8 (2011), 872–882.

Maingard, J.: "Imag(in)ing the South African Nation: Representations of Identity in the Rugby World Cup, 1995", *Theatre Journal*, 49, 1 (1997), 15–28.

Majumdar, B. and Brown, S.: "Why Baseball, Why Cricket? Differing Nationalisms, Differing Challenges", *The International Journal of Sport History*, 24, 2 (February 2007), 139–156.

Marais, H.C.: "Herkomspatrone van Stellenbosch se Toprugbyspelers", *Geo-Stell*, 3 (1979), 45–53.

Merrett, C., Tatz, C. and Adair, D.: "History and its Racial Legacies: Quotas in South African Rugby and Cricket", *Sport and Society*, 14, 6 (2011), 754–777.

Mordant-Bexiga, M.: "Rugby, Gender and Capitalism": 'Sportocracy' up for Sale?"*Agenda*, 25, 4 (2011), 69–74.

Munro, W.A.: "Revisiting Tradition, Reconstructing Identity: Afrikaner Nationalism and Political Transition in South Africa", *Politikon*, 22, 2 (1995), 5–33.

Nadar, S.: "Palatable Patriarchy and Violence Against Women in South Africa – Angus Buchan's Mighty Men's Conference as a Case Study of Masculinism", *Scriptura*, 102 (2009), 551–661.

Nalapat, A. and Parker, A.: "Sport, Celebrity and Popular Culture: Sachin Tendulkar, Cricket and Indian Nationalisms" in *International Review for the Sociology of Sport*, 40 (2005), 433–446.

Nasson, B.: "'Not Quite Fair Play, Old Chap': The Complexion of Cricket and Sport in South Africa," *Kronos*, 35 (2009), 248–256.

Nauright, J.: "Global Games: Culture, Political Economy and Sport in the Globalised World of the 21st Century", *Third World Quarterly*, 25, 7 (2004), 1327–1336.

Nauright, J.: "White Man's Burden Revisited: Race, Sport and Reporting the Hansie Cronjé Cricket Crisis in South Africa and Beyond" in *Sport History Review*, 36, 1 (2005), 61–75.

Nixon, R.: "Apartheid on the Run: The South African Sports Boycott", *Transitions*, 58, 1992.

Nöthlingh, F.J.: "Soccer in South Africa: A Brief Outline", *Kleio* (1982), 28–41.

Petryszak, N.: "Spectator Sports as an Aspect of Popular Culture – An Historical View", *Journal of Sport Behaviour*, 1, 1 (February 1978), 14–27.

Posel, D.: "Social History and the Wits History Workshop" in *African Studies*, 69, 1 (2010), 29–40.

Rahn, W.M., Kroeger, B. and Kite, C.M.: "A Framework for the Study of Public Mood", *Political Psychology*, 17, 1 (1996), 29–58.

Robolin, S.: "Of Colour and Blindness in *Invictus*", *Safundi: The Journal of South African and American studies*, 13, 1–2 (2012), 115–150.

Ryan, G.: "Few and Far Between: Maori and Pacific Contributions to New Zealand Cricket", *Sport and History*, 10, 1 (January 2007), 71–88.

Scalmer, S.: "Cricket, Imperialism and Class Domination", *Working USA: The Journal of Labour and Society*, 10 (December 2007), 431–442.

Scholtz, G.J.L. and Olivier, J.L.: "Attitudes of Urban South Africans Towards Non-racial Sport and their Expectations of Future Race Relations – A Comparative Study" in *International Review for Sociology of Sport*, 19 (1984), 129–142.

Sen, S.: "Enduring Colonialism in Cricket: From Ranjitsinhji to the Cronjé Affair", *Contemporary South Asia*, 10, 2 (2001), 237–249.

Simons, J.: "The 'Englishness' of English cricket", *Journal of Popular Culture* 29, 4 (Spring 1996), 41–50.

Skipper, J.K.: "The Sociological Significance of Nicknames: The Case of Baseball Players" in *Journal of Sport Behaviour*, 7, 1 (February 1984), 28–37.

Strelitz, L. and Steenveld, L.: "Sport en Nasiebou in Suid Afrika: Die Betekenis van die 1995 Rugby Wêreldbeker", *Equi Novi*, 17, 2 (1996), 137–38.

Taylor, M. and Taylor, R.: "Something for the Weekend, Sir? Leisure, Ecstacy and Identity in Football and Contemporary Religion", *Leisure Studies*, 16, 1 (1997), 37–49.

Tunstall, S.M. and Penning-Rowsell, E.C.: "The English Beach: Experience and Values", *The Geographical Journal*, 164, 3 (November 1998), 319–332.

Van der Merwe, F.J.G.: "Afrikaner Nationalism and Sport", *Canadian Journal of Sport*, 22, 2 (December 1991), 34–46.

Van der Merwe, F.J.G.: "Sport and Games in the Boer Prisoner-of-War Camps during the Anglo-Boer War, 1899–1902", *International Journal of the History of Sport*, 9, 3 (December 1992), 439–545.

Welsh, D.: "Urbanisation and the Solidarity of Afrikaner Nationalism", *Journal of Modern African Studies*, 7, 2, (1969), 265–276.

Young, T.: "The Sociology of Sport: Structural Marxist and Cultural Marxist Approaches", *Sociological Perspectives*, 29, 1 (January 1986), 3–28.

Unpublished theses and papers

Bolligelo, A.: "Tracing the Development of Professionalism in South African Rugby, 1995–2004" (Unpublished M.A. mini dissertation, Stellenbosch University, 2006).

Botha, M.E.: "Partikuliere Volksorg in die Afrikaanse Volkskultuur met Verwysing na die ATKV (SAS en H), 1930–1964" (Unpublished D.Phil thesis, Potchefstroom University, 1970).

Cilliers, J.: "Preaching Between Assimilation and Separation: Perspectives on Church and State in South African Society" (Unpublished paper, Homiletics Seminar for Danish Pastors, Copenhagen, June 2008).

Johns, K.: "A Second Innings for Cricket: The Political Economy, Nation-building and Cricket Development Programmes in South Africa" (Unpublished M.A. thesis, University of the Witwatersrand, 1995).

Kok, F.J.: "Die Taak van Kultuurorganisasies in Minderheidsgroepe met Besondere Verwysing na die ATKV" (Unpublished D.Phil thesis, Stellenbosch University, 1992).

Lange, L. "The Making of the White Working-Class: Class Experience and Class Identity in Johannesburg, 1890–1922" (D.Phil thesis, University of the Witwatersrand, 1998), pp.163–259.

Lapchick, R.E.: "The Politics of Race and International Sport: the Case of South Africa" (Unpublished D.Phil. thesis, University of Denver, 1973).

Le Roux, W.G.: "Die Vermaaklikheid en Ontspanning van die Armblanke Kind in Kaapstad" (Unpublished MA dissertation, Stellenbosch University, 1940).

Louw, A.M.: "Sport Transformation in South Africa: A Critical Analysis of the Applications of Affirmative Action in Professional Sport" (Unpublished paper, International Association of Sport Law, XI, Annual Congress, Johannesburg, 2005).

Nauright, J. and Black, D.: "Much More Than a Game: Springbok-All Black Rugby, Sanctions and Change in South Africa, 1959–1992" (Paper, 1993).

Nell, I. and Cilliers, J.: "Within the Enclave: Profiling South African Social and Religious Developments" (Unpublished paper, Stellenbosch University, 2011).

Odendaal, A.: "The Hundred Years' War: Brown balls, Bronzed Colonials and the Persistence of Colonial Biases in 21st Century Rugby Cultures" (Plenary address to the conference on "Afrikaners, Anglos and Springboks, 1906–2006" London, 25 September 2006).

Pearson, P.: "Function, Familiarity or Fun? Nicknames in Rehoboth, Namibia" (African Studies Institute paper, University of the Witwatersrand, October 1988).

Peires, J.B.: "*Facta non verba*: Towards a History of Black Rugby in the Eastern Cape" (Unpublished paper, History Workshop, University of the Witwatersrand, 1981).

Pretorius, I.P.W.: "Senior Rugby in Pretoria, 1938–1989" (Unpublished MA dissertation, University of South Africa, 1989).

Rademeyer, J.S.: "Die Rol van Sportisolasie as 'n Faktor in die Daarstelling van 'n Nuwe Politieke Bedeling in Suid-Afrika" (Unpublished D.Phil thesis, University of the Orange Free State, 2003).

Saaiman, G.B.: "Sport en Politiek: Suid Afrika se Sportisolasie en die Invloed op die Binnelandse Politiek" (Unpublished M.A. dissertation, University of the Orange Free State, 1981).

Snyman, D.: "Deep Heat Heroes and Forgotten Fields" (Manuscript, 2007).

Stander, G.B.: "Die Geskiedenis van Matie-Krieket" (Unpublished M.A. thesis, Stellenbosch University, 2000).

Tayler, J.A.: "With the Shoulder to the Wheel: The Public Life of Erika Theron" (Unpublished D.Litt et Phil dissertation, University of South Africa, 2010).

Van der Horst, F.: "The South African Council on Sport: The Sports Wing of the Liberation Movement" (Unpublished paper, Sport and Liberation Conference, University of Fort Hare, East London, 15 October 2005).

Van Rensburg A.P.J.: "Op die Voorpos: die Verhaal van die Stigting, Strewe en

Prestasies van die ATKV (SAS en H) (Unpublished manuscript, Institute of Contemporary History, Bloemfontein, 1969).

Van Staden, N.: "Gereformeerd en Charismaties? 'n Liturgiese Ondersoek na Kontemporêre Tendense in die Nederduits Gereformeerde Kerk, (M.Div thesis, Stellenbosch University, 2007).

Williams, J.G.: "Sosiologiese Ondersoek na Bepaalde Aspekte van die Maatskaplike Milieu en Leefwyse van 'n Groep Provinsiale Rugbyspelers" (Unpublished M.A. dissertation, University of Pretoria, 1976).

Winch, J.: "Sir William Milton: A Leading Figure in Public School Games, Colonial Politics and Imperial Expansion, 1877–1914" (Unpublished D.Phil thesis, Stellenbosch University, 2012).

Newspapers and magazines

Beeld
Business Day
Cape Argus
Cape Times
Citizen
City Press
Daily News
Daily Maverick
Democracy in Action
Die Afrikaner
Die Burger
Die Kerkbode
Die Suid-Afrikaan
Die Taalgenoot
Die Transvaler
Die Voorligter
Die Vrye Afrikaan
Eastern Province Hearald
Economist
Evening Post
Finansies en Tegniek
Frontline
Huisgenoot
Insig
Leadership SA
Living
Mail and Guardian
Millennium Magazine
Natal on Saturday
New Nation
New Statesman
Oosterlig
Post Natal
Pretoria News
Productivity SA
Rapport
Rugby
Rugby 15
Rugby 15 International
Rugby World South Africa
SA Protea Cricket Annual
SA Rugby
SA Rugby News
SA Sports Illustrated
Saturday Star
Sidelines
South African Cricket Review
South African Cricketer
Sunday Independent
Sunday Paper
Sunday Times
Sunday Times Inside
The Citizen
The Friend
The Guardian Weekly
The Independent
The Hindu
The Sportsman
The Star
The Sunday Independent
The Telegraph
Time
Trek
Vigor
Volksblad
Vrye Weekblad
Weekend Argus
Weekly Mail
Weekly Mail and Guardian

Internet sources

Lombaard, C.: "Die Charismatiserende Afrikaanse Kerke – Enkele Gedagtes", 1 January 2005, http://www.teo.co.za. (Accessed 4 February 2012)

Terreblanche, S.: "Mag en onverdiende rykdom in SA", http://www.vryeafrikaan.co.za/leesphp?id=815. (Accessed 20/2/2012)

Opening address by Minister M.S. Stofile, Sandton Convention Centre, 7 June 2005, http://www.info.gov.za/speeches. (Accessed 7 November 2007)
Parliamentary Monitoring Group, South African Rugby Union transformation plan progress report, 23 May 2012, http://www.pmg.org.za.report. (Accessed 24 May 2012)
"Transformation in rugby", April 2004, http://www.litnet.co.za/seminar/ollie.asp. (Accessed 1 September 2004)
"Montpelliers swoops on 'quota' victim", http://www.planet-rugby.com. (Accessed 24 October 2007)
http://www.keo.co.za/2006/02/15-sas-professionalism-promotes-mediocrity. (Accessed 21 July 2006)
http://www.iol.co.za/news/south-africa/-more-than-70 000-gather-at-Loftus for Jesus. (Accessed 7 February 2012)
www.http://za.wowcity.com/centurion/locbus2/2608424657405141430/n-g-kerk-moreleta-park. (Accessed 8 February 2012)
www.http://moreleta.org.video/video/search?q=Matfield

Archival sources

Central Archives Pretoria
TA, C 58 Dog Racing Commission, 1942

Dutch Reformed Church Archives, Pretoria
Synod Minutes, 1943

Institute of Contemporary History, Bloemfontein
ATKV Papers, Verslag van Hartenbosbestuur, 1953
Archives of the Federasie van Afrikaanse Kultuurvereniginge

University of South Africa
United Party Archives

University of the Witwatersrand
South African Cricket Board Archives

Stellenbosch University
South African Rugby Board Archives

Interviews and personal communication

B. Sieberhagen, 6 January 1994, Stellenbosch.
Joel Stransky interviewed by Alana Bolligelo in Cape Town, 11 April 2005 (Transcript in private collection).
Ewie Cronjé, Bloemfontein, 5 September 2008.
Dawie de Villiers, Stellenbosch, 3 April 2013.
M.C. Edmonds, Pretoria, 5 August 2000.
E. Griebe: statistician of SA Rugby. E. Griebe to author, 16 February 2012.

Index

Abass, Abdullah 102
Adam, Heribert 142
affirmative action *see* race and racism
Afrikaanse Taal en Kultuur Vereniging *see* Hartenbos
Afrikaner Broederbond 75, 91
Afrikaners
    Afrikaans language 38–42, 90, 151, 215
    Afrikanerdom 26, 28, 43, 47, 49, 52, 55, 67, 76–79, 89, 187, 190, 192, 213
    Boere/Boers 49–50, *53*, 55, 65, 72, 90, 115, *147*, 154, 194–197
    elite 55, 62–63, 75, 168, 169, 197, 201
    historiography 9–14, 26, 39, 49, 52, 78, 81, 130–131, 214, 216
    ideology 8, 12, 24, 28, 36, 40, 47, 49, 51, 61–64, 75, 78, 92, 100, 129, 149, 161
    nationalism 11, 14–15, 34, 40–41, 45, 47, 51–55, 60–64, 72–73, 94, 123, 145, 170
    popular culture 11, 33, 68, 70–72, 78–79, 219–220
    poverty 15, 19, 20–23, 28–30, 33, 35, 39, 41, 43, 73, 125, 168
    railwaymen 35, **37**, 39–46, 51
    Reddingsdaadbond 73
    volk 15, 24, 29, 40–43, 47–51, 54–55, 61, 70, 72, 78–80, 182, 187, 194
    volkspele 26, 49–50, 55
    Voortrekkers 41, 49–50, 61–62, 83
Anderson, Benedict 51, 69
Andrew, Rob 156
Andrews, Keith 176
apartheid 7–8, 46, 60, 76–79, 100–102, 110–112, 116–119, 133–137, 141–143, 152–153, 211, 220
    anti-apartheid movement 8, 11, 93, 95–99, 102, 104–107, 111, 134, 165, 167, 173, 205
    post-apartheid 131, 137, 187, 190, 211, 213
Aplon, Gio 185
Australia 59, 66, 77, 83, 96, 118, 123, 156–158, 203–204, 208–211

Badela, Mono 77
Balfour, Ngconde 163
Basson, Willie 203
Batoyi, Shamila 214
Bedford, Tommy 91
Blackwell, Leslie 20
Boipatong massacre 119–121, 123, *147*
Botha, Naas 118
braais 90, 176, 206

brands and branding 143, 164
Buchan, Angus 184–185

campaigns 31, 33, 74, 98, 134, 136–137, 184
Christie, Kitch *133*–134
Claassen, Wynand 11
Claassen, Johan 97
Coetzee, J.M. 139
Collins, Tony 9–10
commercialisation 18–20, 53, 107, 156–158, 162, 169–174, 190, 194, 198, 208
Craven, Danie 55–57, *67*, 69, 75–76, 85–86, 97, 101–114, 124, 155–156, 171
cricket 7, 12, 94, 192, 194, 197–198, 204, 211–215, 219–220
    administrators and officials 194, 204
    betting 214, 216
    Empire's game 94, 193, 195–198
    international 207–208, 210, 216
    Nuffield 202
    politicians 94, 113, 197, 199, 203, 205, 207, 210, 212
    schools 197–198, 200–202, 206
    tests 195, 203, 208
    tours 94, 114, 194, 196–197
Cronjé, Hansie 201, 207, 211–*216*, 217, 220

Dalton, Andy 105
Desai, Ashwin 171
De Beer, Jannie 180–181
De Klerk, F.W. 109–111, 142
De Klerk, Jan 110
De Villiers, Dan 75–76
De Villiers, Dawie 96, 110
De Villiers, Fanie 202
De Villiers, Peter 184–185
De Villiers, Pieter 194
dog racing 14, 24, 26, *27*–29
    abolition of 30–31, 33
    anti-animal cruelty 16, 30, 33
    associations 17–18
    betting 15–20, 23, 25, 32
    commission of enquiry 18, 30–31
    coursing 15–16
    licencing 16–17
    mechanical hares 15–16
    punters and patrons 16, 18–20, 22, 25, 31–32
    profits 17, 19
    tracks 17, 20
D'Oliviera, Basil 94
Dobson, P. 103
Donald, Allan 201–202

237

Dreyer, Nelle 87–88
Du Plessis, Morné 80, *133*–135, 148–149

elitism 62–63, 75, 80, 155, 161, 171, 168–169, 176, 186, 197, 201, 205–206, 216
Engelbrecht, Jannie 124
Erasmus, Frikkie 149
ethnicity 14, 24, 31, 46–53, 68–69, 78, 91, 94, 119, 136, 138, 187, 197, 206–217, 220

Ferasse, Albert 101
First World War (1914–1919) 16, 36, 59, 73
foreigners and foreignness 14, 41, 48–49, 51–52, 194
Fraser, Malcolm 210
French, Joe 123

gambling 15–16, 19–23, 25–26, 31
games
  jukskei 50, 62
  putt-putt 49–50
  wapadspele 50
gender 22, 81, 87, *88*–89, 91–92, 150, 180
  masculinity 11, *27*, 81–85, *88*, 90–92, 185, 220
  women 22–23, 65, 81, 85–90, 171, 181
Gentles, Tommy 84
George, Mluleki 118
Giliomee, Hermann 12
Great Depression 16, 23, 35, 125
Great Trek centenary celebrations (1938) 26–*27*, 28, 41, 50, 55, 61, 78
Greyling, Piet 96
Griffiths, Edward 132–134, 137, 139, 147, 149, 209
Guelke, Adrian 109
Guttman, Allen 143

Hartenbos 12, 33, *39*, *45*, *48*, 219–220
  Afrikaanse Taal en Kultuur Vereniging (ATKV) 38–*39*, 40–*45*, 46, 50, *53*
  Afrikaner resort 11, 33–35, 42, 44, 46, 50
  Boeretroos Restourant 53
  development 35–46
  estate *42*, 46, *48*
  housing 44, *48*
  project 43, 44, 47
  visitors **45**–46
Hain, Peter *95*, 97–98, 102
Haswell, R.H. 18
Hendriks, Pieter 137
Hobsbawm, Eric 70
Hofmeyr, J.H. 197
Hogg, G. 66
Holt, Richard 10

imperialism 36, 61–63, 91–92, 193–194, 196, 203
International Rugby Board (IRB) 101, 105–107, 124, 132
Irwin, Mark 179

James, Wilmot 129

Keating, Frank 60
Kellas, J.G. 64
Keohane, Mark 158, 169
Klaaste, Aggrey 146
Klopper, Henning 39
Komphela, Butana 161, 165
Koornhof, Piet 101–102
Kotze, J.J. 195–196
Kotze, G.P. 194
Kruger, Paul 194

Laidlaw, Chris 68, 86, 104
leisure 7–13, 15–16, 21, 23–26, 33, 41, 47, 49–50, 76, 78, 145, 220
Le Roux, J. 74
Loriston, Cuthbert 100–101
Louw, Chris 190
Ludeke, Frans 186
Luyt, Louis 105, 107–108, 122, 124–127, 131–133, 137, 147, 149–150

MacClancy, Jeremy 9
Malan, D.F. 197
Malan, Magnus 81
Mandela, Nelson 114, 118, 128–130, 134, 138, 143, *144*–145, 150–151
Manuel, Trevor 148
Markgraaf, André 150, 163
Markötter, A.F. 55, 73
Matfield, Victor 186, 189
McGregor, Liz 91
McKeever, Tony 165
McKibbin, Ross 26
Meads, Colin 105
media 34, 68–69 104–105, 108, 127, 130, 133, 143, 149, 152, 157, 169–170, 180, 182–183, 187
  books 130, 151, 185, 189, 204
  journalists 53, 78–79, 85–86, 90–91, 116, 129, 132, 135, 142, 145, 153–154, 159–160
  motion pictures 130, 157
  newspapers 27, 29, 70, 125, 129, 136, 173
  television 78, 96, 128, 135, 138, 154, 157–159, 170–172, 179, 183
Meeser, F.C. 18
Meiring, A.M. 31
Meyer, Heyneke 186
Middleton, Norman 94
Montgomery, Percy *175*
Morkel, Albert 206
Morkel, Albie 202
Morrell, Rob 82
Mulder, Japie 178
Murdoch, Rupert 157

Nasson, Bill 217, 222
national anthems 120–124, 126, 135

Index

national flags 50, *121*–123, 148, 151
National and Olympic Sports Congress (NOSC) 111
New Zealand 59, 63, 66–68, 75, 82–84, 96–99, 101, 105–109, 118, 128, 179, 198
nicknames 22, 56, 71–72, 172, 195
Nicol, Rev. William 25, 31
Noakes, Tim 140
Nourse, Dudley 197

Odendaal, André 7, 206

Patel, Ebrahim 106, 112, 114, 117, 124
Pelser, Martin 66
Phillips, P.H. 98
Pickard, Jan 111
Pienaar, A.J. 74
Pienaar, Francois 128–130, *133*–134, 144, 149, 183
Pienaar, J.J. 32
platteland 14, 56–57, 103, 114, 118, 171–172
political parties
    African National Congress (ANC) 107–114, 120–123, 134, 138, 142–142, 150, 155, 159, 170
    Labour Party 38
    National Party (NP) 12, 21, 32, 38, 64, 75, 93–94, 108–109, 112, 119, 151, 197, 205, 213
    Progressive Federal Party (PFP) 103, 134
    United Party 32–33, 72, 75, 203
political transformation 103, 142, 150, 158–161, 163, 168, 170–171, 191
Pollock, Peter 204

Qunta, Vuyisa 160

race and racism 87, 100–101, 103–104, 112, 160–162
    affirmative action and redress 151, 159, 161
    "non-white" 94, 159, 166
    transformation 103, 142, 150, 158, 160–161, 163, 168, 191, 199
    white supremacy 87, 118–119
rainbow nation 130, 136, 138–140, 148, 151
Ramsamy, Sam 106
recreation 8, 22–23, 59, 62, 113, 142, 200
religion 41, 56, 61, 73, 155, 180–182, *183*–189, 191
    charismatic churches 184–190
    clerics, *dominees* and *predikante* 14, 25, 29, 56–57, 182, 187, 189, 197
    Christianity 31, 59, 181, 184–186, 215
Roos, Paul 196
Roux, Jurie 168
Roux, Mannetjies 71, 95
rugby
    amateur 66, 127, 155, 163, 168, 171–173, 176–180, 186

clubs 55–59, 64, 72–74, 98, 101, 108, 155, 171–175
coaches 100, 105, 115–116, *133*–135, 150, 162–164, 172, 184, 186
Currie Cup 77, 107, 156, 166, 169, 203
development programmes 55, 103–104, 114–117, 149–150, 167
intervarsity 64–65, 87
league 115, 156, 166–167, 175–176
professional 66, 88, 91, 127, 155, 157–160, 163, 176–186, 189, 190–191
spectators and supporters 68–69, 83–85, 89–91, 96–97, 99, 110, 115, *121*–123, 148, 172–173
sponsors 80, 105–106, 126, 154, 162–167, 169, 173, 177, 190
stadiums 71, 77, 107, 121–123, 126, 128, 130, 141, 149, 167, 183, 191
statistics 66, 81, 103, 115, 159–160, 165–166, 174–175, 179, 185
subculture 71, 88, 90, 92, 99, 122, 146, 155, 173–174
Super Rugby 164–167, 169, 175, 183
tests 65, *67*, 71, 79, 84, 86, 96, 116, 120–121, 123, 135, 148, 160, 181, 195
tours 56, 59, *65*–69, 75, 79, 83–86, 93–94, *95*–101, 105–107, 109, 111
unions 73–75, 77, 114, 118, 123, 132, 155, 161, 165–169, 172–174, 177, 180, 190
World Cup tournaments 116, 118–119, 126–128, 131–132, 137–154, 160, 178, 180, 191
rugby teams *see also* Springboks
    All Blacks 66, 68, 80, 82, 86, 93–94, 96, 105, 118, 120, 124, 128, 147–149, 156
    Blue Bulls 174, 183–184, 186
    British Lions 65, *67*, 69, 71
    Gauteng Lions 166, 174, 184
    Jaguars 105
    Leopards 100–101
    Maties 56–*57*
    Proteas 100
    Pumas 105
    Sharks 174
    Wallabies 118, 123
    Western Province 56, 59, 73, 111, 114, 136, 174
Rupert, Johann 164

Sanderson, H.J. 74
Schoeman, Ben 21
schools 14, 22, 24, 30–31, 39–40, 43, 56–57, 106, 200–201
    cricketing 197–198, 200–202, 206
    rugby 11, 59, 64, 82, 89, 108, 167–170, 172, 177
Second World War (1939–1945) 45, 72, 74
Slabbert, Frederik van Zyl 56, 145

slogans 98, 136, 141, 148
Smith, Adrian 109
Smuts, Jan 197
Snyman, Dana 173
soccer 66–67, 117, 126, 153, 159, 165, 198
social classes 29
  blue collar 66
  bourgeouise 76
  middle class 24, 28–30, 33, 59, 66–68, 82, 87, 91–92, 125, 200 219–220
  upper class 168, 193, 197, 219
  white collar 66
social work and welfare 21–22, 24, 28–30
South African Council of Sport (SACOS) 94, 117, 173
South African Railways 35–**37**, 38–40, 46–47
South African Rugby Association (SARA) 101
South African Rugby Board (SARB) 70, 74, 89, 100, 105, 137
South African Rugby Federation 100
South African Rugby Players' Association 180
South African Rugby Union (SARU) 101–103, 106, 112–114, 118–119, 166–168, 172
South African War (1899–1902) 36–37, 72, 194–196
Soweto uprising (1976) 102, 146
Spies, Pierre 185
spirituality 25–26, 41, 48, 52, 185, 187–188, 190, 213–214
sport
  administrators 98, 105–108, 111–116, 119, 127, 132, 136, 150, 163, 172–173, 176, 204
  boycotts 8, 11, 93, 97–98, 101–102, 106, 108–111, 134, 207–208, 210–211, 220
  heroes 83, 89, 95–96, 173, 179, 181–182, 204, 208, 212–213, 215, 218
  historians 8–10, 109, 140, 182, 206, 217–218
  "multi-national" 99–101
  politics 8, 23, 70–73, 92, 97–98, 103, 111, 118, 122, 133–135, 158–160, 166, 196, 208–211
  professional 66, 88, 91, 127, 155, 157–160, 163, 176–186, 189, 190–191
  sponsorship 80, 105–106, 126, 154, 162–167, 169, 173, 177, 190
sporting codes 7, 94, 110, 112–113, 156, 160, 201
Springboks *see also* rugby teams
  Amabokoboko 136, 146
  captains 11, 80, 91, 96, 110, 128, *133*–134, 149, 196, 204

emblem 118–119, 136
jerseys 77, 120, 128, 136, 166
selections 99, 124, 159, 162
teams 71, 81–85, 96, 98, 128, 141–147, 158–159, 168–170, 199
Stellenbosch 28, 54–56, *57*–58, 65, 73, 75, 87, 89, 91, 135, 164, 195, 219
Stofile, Rev. Arnold 112
Stofile, Makhenkesi 159–160, 163
Stofile, Mike 161
Stransky, Joel 128, *133*, 149, 153, 157
Struna, Nancy 10
symbolism 34, 41, 44, 50, 61, 70–71, 80, 91, 118–123, 143, 152, 196, 198, 211–213, 215
Symington, Johann 181–182

Tendulkar, Sachin 217
Terreblanche, Eugene 78
Theunissen, N.J.H. 195
Tobias, Errol 101
townships 19, 77, 104–106, 115–117, 119, 121, 129, 136
Tromp, Henry 137–138
Tshwete, Steve 113–114, 117, 120, 122–123, 143
Tutu, Desmond 136

Uitlanders see foreigners and foreignness
University of Cape Town 54, 87
University of Pretoria 58, 64
University of Stellenbosch 28, 54–57, 73, 75, 87, 91, 135, 195, 219
University of the Witwatersrand 64
urbanisation 14–15, 21, 23, 25, 27, 58, 61, 71, 119, 172, 189
Uys, Pieter-Dirk 141

Van der Merwe, Peter 204
Van der Westhuizen, Jaco *183*–184
Van der Westhuizen, Joost 178
Van Graan, Barend 186
Van Onselen, Charles 28
Van Zyl, Corrie 201
Verwoerd, H.F. 26, 28, 93, 213
Viviers, Gerhard 69, 97
Voortrekkers see Afrikaners
Vorster, B.J. 93–94, 99, 101, 206
Vrededorp 21–22, 28

Watson, Cheeky 103, 165–167
Watson, Luke 165–166
Wessels, Kepler 201, 207–208, *209*–211, 214, 217, 220
White, Jake 164
Williams, Chester 136, 149

Yssel, Gert 181